NORTHROP FRYE ON MYTH

NORTHROP FRYE
ON MYTH

FORD RUSSELL

ROUTLEDGE
NEW YORK AND LONDON

First paperback edition published in 2000 by
Routledge
29 West 35th Street
New York, NY 10001

Published in Great Britain by
Routledge
11 New Fetter Lane
London EC4P 4EE

Routledge is an imprint of the Taylor & Francis Group

Copyright © 1998 by Ford Russell
Previously published as vol. 1166 in the Garland Reference Library of the Humanities

Library of Congress Cataloging-in-Publication Data

Russell, Ford.
    Northrop Frye on myth / Ford Russell.
            p. cm.
        Includes bibliographical references and index.
        ISBN 0-8240-3446-5 (alk. paper)
        ISBN 0-415-92905-9 (pbk.)
        1. Frye, Northrop. Anatomy of Criticism.   2. Literature—
History and criticism—Theory, etc.   3. Myth in Literature.   I. Title.
II. Series.
PN75.F7R87   1998
801'.95'092—dc21   97-18441
                                                              CIP

10 9 8 7 6 5 4 3 2 1

Printed on acid-free, 250-year-life paper
Manufactured in the United States of America

In a strict sense, Northrop Frye is not a theorist of myth. He is a theorist of the mythic origin of literature—specifically, Western literature. For him, Western literature originates in biblical and classical myth—specifically, hero myth, and hero myth tied to ritual. Frye is certainly not the first to root literature in myth. Indeed, he is indebted to James Frazer for his myth-ritualist scenario, and the linkage of literature to myth and ritual goes all the way back to Aristotle. But whereas most other myth-ritualists confine themselves to the origin of a single literary genre such as tragedy, Frye derives all of the main literary genres—romance, comedy, and satire, as well as tragedy—from myth and ritual.

Ford Russell goes far beyond other scholars, not merely in devoting a whole book to Frye's theory of myth, but, more important, in tracing the many sources of Frye's theory. Rather than confining himself to Frazer, as is commonly done, he works out the equal influence on Frye of Oswald Spengler, Sigmund Freud, C.G. Jung, and especially Ernst Cassirer, who, according to Russell, was the fullest and most direct influence on Frye. Systematically comparing each of these figures with Frye, as well as with one another, Russell shows how they contributed to Frye's ideas, terms, and typologies. He shows how Frye uses these thinkers to develop his own theory.

Russell simultaneously demonstrates how, as he likes to put it, Frye adapts whatever he adopts. Frye picks and chooses what he takes from each thinker, somehow manages to reconcile their seemingly incompatible views, and most of all transforms into literary criticism the tenets of the disciplines from which the thinkers hail. Anthropological (Frazer), psychological (Freud, Jung), cultural (Spengler), and philosophical (Cassirer) categories are made into literary ones. In fact, Frye reads anthropology, psychology, cultural morphology, and philosophy *as* literary criticism. And so he must, committed as he stalwartly is to the autonomy of literature. As obsessed as Frye is with the mythic origins of literature, he does not equate myth with literature. On the contrary, he insists on the irreducibly literary nature of literature. He seeks to establish that literature grows out of myth, not that literature is myth.

Russell does not limit his analysis to Frazer, Freud, Jung, Spengler, and Cassirer. He continually discusses other sources, ranging from Aristotle and Origen, to Kant and Vico, to Robert Graves, and from Joseph Campbell to Paul Ricoeur. He by no means neglects William Blake, whom some scholars deem the chief influence on Frye. Russell's consideration of all influences is not merely thematic but also biographical; he tries to determine whom Frye actually read, not simply whose views are akin to Frye's. Russell's overarching aim is to work out how all of the figures he discusses enabled Frye to link biblical and classical mythology to literature, which is to say to secular literature. For Frye, the shift from myth to literature is the shift from religious literature to secular literature. At the same time, secular literature recreates the religious mythology from which it derives.

Russell concentrates on the *Anatomy of Criticism,* indisputably Frye's key work on myth. However, much of the rest of Frye's corpus does get considered, in helping to explicate the *Anatomy.* Russell explicates in detail Frye's actual theory of myth. He is particularly adroit at charting Frye's myriad classificatory schemes. Russell's book provides the most thorough presentation so far of Frye as a theorist of myth.

In addition to delineating the theory of myth in the *Anatomy,* Russell delineates the myth *of* the *Anatomy:* the myth of the "ideal reader." Russell maintains that Frye's true hero is not only the subject of hero myths but, at least as much, the sophisticated reader of literature, who undertakes a quest as bold and as formative as that of any mythic hero.

To Cristabelle

CONTENTS

PREFACE

What Northrop Frye calls the "communism of convention" affects the beginnings of books (*AC*, 98). A commentator's preface normally suggests that he has done what no one before has or has been more comprehensive in his coverage. The *hubris* that the preface expresses is followed by the humility of acknowledgments extended to everyone. Some commentaries grudgingly concede that other works on their subject exist perhaps because the anxiety of influence applies to our works as much as to the figures we study. There is anxiety not only about the relationship of our work to the developing body of commentary but also about the place of our chosen figure in the field. The marginalization of Frye in contemporary literary studies seems to elicit a running commentary in works on him.

The question of Frye's place in his field is much like the case of the various myth theorists with whom I compare him. What is Oswald Spengler's place in historical studies, James Frazer's in contemporary anthropology, or Ernst Cassirer's in present-day philosophy? Each has died in his own field or tends to lack followers within it, like Frye. They sought to found, revolutionize, or reform a field of study, as Frye attempted in *Anatomy of Criticism*. From one point of view, the *Anatomy* brings the works of the moderns into the literary criticism of the 1950s, not only those of Joyce and Eliot but some of the works of our myth theorists, who affected their cultural milieu. Forty years later, though, the *Anatomy* is beginning to look more like the most traditional literary critical work the century produced. It can be compared with projects of restoration such as those of Hans-Georg Gadamer and Paul Ricoeur. As any work purporting to be foundational must, *Anatomy* attempts to ground itself in Aristotle's *Poetics*, but it also endeavors to work from Biblical hermeneutics. The first essay restores what Frye encountered in William Blake: prophetic poems that have the Biblical landscape as the setting for characters and situations. The *Anatomy* widens this landscape to include Classical mythology, and from this common mythic ground there emerges a sequence of horizons or periodizations adapted from Spengler into a sequence of writing and reading cultures.

Frye's second essay begins at the point at which Cassirer's *Mythical Thought* ends: with medieval hermeneutics. Though each of Frye's essays presents itself as the "theory" of something, it might be better now to perceive them relative to the practices in which they invite us to participate. Frye's proposal, in the light of our modern conflict of interpretations, was to start from what was a single "tradition of interpretation" (Smalley, 6). Frye points to a single figure, Dante, in this thousand-year tradition, perhaps for the reason Cassirer suggests. What Frye calls the "scheme of literal, allegorical, moral, and anagogic meanings," and which he says was "taken over from theology and applied to literature," is congruent with Cassirer's observation that this practice serves not only Dante's "theology," but also "his poetics" (*AC*, 72; *Mythical Thought*, 256).

Frank Kermode recognized long ago that Frye's second essay correlates the thought of Cassirer with Aristotle. The essay on symbolism also makes a place, in the area of "archetypal criticism," for Frazer and for Freud and Jung. They are situated within a larger framework that starts from medieval hermeneutics, so that, with hindsight, we can perhaps now begin to see them as Frye does. Their "new forms of allegorical interpretation" have a history, and that history, within Western literature, is relatable to Biblical hermeneutics as it is to the Greco-Roman allegorization of myth ("Allegory," 6). Their quest for subcultural or subconscious patterns of meaning beneath the manifest is a modern version of what Origen introduces into Biblical hermeneutics in the third century when he finds hidden underneath the surface events of the Bible a mega-narrative of forms and types.

Like the others, the third essay is relatable both to its own time and to earlier times. The manual of literary imagery is akin to the projects of other myth theorists: the "grammar of literary symbolism" that Jung studies in *Psychology and Alchemy* and that Frye thinks applicable to writers in the tradition of quest-romance and which for him is an extension of "Biblical typology" (*NFCL*, 128). Other projects include *The Dying God* in Frazer and *The White Goddess* of Robert Graves. Frye feels, however, that "there is something dismally corny about isolating a myth" in the way they do (*NFCL*, 233). Here again Frye sets modern myth theorists within a tradition. Graves can be placed in the line of "the solemnly systematic mythographers" in "the tradition of Apollodorus and Nataliss Comes and George Eliot's Casaubon," but Frye assigns him "to the tradition of the writers who have turned mythical erudition into satire," such as Apuleius or Rabelais, along with the "exuberantly hyperbolic Celtic mythical poets" on whom *The White Goddess* focuses (*NFCL*, 234). Graves' "white goddess myth" is for Frye an "ironic myth" affecting the story type of satire (*NFCL*, 234-35); the "ritual of the killing of the divine king in Frazer" is in the *Anatomy* the "form" underlying literary "tragic and ironic structures" (*AC*, 148). In Graves' poetry, Frye finds myth present as a "kaleidoscopic chaos of human fragments" (*NFCL*, 234). Later on, he speaks of "myth-making" as "a putting together of bits and pieces" out of whatever a writer has been reading (*GC*, xxi). This assumption greatly complicates the *Anatomy*'s streamlined portrayals of writers through time displacing myths, his archetypal critics as those who restore them, and with both engaged in a return to myth.

The later portion of the third essay, Frye's circle of story types, is also relatable to its own time. Like H. Richard Niebuhr's *Christ and Culture*, which draws upon Carl Jung's *Psychological Types* to "supplement and in part to correct Ernst Troeltsch's *The Social Teachings of the Christian Churches*" (Niebuhr, xii), Frye draws upon what he thinks of as Jung's personal private myth of individuation and upon *Psychological Types*. Jung's four experiential types become Frye's four story types. On the one hand, Jung presents an allegory of psychological development into maturity and on the other a purely relational, comparativistic, or synchronic arrangement of types. Frye, too, constructs an ideal reading process that has both developmental and synchronic, both allegorical and typological dimensions.

However, in this and his other typologies, Frye's effort need not be confined to Jung. The last chapter of this book compares Frye's Biblical hermeneutics with Origen's. Frye's books on the Bible and literature books are productively compared with the initial effort, within Biblical hermeneutics, to enjoin the allegorical habits of reading Origen inherited from Philo with the universalization of typology. The assumption of the *Anatomy* is that readers move through some "death and rebirth process"; this is Origen's cardinal rule for reading since he says that the reader has to die to the literal to rise to the spiritual sense of Scripture. Where Origen says that the entire narrative of Scripture consists of a continuous subterranean sequence of forms and types, the *Anatomy* has a reader who becomes capable of recognizing archetypes from Classical and Biblical myth in corresponding antitypes occurring in secular literature.

The development of Frye as a student of myth is similar to that of Joseph Campbell. Both started reading Frazer and Spengler as well as Freud and Jung. A major difference is that Frye's experience of reading Blake in the light of the Bible dislodged him from the historical framework that he says Campbell settled into; Frye quite early exchanged it for a mythological framework that includes and grows out of Classical and Biblical myth. Both begin as comparativists, but, from his early experience of reading Blake to his book on Blake through his Bible and literature books, Frye situates himself and us within Western civilization or its sacred and secular texts. His chosen and perennial focus is "the meeting point of the sacred book and the work of literature" within our civilization as a whole (*GC*, 216). Frye regularly says that all his ideas came from Blake, which is perhaps true to the extent that much of Blake comes out of the Bible, though even his study of Blake is partially informed by the several allies he brings to his commentary on the prophetic poems: Frazer and Spengler. Even the much reduced final version of *Fearful Symmetry* teems with allusions or observations based upon them. *Anatomy of Criticism* a decade later is, unsurprisingly, indebted on the topic of myth itself to the theorists closest to his own field: Cassirer and Spengler.

The Critical Path turns to their common mentor, Giambattista Vico, who he says presents a "theory of culture" outlining "secular history" while "avoiding the whole of the Bible" (*GC*, xix). Harold Bloom's recent *The Western Canon* has a Viconian version of secular history applied to literary history. But Frye does with Vico, in his Bible and literature books, what he had done in *Anatomy* with each of our five myth theorists. The principle is that, with each of them, he performs some major adaptation of whatever he adopts from them. In other words, he elicits, usually from one or several of their individual works, some typology for literary studies. The adaptation of Vico is that his framework is expanded by Frye so that it coincides with the Bible as the great code for the rest of Western literature and thus allows us access to literary works sharing scriptural power because they, too, are informed by myth and metaphor.

The relationship of the *Anatomy* to the five myth theorists is indispensable to understanding it. Freud and Jung, despite their antagonisms, become like reconciled brothers within its pages. Together they provide Frye with a dual vision of what writers (Freud) and readers (Jung) do with myth. Freud affects his account of the writer as the shaper of myth. Writers draw upon the myths of our Greco-Roman and Judeo-Christian foundational cultures and they recreate it within the writing cultures. These writing cultures are adapted by Frye from Spengler, though perhaps even those eras or periodizations are the creations of writers (*FI*, 147). The counterpart to the writers' recreation of myth is his Jungian account of the reader's assimilation of archetypes. An "archetype" for Frye is any significant pattern that a reader recognizes in a secular literary work on the basis of his responsiveness to our dual heritage of myth.

Most literary critics "have one figure that they use as a Vergilian guide through [the] contradictory mazes" of thought since the Romantic era (*TLS*, 52). Frazer serves as Frye's guide to the infernal regions beneath his circle of story types. The "ritual of the killing of the divine king" in *The Golden Bough* becomes in the *Anatomy* the "radical demonic form" operative upon "the tragic and ironic structures" just above it (*AC*, 148).

Cassirer is the last of the myth theorists that Frye read. He read him while he was writing *Anatomy*. He influences Frye on myth more than the others save for Spengler. Cassirer and Frye were the only major thinkers in the old humanities who chose to make myth a major category. Cassirer is Frye's predecessor in undermining many of the assumptions of social scientific theorizing on myth: the reification of theory over practice, delimited causal thinking, the introduction of subject and object frameworks, and so on. For instance, "the relation of subject and object" is applied all the way through the culminating chapter of *Psychological Types*, and becomes like a straitjacket that makes his discussion nearly "opaque" (*Portable Jung*, 180; *MM*, 178). Cassirer is helpful to the *Anatomy* in providing a containing form for his second essay. His adaptation of Cassirer is similar to an adaptation of Spengler, in the first essay, and to an adaptation of Jung, in the third essay, in that these become the devices by which Frye organizes these essays. Yet the difference between Frye's relationship in the *Anatomy* to Cassirer and to the other myth theorists is that they tend to affect portions of the book, while Cassirer is continually present.

Kierkegaard said that, though life as lived can only go forward, we understand it only by moving backward. If we look at the final Bible and literature book, we can see that Frye has entered into the allegorical and typological tradition of Biblical hermeneutics. Prior to them, there is the Frye who works from his adaptation of Vico, the common mentor of Spengler and Frazer. With the *Anatomy,* we find that Frye has at once entered into the conventions and practices of Frazer, Freud, Jung, and Spengler yet has already begun his departure from them with some help from Cassirer. With *Fearful Symmetry*, his chief allies were Frazer and Spengler, and perhaps his main difficulty was in getting beyond them. If we go back to some of the papers Frye wrote as a student, we find Frye continually reworking "ideas drawn from Frazer and Spengler which contain an embryonic version of many of the principles that Frye developed much more extensively in *Anatomy of Criticism*" (*NFN* 6 [Fall 1995], 2).

Most of my book is a commentary on the *Anatomy.* Hence the focus is confined to one stage of Frye's thought and one book among some thirty of them. The study of Frye on myth in the *Anatomy* does not necessarily "embalm" his book "in a sarcophagus" of the species of myth criticism that he and others practiced within the literary criticism of the 1950s (*WP*, xvii). As an effort to clean up the Augean stables of literary criticism, the *Anatomy* has been as unsuccessful as the efforts of the other myth theorists in their fields. Robert D. Denham's thoughtful probing of the validity of Frye's approach in relation to other literary critical methods elicits the same problems as other theorists face in their fields. A. C. Hamilton's defense of *Anatomy of Criticism* as a playing field for literary criticism in our time has also been very helpful to me. Still, I am less interested in defending the Frye who seems to make of literary criticism an autonomous discipline than in defending the Frye who is as integral to Biblical as he is to literary studies. The study of Frye's relationship to other myth theorists has largely been ignored in other studies of Frye. Perhaps it is because focusing upon figures such as Spengler does not enhance academic reputations. Or maybe it is more entertaining to relate Frye to the new constellation of Gallic and other continental stars who have replaced our myth theorists in the literary critical heavens during the last generation. In any case, the Frye of the *Anatomy* does what he says most imaginative writers do. He enters into a set of practices that were ongoing at the time he started writing and expresses himself through them. The project of the *Anatomy* is to enter into their thought and relate them to extant practices within literary criticism and reconcile them to each other: he reconciles Freud with Jung, sets Frazer's ritual as the demonic counterpart to the Christian myth of death and resurrection, reconciles Spengler with Toynbee, and relates Cassirer to Aristotle.

"The Theory of Myths," the third essay of the *Anatomy*, is probably neither a "theory" nor about "myth" itself. Instead, it presents "some of the structural principles of Western literature" when read in the light of its "Classical and Christian [mythic] heritage" (*AC*, 133). His survey of literary imagery on the basis of Revelation and his study of literary traditions, or "*mythoi*," are designated as "the practice of archetypal criticism," which is our "habit of imaginative reading" literary works in the light of our dual mythic heritage (*AC*, 112; *NFCL*, 138). "Myth," for Hans-Georg Gadamer, "is the technical term for the form in which religious texts speak." Myth is for Frye the term for the form in which secular literary works speak as well.

The attempt to record one's indebtedness to others is indispensable. It is an exercise from which one learns the futility of fairness and is as tedious for readers as the catalog of ships in Homer or Biblical genealogy. I am grateful to others who have written on Frye, especially to Robert D. Denham for reading, commenting upon, and offering constructive advice on an earlier version of my manuscript. Like anyone else writing on Frye, I have found his critical and bibliographical works to be of inestimable help to my work. A. C. Hamilton's book and articles on Frye have also been invaluable. Frank Kermode's observations on Frye have often provided points of departure for my study of him. As every commentator has his own heroes, I may as well confess that my own are Cassirer, Hans-Georg Gadamer, and Paul Ricoeur.

Frye suggests that literary education should begin with the Bible and proceed to Classical mythology. My own education began with the Greek myths my father recounted as bedtime stories. Bible stories came later and settled on top of the myths, so that characters like Abraham entered an imaginative landscape already occupied by Greek heroes. During college, I took three Classical mythology courses, but the one that made an impression consisted of sequential tellings of one myth after the other in the same way Frazer recounts dying god myths; and my reception of them, in Gadamer's phrase, was one of "naïve assimilation," not much different from the first naiveté of the bedtime stories.

My introduction to Frye came in a Milton class in 1970 when the teacher casually remarked that "we should be grateful to Northrop Frye because he thinks we can understand him." Taking this remark literally, I spent the week of spring vacation reading the *Anatomy*. My reader response was that the first essay did seem comprehensible, but that the rest of it, especially "The Theory of Myths," felt like the experience of being lost in an expressionistic fogbank.

During five years in the later 1970s at a Presbyterian seminary, I read Frye somewhat as he had read Frazer in a similar setting. David Reeves, then senior New Testament professor at McCormick Theological Seminary in Chicago, helped initiate me into his practice by which thinking mythically and thinking imaginatively become indistinguishable. I would also like to express my gratitude to K. K. Collins and Thomas J. Hatton, under both of whom I studied at Southern Illinois University at Carbondale during my decade there in the 1980s.

Among others to whom acknowledgments are due are the late Robert Boling, Stan Bomgarden, Richard Bryant, George Goodin, Christopher Hamilton, Paul Pimomo, Manuel Schonhorn, the late Joseph Sittler, Stephen Tyman, David M. Vieth, and Don Wardlaw. A Dissertation Research Award from the Graduate School of Southern Illinois University allowed me to spend a year in the late 1980s on Frye. Robert A. Segal provided editorial comments. Bruce Ormsby Adam processed several drafts of the manuscript. Mike and Gloria

Hughey processed the final draft. What I owe to my wife, Cristabelle, is, in her native language, *utang na loob*, a debt of honor that, like all such debts, can never be repaid.

ABBREVIATIONS

AC	*Anatomy of Criticism*
C&R	*Creation and Recreation*
CP	*The Critical Path*
DV	*The Double Vision*
EI	*The Educated Imagination*
EAC	*The Eternal Act of Creation*
FI	*Fables of Identity*
FS	*Fearful Symmetry*
FT	*Fools of Time*
GC	*The Great Code*
HH	*Harper Handbook to Literature*
MC	*The Modern Century*
MD	*The Myth of Deliverance*
MM	*Myth and Metaphor*
NFCL	*Northrop Frye on Culture and Literature*
NFIC	*Northrop Frye in Conversation*
NFShx	*Northrop Frye on Shakespeare*
NP	*A Natural Perspective*
OE	*On Education*
RE	*The Return of Eden*
RW	*Reading the World*
SER	*A Study of English Romanticism*
SS	*The Secular Scripture*
St. S	*The Stubborn Structure*
SM	*Spiritus Mundi*
TSE	*T. S. Eliot*
WP	*Words with Power*
WGS	*A World in a Grain of Sand*
WTC	*The Well-Tempered Critic*

"Allegory"   Entry in *Encyclopedia of Poetry and Poetics*, ed. Alex Preminger and others (Princeton: Princeton University Press, 1965) 12-15.

"E-CS"   "Response," *Eighteenth-Century Studies* 24 (Winter 1990-91), 157-72, 243-49.

"LC"   "Literary Criticism," in *The Aims and Methods of Scholarship in Modern Languages and Literatures*, ed. James Thorpe (New York: Modern Language Association, 1963), 57-69.

"L&M"   "Literature and Myth," in *Relations of Literary Study: Essays on Interdisciplinary Contributions*, ed. James Thorpe (New York: Modern Language Association, 1967), 27-55.

LNF   *The Legacy of Northrop Frye*, eds. Alvin A. Lee and Robert D. Denham (Toronto: Toronto University Press, 1994).

"M&P"   "Myth and Poetry," in *The Concise Encyclopedia of English and American Poets and Poetry*, eds. Stephen Spender and Donald Hall (New York: Hawthorn Books, 1963), 225-28.

NFMC   *Northrop Frye in Modern Criticism*, ed. Murray Krieger (New York: Columbia University Press, 1966).

NFN   *Northrop Frye Newsletter*, ed. Robert D. Denham. 1 (Fall 1988-).

TLS   "In the Earth, or in the Air?" *TLS*, 17 (January 1986), 51-52.

CHAPTER ONE

LIFE AND WORKS

The early life of Northrop Frye resembled what he called "the commonest formula of Canadian fiction (*OE*, 175). "Childhood and adolescence are passed in a small town," he said, and adulthood is attained with "the entry into a more complex social contract" (*OE*, 175). Born July 14, 1912 at Sherbrooke, his family moved to nearby Lennoxville; these towns are just north of Vermont in the province of Quebec. They settled in Moncton when he was eight. Located in the Maritime province of New Brunswick, Moncton is northeast of Maine.

He received only eight years of public schooling. His mother gave him what is now called a "home education." He was then placed in grade four; high school graduates there left after grade eleven. His family's economic circumstances declined during his youth so that even the possibility of a college education was in question. His further education was dependent upon a continuing sequence of awards, scholarships, or fellowships. A local business college provided a scholarship for the best high school English student, so he took some courses before entering the University of Toronto the next year, in 1929. His student years there coincided with the Great Depression; his teaching career began a decade later, in 1939, the year World War II commenced. Toronto, where he taught for over fifty years, provided the setting for most of his professional life. He continued teaching after 1978, when he might have retired, until his death on January 23, 1991, at the age of 78.

Frye enrolled in 1929 at Victoria College, which is one of a federated group of three liberal arts colleges within the University of Toronto. They were differentiated by their religious affiliation. Victoria received students from the recently formed Church of Canada, which included Methodists like Frye, Congregationalists, and Presbyterians. Entering students chose a four-year honors program or a three-year pass program. Due to the brevity of his formal schooling, Frye was placed on probation in the easier pass program. The next year he was reassigned to the honors program. The coursework Frye took emphasized philosophy, with a secondary concentration upon English literature.

After his B.A. in 1933, he continued at Emmanuel College for another three years. Emmanuel is connected with Victoria, because both are affiliated with the United Church of Canada. His coursework prepared him for ministry. When he received a second Bachelor's degree, he was ordained. A fellowship, however, now allowed him two further years of English studies at Merton College, Oxford. In 1937, he married Helen Kemp (a marriage which lasted until her death some fifty years later in 1986). His undergraduate studies at Oxford "covered English literature down to 1830" (*SM*, 4); these studies had a provision by which they could later count as or be "automatically transmuted into an M.A.," which he received in 1940.[1] When he resumed as Lecturer at Victoria in 1939, he had accumulated three Bachelor's degrees. As he observed, he was "deflected from everything that could conventionally be described as research" (*SM*, 3). Frye, as a younger man, viewed his education ironically. His primary schooling was "penal servitude" (*WGS*, 330), his high school was "primitive" (*NFIC*, 45), and, upon the completion of his higher education at Oxford, he felt relieved to have "ended the compulsory time-waste period"; he was also glad to have avoided "jumping through the hoops" of graduate school, "and turning Ph.D. cartwheels to amuse [his] elders."[2]

Such remarks became subdued as he advanced through the positions of Assistant (1942), Associate (1947) and full Professor (1948); and with the successive administrative posts of English Department Chair (1952), Principal of his College (1959), University Professor at Toronto (1966), and Chancellor of Victoria and Emmanuel Colleges (1978). He received some of the most distinguished awards available to a Canadian and some three dozen honorary doctorates. Though his life is identifiable through what he called "the layer of personae"—the many public roles he had as teacher, administrator, and international lecturer—it is perhaps more interesting to glimpse him as he was initially trying out different social roles and considering his vocational choices (*OE*, 211).

He appears to have considered writing, preaching, and teaching as his main options. From an early age, he began thinking of himself as a writer. If one could excavate the past of almost any English teacher, probably some long-buried sheath of poems or batch of stories will eventually be brought up, as has recently been done with Frye. Though he wrote some poems, he focused upon short fiction; six stories appeared in Victoria's literary magazine and in *Canadian Forum* between 1936 and 1941.[3] His fertile mind continued to conceive of plots, characters, and ideas for novels from about 1935 through the rest of his life. His senior colleague at Victoria, poet E. J. Pratt, advised him to establish his academic reputation and then return to writing (Ayre 1989, 166-69). The one fragmentary novel so far recovered deals with the topics Frye knew well, religion and education, and its main character is a clergyman.

The possibility of ministry seems to have been his mother's idea. Frye thought her religious training and desire for him to enter ministry was "very much dominated by her father," a Methodist preacher (*WGS*, 329). She envisioned him as a "symbol of her father," and "dragged" him off for talks with an "appalling series of parsons" (*NFN* 5 [Summer 1993], 26). Their conversations centered on his aptitude for ministry. Perhaps he felt unfit for the administrative leadership, the initiative expected in establishing and maintaining multiple programmatic activities in areas such as Christian education, evangelism, and stewardship. He may also have felt uncomfortable with the intimacy pastoral care requires. Yet he was perhaps attracted to the core activity of preaching or proclamation.

There was, he said, a "strong evangelical religious streak in the family," which he inherited through his mother from her father, who had been a circuit rider (*WGS*, 328). Frye describes his grandfather's duties with a sense of pathos, perhaps identifying him with the figure he himself might have become. The grandfather thought that the rural outpost that he was "assigned by his bishop" was the place "that God had called him to, and he didn't realize that he was [denominationally] in with a bunch of pushing entrepreneurs who were grabbing all the soft spots in the bigger cities" (*NFIC*, 41).

Methodism seems to us merely another species of mainline Protestantism. David Cayley, however, designates the Methodism Frye was brought up in as "radical" Protestantism, by which he means that it drew its "inspiration directly from the Bible without priestly, liturgical or doctrinal intermediations" (*NFIC*, 3). He also deems it "authoritarian," though it is more likely anti-authoritarian," and populist.

Through at least the age of twenty-one, Frye planned to enter the ministry. He announced his decision to his family (*WGS*, 330) and defended it as a career choice to his fiancée (*NFN* 6 [Fall 1994], 8). While he felt ministry would allow him to exercise his desire to be a writer, he expressed doubts about the possibility of teaching. Preaching and teaching are, he told his fiancée, two possible "Fates" who are pulling in opposite directions" and leaving Frye uncertain "which one is God" (*NFN* 6 [Fall 1994], 9). A "professor," according to his metaphor, is an "orchid," or "highly cultivated" plant, since it has "no roots in the ground" and is "cut off from life" (*NFN* 6 [Fall 1994], 8). Frye at twenty-one has the undergraduate's normal suspicion that research and specialization are divorced from the "community of live people" (*NFN* 6 [Fall 1994], 8).

What he came to regard as the decisive episode that propelled him towards his profession occurred one icy February evening in 1934.[4] He was working on an assigned paper the night before it was due, as most students do. Seated in an all-night cafeteria, and probably with the help of many cups of coffee, sometime well after midnight, a revelatory insight occurred to him. The task was on Blake's poem *Milton*. He set out to compare the poets. His initial assumption was that the poets were "connected by their use of the Bible"; the eventual insight was the discovery that a "mythological framework" contained both poets (*SM*, 17). One might say that the question of "the historical period" to which the poets belonged had impeded Frye and is inherently perplexing. Milton is one of the last Renaissance poets living into the Restoration era; he himself perhaps conceived of himself as the last, best writer of the Reformation. Blake is a first-generation Romantic poet but can be placed in the company of later eighteenth-century poets, as Frye suggests in an essay on this period, "Towards Defining an Age of Sensibility," (*FI*, 130-37). Frye seems to have departed from such historical categories and arrived at a transhistorical, or "mythological," superhighway that starts from the Bible and runs straight through such intensely Biblical poets as Milton and Blake.   The real point, which made it a revelatory experience for Frye, was that he experienced himself entering imaginatively into the Biblical landscape. His description of the experience, that it was "a vision of coherence," that in the middle of the night "suddenly the universe just broke open," and that he was never "the same man again," lends itself to a variety of interpretations (*NFN*, 3 [Winter 1990-91], 5).   It can serve as a self-image for Frye as the "great twentieth-century reader" rather than as "a poet like Milton or a ... visionary like Blake" (*NFN* 5 [Summer 1993], 27). His reading experience, in our present context is a "chance happening" that was "transformed into a destiny by means of a choice" to write what became the book on Blake thirteen years later, a choice constantly renewed in subsequent books (Paul Ricoeur, *OAA*, 25).

It is helpful to add to our sketch of his life and vocation a survey of some of the books he encountered when young. His adage about the Bible is applicable to his own exposure to it through his mother. The Bible "should be taught so early and so thoroughly," he said, "that it sinks straight to the bottom of the mind, where everything else that comes along can settle on it" (*EI*, 110). A family picture his biographer mentions displays Frye clutching to himself a copy of John Bunyan's *Pilgrim's Progress*, a work that places its hero, "Christian," on a Biblical path leading him through the secular world around him. Frye recalled that "several shelves" of the family's library were "portly theological volumes" previously belonging to his clergyman grandfather (*SM*, 48). Another "whole shelf" consisted of "children's adaptations of the classics" (*NFIC*, 41). Sets of the works of Dickens and Scott and works by other novelists were in the family collection, which was not added to after 1910, presumably because they could not afford further acquisitions. An aunt, however, brought them a few books by Wells, Ibsen, and Shaw, and he read more of their works at the public library (*WGS*, 328). One of his high school English texts was a collection of seventeenth-century lyrical poetry. His exposure to the early Milton and to Donne may account for their presence on a list of favorite writers which he compiled toward the end of his stay at Victoria: "Donne, Milton, Bunyan, Swift, Blake, Dickens, Browning, and Shaw" (*NFN* 6 [Fall 1994], 24). This evaluative canon of his "heroisms in literature" can be expanded to include the "culture heroes of his student days," anthropologist James Frazer and metahistorian Oswald Spengler (*SM*, 111). He found Frazer's *Golden Bough* "hidden behind" the circulation desk of the Moncton Public Library because he had a job there when it opened in his mid-teens (Ayre, 124). He "picked up Spengler's *Decline of the West*" as an undergraduate at Victoria (*NFIC*, 61).

The salient feature of his entire higher education is the layered sequence of his readings of the works that were then considered to constitute the English literary tradition. The honors program had been devised by a philosophy teacher on Victoria's faculty. The "curriculum" he prescribed had "set courses and authors for each year, so that a student would progress through four hundred years of English literature and European [philosophical] thought" during his four years (Denham 1991, 17). While training for ministry at Emmanuel, Frye claimed he "perhaps spent more time doing English literature than theology" and that his interest in theology was displaced by his interest in Frazer's *Golden Bough*. While at Emmanuel, he took some graduate courses over at Victoria, and was more fascinated by Frazerian applications to the Bible and literature than by his theology courses. The two years at Oxford comprised a "hard program of reading" which covered English literature" from its beginnings "down to 1930" (*SM*, 4). Moreover, his early teaching duties reinforced his comprehensive readings. Initially assigned courses in four different periods, he soon found himself teaching "everything in English literature from Chaucer on." Though his work on Blake's book was arrested by his "preparing for his lectures," they may have implicitly entered into his depiction of Blake as a typical expression of the English literary tradition from Chaucer down to Blake (*NFIC*, 51).

Our portrait of the literary critic as a young man requires a glimpse of him as person. As an adolescent, he appeared to a peer at Moncton as a "tall, thin youth" with "wildly blowing reddish hair," which epitomized his "artistic eccentricity" (*WGS*, 334), though he was in fact of medium stature with blond hair. He seemed remote, bent on some special purpose, with "his books stacked under an arm," absorbed in his own thoughts, and looking "straight ahead and determined" (*WGS*, 334). When Frye, in later years, heard this account of him, he called it a "fairly sharp perception" (*WGS*, 334). It helps suggest the "extraordinary aloofness" by which analytical psychologist Carl Jung designates the person who is introverted and intuitive.[5] A characteristic calling for this kind of person is that of artist and writer, who are themselves, at least in our extended Romantic era, the modern descendants of the Biblical prophets. In choosing to study Blake, Frye selected what Jung would call a "type" of personality he himself had.

Writer Richard Kostelanetz, who interviewed Frye when he was in his early sixties, supplies a character sketch (432). He was "medium in height and build." His hair, which remained wavy, had become gray. His forehead was "relatively unlined." He wore "wire-framed, rimless glasses." The face seems "relatively unlined" to Kostelanetz, with "soft jowls" around the thin lips. "His mouth opens only slightly when he speaks" and his speech is uttered in a relatively monotone voice. His manner seemed "reserved" and "a bit inscrutable"; Frye used the word "reclusive" in reference to his lifestyle.

Another writer said the impression made upon her by his lecture room style was that of "a magician."[6] As she saw him in 1960, Margaret Atwood said she felt the desire "to go around behind" where Frye was speaking "or look under the table to see how he did it." He started by standing "in front of the room" behind a table, then "took one step forward, put his left hand on the table, took a step back, put his right hand on the table" and "repeated the pattern" as, all the while, "pure prose," in book form, "issued from his mouth." Hearing the outpouring of words was like "seeing a magician producing birds from a hat." Many of his students seem to have regarded him as the figure Jung designates "the magician," "counselor," or "wise old man."

Frye recalled that his father was "always of rather retiring disposition," and his mother was even more so: she gradually became "extremely deaf and withdrawn and introverted" (*NFIC*, 42). A sense of Frye's isolation or introversion recurs throughout the settings and stages of life. Even at Victoria, where he entered almost zestfully into many student activities, he experienced himself as set apart socially and as one of the "church students" bent upon ministry (*NFN* 6 [Fall 1994], 16). Yet at Emmanuel it seemed to him that most of his fellow students "regarded me as somebody who just stood outside what they were standing for altogether"; also, his Methodist heritage contrasted to the "dominating *ethos*," there, which was "Presbyterian and doctrinal" (*NFIC*, 60).

A recurring topic of discussion with the various ministers to whom he was "dragged" by his mother during summer vacations from college was his aptitude for their vocation. To one of them he confessed he "worried" about his "own personal cowardice"; temperamentally, he was "easily disheartened by failure, badly upset by slights, retiring and sensitive" (*NFN* 6 [Fall 1994], 13). The clergyman's response to this self-abasement was the suggestion that he "put on the armour of Christ"; Frye thought this Pauline injunction "good advice," though adding that a "thick skin" was his basic need.

Very different from this self-depiction of himself as a social craven (very natural for a twenty-one year old in the process of developing a persona or social role) is the perception of himself as "one of Jung's feeling types, a sensor of occasions" (*NFN* 5 [Summer 1993], 35). A "sensor of occasions" is exemplified by the chairperson with an aptitude for "collecting" and expressing "the sense of the meeting" (*NFN* 5 [Summer 1993], 35). An introvert will usually rely upon either extraverted "thinking" or "feeling," according to Jung. A gloss Frye wrote upon this pair of types contrasts a "hard-driving aggressive person" to someone who depends upon his feelings; the choice in fact for Frye is actually between "aggressive" and "receptive" forms of thinking (*MM*, 178). With the help of Frye's identification of himself as "one of Jung's feeling types," he can be seen, in his own terms, as a "receptive" thinker. Nuancing these terms is quite productive for the understanding of a dimension of his character such as the glowing picture of himself as a "professional rhetorician, the saviour of occasions, the person in constant demand for convocation addresses ... and church services" (*NFN* 5 [Summer 1993], 35). On these occasions, Frye displayed his capacity for being relational as well as using his intuitive perception of what the particular situation or audience required. The impression he usually made upon others was that of an unpretentious, deferential, and patient person. He was probably congenial with those with whom he was intimate (the nickname they used, "Norrie," seems to fit). There is a slightly pastoral cast in the concern he displays for those around him.

If Frye was right in saying that he was "one of Jung's feeling types," then he was unlikely or rather less likely to be an "aggressive" thinker—the kind of person who is often abrupt, assertive, and, as he says, "impatient with the untidiness of people who never seem to understand that the shortest distance between two points is a straight line"—a linear thinker (*MM*, 178). Harold Bloom's characterization of Frye as a "reconciler not a quarreler" is apt (1957, 133). Moreover, as a "receptive thinker," he characteristically relies, works through, or is responsive to others' thought. Somewhat as a poet relies upon Muses, Frye often expresses himself through intellectual mentors: some are the poets and others are myth theorists.

The least developed element in Frye's character is "extraverted sensation." His classmates at Moncton perhaps recognized this deficiency in nicknaming him "the Professor," for they perceived someone who, as he says, was "never very well coordinated" and retained a lifelong disinterest in sports (*WGS*, 324). Nonclassical music was dismissed by him as "an evil spirit trying to get born and not succeeding" (*RW*, 178). He never learned to drive a car. He seems to have regarded external nature largely with indifference.

The real Northrop Frye is the books he bequeathed us. Fifteen of the thirty books to have been published by the time of his death in 1991 or thereafter have the words "study" or "essay" in the title or subtitle. His more important or extended works deploy one or the other of these terms:

> *Fearful Symmetry: A Study of William Blake* (1947)
> *Anatomy of Criticism: Four Essays* (1957)
> *A Study of English Romanticism* (1968)
> *The Critical Path: An Essay on the Social Context of Literary Criticism* (1971)
> *The Secular Scripture: A Study of the Structure of Romance* (1976)
> *The Great Code: The Bible and Literature* (1982)
> *Words with Power: Being a Second Study of "The Bible and Literature"* (1990)

Notice that the last subtitle suggests that this book's predecessor is also a "study." In the first book on our list, he says that "a study" of Blake's "relation to English literature is" what he has "attempted" (*FS*, 3). The second book begins by defining "essays" as "attempts": "this book consists of 'essays,' in the word's original sense of a trial or incomplete attempt" (*AC*, 3).

He attempts in the first book to place Blake in the central line of mythopoetic poets, in defiance of the then existing body of Blake criticism, which usually cast the poet as an eccentric and dismissed his "prophetic" poems as an anomaly. Frye's second book assays to introduce his and others' myth criticism into the body of extant literary critical methods or practices. This effort is only part of his ambitious attempt at a "systematic study of the formal causes of art" (*AC*, 29). The four story types, in *Anatomy*, are continuous literary traditions. *A Study of English Romanticism* revises that assumption. The four story types are now said to have been transformed (*SER*, 35): his thesis is that the era introduced an elemental "change in the structure of literature" (*SER*, 4). In *The Critical Path*, "the social function" of literary criticism is explored through a review of traditional defenses of literature and education until arriving at questions of political and non-ideological myth. He articulates a dual vision of a "myth of concern" continuously modified by a "myth of freedom." *The Secular Scripture* treats prose romances, focusing especially upon foundational Greek, Roman, and Christian texts. He reverts to the assumption of the *Anatomy* that there is a continuous tradition of romance, but he now considers it less as the direct descendant of Biblical and Classical myths than as itself an autonomous mythic structure—a secular scripture. The titles, *The Great Code* and *Words with Power*, suggest that the Bible has continuously informed secular literature and presents metaphors to live by even today.

Each of these seven books opens something unattempted in any previous work. Yet it is still a matter of convenience to frame his works by means of a set of distinctions he often applied. He observed that "Kierkegaard divided his works into the 'aesthetic' or 'literary'" and a later stage "where he spoke in his own name as an 'ethical' writer or teacher" (*WP*, 116). "Poetic," a term intermediate between "aesthetic" and "literary," is my choice for designating the initial stage of Frye's works.

Fearful Symmetry aims "to establish Blake as a typical poet and his thinking as typically poetic thinking" (*FS*, 424). "Poetic" was the term Frye desired to use as part of the title for what became, courtesy of Princeton University Press, *Anatomy of Criticism*. His earliest working title was *A Defense of Poetics*, which has the merit of placing his book within the generic grouping starting with Philip Sidney's *A Defense of Poetry*, which in turn stems from Aristotle's *Poetics* (Ayre, 253). Another of the author's choices was *Essay on Poetics* (Ayre, 238). This title points towards the attempt at producing a work that is grounded in Aristotle yet expressive of our era. Another of his choices, *Structural Poetics: Four Essays*, seems to place his literary critical effort within a broad front of structuralist efforts in related fields; and the subtitle points to the uniform attempt, across the four parts of his book, to recreate an existing area of study into his own synthetic "structure" (Ayre, 252). In any case, the word "poetic" does make its way into *Fables of Identity: Studies in Poetic Mythology* (1963). The word provides a caption, as much as any such word can, for the works of the first period of his writing career.

The contrast between "poetic" and "ethical" elicits certain changes. The impersonal tone modulates into a more personal voice. His earliest books bristle with the word "theory" and frequently employ a pseudo-logical jargon. Perhaps several of Frye's generic definitions provide another difference. His earlier books present themselves in what he calls the "the Aristotelian treatise-book form" (*NFCL*, 172), while later works are often more like what he designates as "a teacher's book [which] adopts bewilderingly complex means in order to produce an effect of massive simplicity" (*NFCL*, 137). He may have learned many of these techniques from writers such as Freud and Spengler, whom he says present "central themes" with "massive simplicity" (*RW*, 323).

Kierkegaard's full division of an author's works concludes with a "religious" dimension that follows from an early "aesthetic" and then from an "ethical" category. Probably the word "Biblical" is more appropriate for Frye's final group of works. He now mentions his "own personal encounter with the Bible" (*GC*, xi). The encounter was continuous from almost the beginning of his life; it was present almost from the beginning of his teaching career, since he very early on regularly taught a course on the Bible. The difference between his first works and his books on the Bible and literature at the close of his career is that, as he says, an early aesthetic attitude produces "comprehensive intellectual systems" (*CP*, 128) where the final books

11

withdraw from the theoretical pretensions of the initial ones, are less academic in orientation, and are guide or "teaching" books.

The rest of Frye's books cannot be subsumed under our three categories. Some of them are popularizations of his major works. He wrote continuously on Blake, who thus receives attention in each of his seven collections of essays.[7] The most sheerly "poetic" of these collections, *Fables of Identity*, opens with a section of four essays related to *Anatomy*. *The Educated Imagination* covers much of the same ground as *Anatomy*, but in the popular format appropriate to what were initially radio addresses. *The Well-Tempered Critic* revises the fourth essay of the *Anatomy*. *Creation and Recreation* and *The Double Vision* are sets of lectures connected with his Bible and literature project.

Frye wrote books on Milton and Eliot. Four more are on Shakespeare. Each of the four consists of genre study, though one places a group of comedies traditionally called "problem comedies" in the light of the Old Testament story of the Exodus or deliverance. The last of the four, *Northrop Frye on Shakespeare*, is a version of his classroom lectures that cuts across Shakespeare's genres.

On Education, among the more "ethical" of his works, collects addresses on that topic from 1957 to 1985. Another later collection, *Reading the World: Selected Writings, 1935-1976*, is divided by editor Robert Denham into sections that roughly mirror many of the emphases over his career: "On the Performing Arts" and "On Painting" are followed by "On Criticism" and "On Literature," and all these might be designated as products of his relatively "poetic" area of interest. The "ethical" dimension appears in the groups "On Education" and "On Culture and Society." The area that Kierkegaard calls "religious" is represented by "On Religion" and his sermons.

CHAPTER TWO

FRYE AND HIS MYTH THEORISTS

Frye's early response to Frazer and Spengler resembles Joseph Campbell's at nearly the same time. Campbell placed *The Golden Bough* among the company of books he considered as personal bibles. He approached Spengler's major work with equal devotion, reading it seven times within the decade after he had encountered it.[1] John Ayre's *Northrop Frye: A Biography* gives us a few glimpses of Frazer and more of Spengler as they affect Frye who came across both their major works quite accidentally. The present chapter is largely a story of how these personal discoveries, as they intertwined with his reading of Blake, led into his book on Blake.

According to Ayre, a public library was established in Moncton in "early 1927" (48). Frye "became a volunteer at the front desk checking books in and out" (48); and there encountered a few volumes of *The Golden Bough*, which the library kept "hidden behind" the circulation desk (124).[2] During his second year at Victoria (1930-31), "he discovered in the small Hart House library," a theater building to which Frye's interest in drama frequently brought him, Spengler's work (65).[3]

The period in which he "practically slept" with the *Decline* "under my pillow for several years" began in his second year at Victoria (*RW*, 321). Rereading it in the early summer of 1931 "set off the first of several epiphanic experiences which turned vague personal ambitions into one great vision," suggests Ayre (68). Frye in fact compares *this* event with the Blake experience (of February 1934). "The same thing happened": "suddenly" a "vision of coherence" came to him in which "things began to form patterns and make sense" as he read the *Decline* (*NFIC*, 48). This is the same interpretation he applies to his experience of Blake, which is also a "vision of coherence" in which "things began to form patterns and make sense" (*NFN* 3 [Winter 1990-91], 5). When Frye adds that he "had two or three nights" with "sudden visions of that kind," he may perhaps be linking the Blake with the Spengler experience.

His reaction to Frazer's *Golden Bough* later in the same year as the Blake experience (1934) is just as hyperbolic or revelatory as his response to Spengler three years earlier. Just as his visceral response to Blake sounds like a conversion experience ("the universe just broke open" for him, so that he was "never... the same man again"), so with Frazer he experiences

> A whole new world opening out ... My ideas are expanding and taking shape so quickly [that] they frighten me; and I get seized with terror sometimes that somebody else will think them out before I do. (Ayre, 106)

In one case, it had felt as if a "universe just broke open," and in the other "a whole new world" was "opening out." He suggests, now interpreting his Blake experience, that such experience may relate to his writing or vocation ("visions of what I myself might be able to do" (*NFN* 3 [Winter 1990-91], 5). After reading Frazer, he even became anxious about priority: he wished to be the first in his newly chosen field of literary studies to apply Frazer's ideas. Among these three intuitive episodes, he says it was the earliest—his summer 1931 reading of Spengler—that provided the "experience I never expect to duplicate," even though his responses to Blake and Frazer during 1934 elicit in Frye closely related accounts or interpretations (*RW*, 321).

Spengler provided a cultural backdrop for the Biblical and literary superhighway that Frye constructs in his first two books: "The sense of the whole of human thought and culture" given by the metahistorian appeared as if "spread out in front of me," like a map. His Blake experience helped him map out a mythopoetic thoroughfare extending from the Bible to Milton and Blake. While Spengler is said to provide a road map spread out in front of him, the Blake experience figuratively allowed him to place himself upon the Biblical landscape. What the response to Frazer adds to the earlier experiences is the sense of a literary critical approach, a mythical approach that, as Frye says, "is the very life-blood of art," and its "historical basis" (Ayre, 106). The dying and rising god pattern is foundational for Frye.

Frye's first several books are expressions of these three early visions. He served as an apprentice to both these sorcerers during the time he worked upon *Fearful Symmetry* and gradually become a master of the artistry of their comparative methods.

While the 1934 Blake paper probably no longer exists, the other student papers he wrote, after encountering Spengler, often are straightforward Spenglerian expositions. A debate reported upon in Victoria's undergraduate magazine said that "Mr. Frye, calling upon his patron saint, Oswald Spengler ... presented a sweeping "survey" of "the whole field of Western culture" (Ayre, 73). His longest paper at Victoria was a 100 page essay on Romanticism, which Ayre says was "faithful to his epiphanic experience" in the summer of 1931 with the *Decline* and is an "overview of Romanticism which was heavily influenced by Spengler's opus" (81).

An essay in 1933 when he was twenty-one takes its ideas straight from Spengler without ever mentioning him. Frye pronounces the need for a "philosophy of history" in any literary historical framework (*RW*, 125). The literary critic is to track "the evolution of art forms" across the landscape of literature which is congruent with his notion that Spengler's work began as a "meditation on the destiny of art forms" (*RW*, 125; *NFIC*, 61). Even though the critic presents an "evolution," he should assume (with Spengler) that "each age has its own inevitable forms of expression" (*RW*, 126). A synchronic species of comparativism enters because, though writers live in different eras, they occupy a "homologous position" (a staple of Spengler's jargon) within their eras, and so authors in one can be compared with those in another era. Thus Henry James, who occupies center stage in our era, is comparable with the central writer of the Renaissance, Shakespeare!

Five years later, in 1938, Frazer's sheerly developmental approach is present in an essay on Surrealism. The Surrealist painters, Frye says, "began to realize that the subconscious speaks a universal ... language" from which "all myths of all religions and all the effective imagery are derived" (*RW*, 36). The threefold repetition of "all" perhaps points toward the universalism of Frazer, and the final verb postulates an origin, a hidden or "subconscious" language that leads out into an immense developmental pattern. Following Frazer and also Freud, Frye conceives of an origin that somehow fans out; in this case, it spreads out into language, religious myths, and art. Frye has chosen to characterize a very complex set of possibilities by positing an origin in the manner of Frazer and Freud, yet in decided contrast to his own later way of thinking.

Around 1941 Frye further clarified his outlook on his Blake project. The context for treating the line of Blake's prophetic poems in their chronological order would avoid placing them in their literary historical period and would instead present "an encyclopedic overview" (Ayre, 176). The intuitive transition of his 1934 Blake paper, the exchange of an historical era for a mythological framework, perhaps crystallized in the decision to adopt a comparative approach. The technique is to compare a particular prophetic poem with others like it on a canvas encompassing both the Bible and an English mythopoetic tradition starting with Chaucer and ending with Blake.

According to Ayre, Frye at this time also had an intuitive "breakthrough" which evoked a "Blakean image at the core of his analysis" (177). "The image of the rebellious" character in Blake named Orc is that of his "overthrowing the senile Urizen" (178). Ayre suggests this image is problematic "because it suggested an ever-repeating natural cycle" (178). From our point of view, this perpetual natural cycle is identical with Frazer's annually dying and rising god: "Orc," from this point of view, is Blake's "Adonis, the dying and reviving god of his mythology" (*FS*, 207). Moreover, "human history, no less than the natural world, has a cyclic rhythm of decline and revival" because every historical culture is an expression of this rhythm (*FS*, 209).

The relationship that Frye perceived between Blake's characters, Orc and Urizen, is cyclical since "Orc becomes the geriatric Urizen" (178). If we retain this "image of the rebellious Orc overthrowing the senile Urizen" (178), then we are no further along than the opening of *The Golden Bough*, where Frazer foreshadows his dying and rising god pattern by displaying the process in which a younger, stronger man would attack, kill, and replace an older one and thus become "King of the Wood" for a time until some younger man "did the same thing to him" (*NFCL*, 86).

The same quandary occurs when the Orc-Urizen relationship is examined by Frye through his Spenglerian perspective. The only thing it continually displays is the movement of Orc through the organic stage of development that Spengler associates with "culture" and becoming Urizen in a final, dead-end stage. Seen this way, "the cycle finally dies in a wild cancerous tissue of huge machinery, a blankly materialist philosophy ... mass wars," and so on which is Spengler's picture of the dead hulk of culture he calls "civilization" (*FS*, 211).

Frye said in 1935 that he had entered into a "Black Hole" almost immediately after his initial Blake paper (*LNF*, 179). He seems to have begun finding his way out of it around 1941 when he says that he "seriously" set to work on what became a sequence of five drafts of the Blake manuscript (*NFIC*, 51).

If Ayre is right in saying that the 1934 Blake paper, the final draft of 1945 of the manuscript, and much of the material in the earlier drafts no longer exist, then statements about the development of Frye's understanding of Blake between 1934 and 1947 are necessarily speculative.

My own speculation is that Frye tended to import his readings of Frazer and Spengler into Blake, that they were helpfully applied to what he calls the Orc-Urizen cycle, and that the "black hole" of which he speaks is his difficulty in showing how Blake transcended that cycle. If Frye were merely a servile follower of Frazer and Spengler, then Blake's prophetic poems could only be displayed as specimens illustrating natural or historical cycles. The advance which may have begun around 1941 perhaps involved a critical departure from or at least a more flexible application of the ideas of "culture heroes" of his "student days" (*SM*, 111).

Like many a romance hero, Frye succeeded upon his third attempt. He submitted several chapters in May or June of 1938 to Faber and Faber at the end of his first year at Oxford. A draft of the manuscript was also rejected by a Canadian subsidiary of Random House in February 1944. A year later, Princeton University Press nearly rejected another draft; following a revision which changed the structure of the submitted draft and deleted 170 pages, *Fearful Symmetry* was published by Princeton in 1947.

The question to address to *Fearful Symmetry*, in a consideration of Frye on myth, is how Frazer and Spengler influenced it. As with the *Anatomy*, anything resembling explicit acknowledgment by any myth theorist comes only decades after the book. A generation after *Fearful Symmetry*, he discovered, as if by coincidence, that "the phrase 'dying god' that he had applied to a Blake character "suggests Frazer" (*St. S*, 189). He adds that "Blake's Druid symbolism has some remarkable anticipations of Frazer's *Golden Bough* complex of symbolism," as if there were only a slight connection between an abstruse spectrum of Blakean symbolism and the entire *Golden Bough*. Similarly, "in Blake's later prophecies, we do find [a] Spenglerian view of history, with a good many of Spengler's symbols attached to it" (*St. S*, 184).

In *Fearful Symmetry*, explicit reference to Frazer and Spengler occurs only once each. In speaking of "the Frazers of their day," Frye refers to a pair of minor mythographers who he thinks affected Blake; he associates them with Rev. Edward Casaubon, the character in George Eliot's *Middlemarch* who fails to produce a *Key to All Mythologies* (*FS*, 174). The hackneyed expression "Spenglerian pessimism" is the sole reference to the metahistorian (*FS*, 219). The technique, in these allusions, is to distance himself from them, perhaps for the reason that few academic reputations would have been served by advertising one's reliance upon them, especially upon Spengler.

Frye regarded the project of his initial book as an attempt "to crack Blake's symbolic code" (*CP*, 13). He acknowledges only that there is some rough connection between his book and the "*Golden Bough* complex of symbolism" or "Spengler's symbols" (*St. S*, 189, 184). The several dozen passages in *Fearful Symmetry* that appear to draw upon either Frazer or Spengler are usually more nearly adaptations than adoptions of their ideas. By contrast, straightforward comparison is deployed when Frye draws upon either Freud or Jung. Freud, who even makes his way into Frye's index, is said to articulate belatedly a "newer Myth of much the same shape" as one in Blake's *Four Zoas*: "the three fallen" characters in Blake's poem, "Urizen, Tharmas and Luvah," whom the poet "identifies with the 'Head,' 'Heart,'" and "'Loins' respectively," correspond to Freud's superego, libido, and id (*FS*, 300-1). Among the glosses of Blake that come from Jung is

Frye's portrait of the development of the "egocentric" man into an individuated self (*FS*, 348-49).

Frye seems to have encountered the writings of Freud and Jung during the 1930s, to have read Jung in depth after *Fearful Symmetry*, and to have assimilated certain of their ideas during the 1940s and 1950s. A diary he wrote during the first half of 1949 is "filled with references to Jung," and one of them indicates an intention of following up an intensive reading of Jung with a close reading of Freud: "I think I've pretty well got the hang of Jung and should start serious work on Freud now" (Ayre, 217). Ayre suggests that he had "seriously returned" to his readings in Jung beginning in "1947-48" following publication of *Fearful Symmetry* (Ayre, 425). Among the reasons for this postponement was his fear that the book might be "overwhelmed by Jungian thought" (Ayre, 425).

By 1957 when *Anatomy* was published, he had written essays on Spengler (in 1936, 1947, and 1955), and reviewed works by Jung (1953) and Cassirer (1954). A popular exposition of Frazer's life and works appeared in 1959. Frye never produced an essay on Freud though his explicit references to him are more frequent than to any of our myth theorists.

As a rule, Frye's references to Freud are more objective, detached, and concrete than his allusions to Jung. Though he says that he was "continually asked" about his "relation to Jung," and especially about the relation of their uses of the word "archetype," he usually distances himself from Jung (*SM*, 117). With Cassirer, to whom he refers least, Frye also maintains an ironic relationship. When, for example, he mentions that "some philosophers" proceed to "replace individual objects with their total forms," he means Cassirer, the philosopher of symbolic forms; when he says that "allegorists represent their total forms by individuals," he perhaps refers primarily to Jung, though Frazer and Freud are often also thought of by Frye as allegorists (*FI*, 249). Frye's relationships to Frazer and to Spengler are the easiest to perceive. They are the figures with whom our study of him as a "myth theorist" begins, not only because he encountered them first but because he offers so many helpful perceptions of their effect upon him. He allows that "their conceptions seem to get into and inform everything I worked on," though he then backtracks and limits their influence (*SM*, 111).

CHAPTER THREE

SPENGLER

A theorist usually employs his key term in a variety of ways. Spengler attaches great significance to his term "prime symbol," for instance, but it is perhaps the most elusive term in the *Decline*.[1] Ernst Cassirer's "symbolic form" has been shown to have four distinct meanings.[2] The term "myth," in the *Anatomy of Criticism*, has a different meaning attached to it in each of its four essays.[3] It is often a productive procedure, when entering into a work or body of work, to notice the interrelationships among the different meanings a theorist assigns to his crucial term.[4] The present essay begins with a brief survey of the meanings Frye gives "myth" in the *Anatomy*. Then, after a biographical sketch of metahistorian Oswald Spengler, I indicate why Frye, as a literary critic, found Spengler a productive influence on the topic of myth.

Frye's procedure in the *Anatomy* is simply to expand the meaning he attaches to myth through the four essays. In the first, he uses it "in the common sense of a story about a god" (33). By the opening of the second essay, "myth" has come to mean "plot" (52) or "narrative" (53, 72).[5] Myth then becomes more complex. In the third essay, he states that there are "two fundamental movements of narrative: a cyclical movement within the order of nature, and a dialectical movement from that order into the apocalyptic world above" (161-62). The halves of this essay differ in that they track one or another of these narrative movements. The first half starts with "the world above," as portrayed in "the book explicitly called the Apocalypse or Revelation, which has been carefully designed to form an undisplaced mythical conclusion to the Bible as a whole" (141). For literary critics, the final book of the Bible "is our grammar of apocalyptic imagery" (141) and the point of departure for Frye's "grammar of literary archetypes" for Western literature as a whole (135).

The argument of the earlier part of the essay is relatively fragmentary. Indeed, Frye's later works can be read as a series of efforts to fill in some of the points this portion of the *Anatomy* presents obliquely. Still, he suggests here that poets do not just receive or inherit "symmetrical cosmology" but help produce it. He argues that there is an analogy between the way "classical mythology became purely poetic" after Christianity replaced it and the way the "Ptolemaic universe" became "a framework of poetic symbols after" it had "lost its validity as science" (161). Notice that the analogy is between the fate of Classical religion and mythology and the fate of Christian literature and mythology. Frye assumes that religion and literature share mythology. One cannot *demythologize* the Bible any more than one can discard the symmetrical cosmology through which Dante and Milton express themselves: the "conception of a heaven above, a hell beneath, and a cyclical cosmos or order of nature in between," is no ornament, but "forms the ground plan" of their works (161).

The second half of this essay proceeds along a different track. His scope is almost entirely confined to an elaborate analogy between the "cyclical movement within the order of nature" and "four main types of mythical movement" that occupy the landscape of literature (162). In this section of the essay Frye has almost entirely severed literature from religion since he is surveying the landscape of the secular literature of the West. This landscape consists of four different kinds of "mythical movement," four distinct "*mythoi*," or story types: romance, tragedy, satire, and comedy. All four are parts of "the quest myth" of the hero. The quest myth constitutes for him a "central unifying myth" (192). Leaving aside the questions of why it is "central" and how it unifies, let us ask what sense of "myth" Frye uses. A note attached to the phrase indicates that he is relating this sense of myth to the body of work done on the hero myth by Joseph Campbell (*The Hero with a Thousand Faces*) and others. These mythographers have studied a variety of religious and legendary heroes and have sometimes included what we would think of as literary figures such as Aeneas along with religious figures and gods. Within his circle of story types, however, Frye restricts himself to literary figures. For instance, he distinguishes romance from myth by insisting upon the humanness of the romance hero and the confinement of his setting to our human world:

> The [hero's] enemy may be an ordinary human being, but the nearer the romance to myth, the more attributes of divinity will cling to the hero and the more the enemy will take on demonic mythical qualities. The central form of romance is dialectical: everything is focused on a conflict between the hero and his enemy, and all the reader's values are bound up with the hero. Hence the hero of romance is analogous to the mythical Messiah or deliverer who comes from an upper world, and his enemy is analogous to the demonic powers of a lower world. The conflict however takes place in, or at any rate primarily concerns, *our* world. (187)

What Frye mentions in the last sentence—that our world is in the middle of higher and lower worlds—helps clarify his phrase "central unifying myth." This "myth" pertains to the natural landscape of the human world that is in between the worlds above and below it. This middle world tends to receive its unity by the imagery from the natural cycle the writer chooses. The writer of romance deploys contrastive imagery, so that his "enemy is associated with winter, darkness, confusion, sterility, moribund life, and old age, and the hero with spring, dawn, order, fertility, vigor, and youth" (187-88). The "archetypal theme" of romance is "conflict," and the writer of romance tends to polarize his imagery in presenting the conflict (192). The "complete form," which is not necessarily found in any particular literary romance but which Frye thinks has the typical episodes of the form as a whole, consists of four elemental episodes, or "archetypal themes" (187-92). His four archetypal themes "may now be seen" (192) in relation to his earlier circular diagram of the natural cycle" (162). The themes may also be seen as Frye's version of a Spenglerian pattern. Spengler's "central symbol" for the whole of Western culture is for Frye "a center with radiating points" (*SM*, 183). Frye situates his four archetypal themes within the complete form of romance in particular and at the hub of his circle of story types. From that center they can be seen as the "seeds" embedded in Western mythology, both Christian and Classical, which gradually develop or radiate outwards into what becomes the landscape of Western literature. For Spengler, every culture, including the West, has a "mother-landscape behind all" its "expression-forms" (*Decline*, II, 278). Western culture began "on the unpromising soil of France" in the Middle Ages with the "sudden and swiftly mounting" appearance of "German-Catholic Christianity," which he also designates as a distinct "mythic world" (II, 288). In Spengler, the seed-ideas of a culture develop through eight or so "expression-forms" such as art and politics. In Frye, literature has four expression-forms or story types. In Spengler, the seed-ideas of a mythic-religious world are all synchronically present, but they move through an organic rhythm of growth, maturity, and decline like everything else in nature. In Frye, there is an initial "mythic mode," in which religious and literary ideas, characters, formulas, and themes are present; subsequently, they move through four distinct stages of development, though the last stage is not, as in Spengler, terminal. Spengler declares that Western culture *is* well into its decline. Frye only suggests that it is possible to look at the whole of Western culture *as if* its entire mythic heritage, as expressed through the four literary traditions of romance, tragedy, satire, and comedy, had come to an end. Spengler's synchronic vision of Western culture presents it as a single work of art, with all its different expression-forms as interrelated units of cultural history moving through the same stages of development and decline. As A. C. Hamilton says of Spengler, the "unifying or mythical shape" of a culture "gives meaning to everything, for everything in a culture—especially the arts—expresses its essential nature. Everything exists within a system of symbolic distinctions; accordingly, each thing is part of a synchronous totality" (Hamilton 1990, 56). Frye's circle of story types is a synchronic apprehension of the whole of Western secular literature.

The fourth essay closes with "myth" seen in relation to sacred rather than secular literature.[6] He ends the essay with a sweeping perspective on the Bible and literature, and, in fact, his vision of both can be found in each of the essays.[7] He shifts from a synchronic perspective to a developmental one. For him, secular encyclopedic and epic forms of literature descend from or develop out of "the definitive myth" of Western culture: the Bible. He now contrasts the secular, or romance quester whom he had treated in the third essay to the "Messianic myth" (317) —the "heroic quest" of Christ (316).

From this rapid survey of the *Anatomy*—of course the essays will be treated in the more detailed fashion they deserve in later chapters— we are now in a position to perceive what Frye does with the term "myth."[8] Initially the subject of myth is any character in a god-story: "God for the [literary] critic, whether he finds him in *Paradise Lost* or the Bible, is a character in a human story" (*FI*, 18). Yet by the end of the *Anatomy* the subject of "myth" is the god-man Jesus Christ, whose story is much the same as the events in "all the dying-god myths," such as Dionysus, yet who is somehow different (192). The "heroic quest" of Christ has the same "stages and symbols" that romantic questers have, yet it is He who is treated as if their prototype because "romantic encyclopedic forms use human or sacramental imitations of the Messianic myth," as in "the quest of Dante in the *Commedia*, of St. George in Spenser, and of the knights of the Holy Grail" in various medieval and Renaissance writers (316, 317). Frye also thinks of myth as plot, though he expands the notion of plot as he goes along: first, to the narrative of any fictional work, then to the total plot of secular literature as a whole, the quest-myth, which he finds in the "complete form" of romance, and, finally, to the creation-through-apocalypse plot of the Bible from Genesis through Revelation.

Perhaps the most distinctive of these meanings is the expressionistic sense Frye gives myth in the third essay. Both his grammar of literary imagery and his circle of story types are playing fields, or landscapes, upon which the expression of the meaning of a reader's literary experience can take place. In a notebook entry he wrote late in life, he describes himself as a "great 20th century reader" and others have frequently made similar remarks about him (*NFN* 5 [Summer 1993], 27). The circle of story types is a chessboard on which one can learn to play; by watching Frye as he positions innumerable works, characters, and virtually any element of literary experience he or a reader can recognize, he invites us to enter into this imaginative game.[9] Frye provides the same kind of exhilarating experience he says Spengler provided for him: "the sense of the whole of human thought and culture spread out in front of one" like a map (*SM*, 194).

Among the five theorists whom Frye had read prior to writing the *Anatomy*, he encountered Frazer and Spengler earliest. On the topic of myth, Spengler is far more significant for him. The reasons are easy to discern. Frazer subsumes myth under religion. Spengler thinks myth and religion together. They are for him fused in his initial phase of any historical culture, the "mythopoetic" era (*Decline*, I, 399). After that, there is a reformation. There follows a period of Enlightenment, which squeezes myth out of religion. Finally, the pale cast of myth is disembodied from religion in a period of "second religiousness" so that only spectral ideas remain, as in theosophy and the occult. Myth, in its organic rather than disembodied form, exists for Spengler when the historical culture is created. He differs from Frazer and most theorists of myth in assigning it entirely to historical and not primitive culture.[10] For a literary critic, concerned primarily with written rather than oral literature, Spengler's assumption about myth is far more productive than Frazer's is.

Spengler was born in the town of Blankenburg in the Harz Mountains of Germany in 1880. Like Frye, he tried his hand at creative writing during his early years. A recurrent theme of his stories is that "an artist cannot fulfill his creative potentialities in a decaying culture" (Fischer, 35).

Though his university studies were principally in the natural sciences, along with mathematics, Spengler also was strongly attracted to the humanities, especially Classics, which was also Frazer's field of study. His doctoral thesis was on the pre-Socratic philosopher Heraclitus. He worked for five years as a secondary school teacher, starting in 1905. The subjects he taught reflect his extensive interests: mathematics, the physical sciences, and German history and literature. When his mother passed away in 1910, he inherited enough to leave his job permanently and resume his passion for writing. Because his interests were so varied, his problem was what kind of writer he would be. His solution was to pack all his interests into a lengthy, two-volume work.

Spengler grasped intuitively the plan of this work all at once in 1912, much as Cassirer conceived the project of writing his philosophy of symbolic forms five years later.[11] As he looked through the window of a bookstore one day, his gaze happened to fix upon the word "fall" or "decline" in a book by Otto Seeck, the *History of the Decline of Antiquity* (Fischer, 43). Spengler then envisioned, by analogy, the project of writing what became *The Decline of the West*. By the time of the outbreak of World War I in 1914, he had completed a draft of his first volume, then expanded and revised it until, after many unsuccessful tries, he found a publisher in 1918. His second volume came out in 1922, and by then the first had sold over 100,000 copies.[12]

These two volumes were entitled *Der Untergang des Abendlandes*, which means literally "The Going Under of the Twilight (or Evening) Lands" or, more freely, "The Twilight and Fall of Cultures." They were translated into English, in 1926 and 1928, as *The Decline of the West*. Frye encountered this work in the spring of 1931 when an undergraduate.[13] For Spengler, the final stage of a culture is its tragic winter-death. The West was now well advanced in the same decline every prior culture had gone through. Frye does not share this tragic perspective on the West. Much more important is the view he takes of Spengler' initial, not terminal, phase of history. For both Spengler and Frye, this period is a "mythopoetic" era. Spengler's initial historical phase and Frye's initial literary or writing culture are equally mythopoetic.

Like some poets, Blake for instance, and like Frye himself, Spengler was an introverted intuitive person. By Kierkegaard's categories, the *Decline* belongs to an "aesthetic" stage. According to Jung, people like him reveal "strange, far-off things" in their art, "shimmering in all colours, at once portentous and banal, beautiful and grotesque, sublime and whimsical" (Jung 1971, 262). Even in 1936, the year Spengler died, Frye spoke of the *Decline* as a work of "massive simplicity" (*RW*, 323). It applied a tragic plot, a "'decline and fall' *mythos*," to our culture; it gave "complete expression to a myth which had been widely accepted" by many "for a century" (*MM*, 9; *FI*, 224). "All" such "myths are oversimplified diagrammatic formulas" which require from us the "qualifying [of] their symmetry" (*MM*, 9).

The formulaic pattern is apparent in the foldout charts in the back of the *Decline*. The left-hand column of these charts has the four seasons descending, so that the similarities among four of the eight historical cultures can be discerned. The initial table begins with the "Birth of a Myth" in every springtime era. "Myth" is here synonymous with his more frequent term, "prime symbol," which is an "oversimplified diagrammatic formula." A Reformation, in summer, is followed by an autumn Enlightenment, and the culmination is the winter-death period of a "Megapolitan Civilization." These cultural developments all have conveniently rounded thousand-year histories. Each is confined to a particular geographical landscape. They are impermeable to influence from cultures adjacent to them in space or preceding them in time.

Spengler's depiction of Classical culture is shaped by Nietzsche, and his portrayal of Western culture stems from Goethe. The *leitmotif* of the *Decline* is the systematic contrast between these cultures. The myths they are born with, their prime symbols, are antithetical. Everything in Classical culture is directed inwards toward the "body," while Western culture starts from a "centre" and expands outwards toward the "infinite" (I, 178). Spengler's contrast is often taken over in Frye's recurrent distinction between centripetal and centrifugal movements.

In the *Decline* the mythic is contrasted to the primitive just as the religious is contrasted to civilization. While other myth theorists think "myths ... are creations of primitive man," Spengler believes that "myth-forming power" begins only when an historical culture does; like Athena emerging from Zeus, this "power" is born fully developed (I, 399). The other dichotomy, the one between living culture and dying civilization, involves their religiosity: "As the essence of every Culture is religion, [so] the essence of every Civilization is irreligion" (I, 358).

Frye develops Spengler on myth and qualifies him on religion. It is mainly Spengler's account of "second religiousness" that Frye finds instructive (*SM*, 195). Metropolitan civilization produces only spectral religious ideas, just as primitive cultures have inchoate fragments of myth. Negatively, second religiousness results in theosophy, the occult, and "New Age" spirituality. Positively, it is more like "second naiveté" in Paul Ricoeur's *The Symbolism of Evil*. Moderns are driven to imagine what the experience of religiosity may have been like in the past. We are as those who know only ourselves, cut off from what had been an organic religious tradition, bringing to it the dead faith of those who now happen to be alive and in quest of what thinkers such as John Ruskin and Jaroslav Pelikan call "the living faith of the dead."

Frye takes from Spengler the idea that the mythopoetic is confined to a single era, the foundational stage of a culture. "The mythopoetic power," according to Spengler, is "limited to particular periods": these "form-worlds of great myth" initiate every culture (I, 399). Besides Spengler's insistence that the mythic is the spontaneous creation of a historical and not primitive culture, there is another thing helpful to Frye: not only does Spengler introduce the mythic into his initial era, but he also dislodges the religious from its dominance there.

In Spengler, Christianity is removed from the later stage of Classical culture and the first stage of Western culture. As Roger Scruton puts it, even though "Christianity has its Magian, its late classical, and its Faustian manifestations, it is," throughout these stages, "the culture, rather than the religion that takes precedence"; in fact, "Christianity is," by this view, "not one but three quite separate religions."[14] Religion becomes but one of his eight areas of cultural activity. In any case, the mythic and the religious go together in both Spengler and Frye. Spengler's "form-world of great myth" and his "great world-image of a new religion" are two ways of saying the same thing (I, 20). Similarly, Frye can speak either of a "mythical" or "theogonic mode" (*AC*, 120).

Though Spengler thinks the mythic originates and is most fully expressed in the springtime stage of every culture, his contrast of Classical to Western makes the Western the exception to this rule. The mythic is continuous throughout Classical culture "from Homer [even] to the [Roman] tragedies of Seneca, a full thousand years, the same handful of myth figures [such as Hercules of Clytemnestra] appear time after time without alteration (I, 13). Though Frye says that the Classical culture went through its own set of stages, he treats it as if it comprised a monolithic and continuous mythical mode. At the center of it, he sets "the Christian Bible," in the "Vulgate tradition" which was continued by the Authorized Version and was thus "familiar to writers in Europe from the fifth century on" (*GC*, xiii). Spengler says that Classical literature and art "handled only the [subject] matter that was ... natural to it, the myth," but Frye places every Western writer in the situation which Spengler says that Classical writers occupy: the matrix or matter of all art is mythic. Spengler thinks that every culture has an indigenous landscape. Life upon that landscape is understandable, primarily, to those who reside upon it. Frye accepts the notion of a landscape, but not the topographical literalism. He returns to the longstanding view that was widely shared prior to what has been called "the eclipse of Biblical narrative." A typical statement of this view is John Calvin's: the Scriptures are the "spectacles" that help us "begin to read" our life in this world "distinctly" (*Institutes*, I, 70). Writers such as Milton or Bunyan allow their readers access to this imaginative landscape, which is resurrected in Blake and re-presented in the *Anatomy*.

"The poetry of the West," for Spengler, like every other area of its culture, is the opposite of the mythically informed Classical pattern (I, 13). The *same* mythic figures recur throughout Classical literature, but the characters of Western literature "are only fully understandable with reference to the historical background" of the distinct and different eras that produced them (I, 13). Parsifal, Hamlet, and Goethe's Faust are the expressions of the successive eras that produced them for Spengler. For Frye, by contrast, "every society is the embodiment of a myth," and writers, among them imaginative writers like Spengler whom we are calling "myth theorists," make and unmake the periods we live in because they "hold" the mythic "thunderbolts that destroy one society and create another" (*FI*, 147).

In Spengler, the prime symbol constitutes the culture. Everyone in a culture perceives through whatever the culture's mythic configuration or prime symbol is. Western culture's prime symbol is a dynamic center expanding outwards or upwards into infinity (I, 178). Or, in Frye's interpretation, Western culture "is strongly historical in sense, with a drive into infinite distance," and which is initially the symbol of a dynamic "center with radiating points" (*SM*, 183). One might say of Spengler what Frye does of Yeats, that a prime symbol, or mythic configuration, contains "the archetypal forms of human life" for a person in his culture (*SM*, 264). Spengler's prime symbol, as will be seen in the chapter on romance, is the core and container of "the archetypal forms," not of human life, "but of human imagination [or] a perfect circle of literary or mythical types" (*SM*, 264).

CHAPTER FOUR

THE MYTHS OF FRAZER AND SPENGLER

In *The Critical Path*, Frye states that he rewrites "his central myth in every book" (9). The reader might reasonably wish that an introduction to Frye on myth would provide an explanation of what he means. What is Frye's core myth? How are his books expressions of it? How can each of his books be a different expression of it? More modestly, how is the *Anatomy* an expression of Frye's myth?

The myth of the *Anatomy*, one might say, is that all literary works exist together upon a playing field that the imagination constructs.[1] His first essay begins with a god who can do anything in the world he desires; the second ends with a reader attaining god-like powers of perception.[2] The theological equivalent would perhaps be the Atonement since the reader who dies into any one work experiences a moment of at-one-ness with everything he has read. Philosophically, the reading of a single work somehow opens an "anagogic," or universal, level of meaning: the categories here have to do with particular and universal, units and unity, the one and the many. Any particular work, when entered into imaginatively, becomes the point of departure for a meditation that leads its reader into an intertextual universe that is purely literary and composed of everything he has previously assimilated. A later chapter will call this "the myth of the ideal reader." The myth is that the lifelong pursuit of reading will at some point involve a reader who is experiencing what his or her entire literary education has been about through some crowning synchronic moment of awareness (*NFN* 5 [Summer 1993], 27). The quest-myth of the *Anatomy* may consist of the reader's search for such epiphanic moments.

Another possibility is that the myth of the *Anatomy* is his assumption that "the mythical backbone of all literature is the cycle of nature" (*NP*, 119). The *Anatomy*'s circle of story types presents all of secular literature as if it belonged within or can be represented by the "natural cycle" (*AC*, 162). His moving circle of story types has its source in the rotation which the seasons undergo: is this the myth?[3]

With these several possibilities in mind, a detour through what Frye says about the myths of Frazer's *Golden Bough* and Spengler's *Decline of the West* helps us elucidate what Frye may mean about the myth of his own works. "Myth," as he applies it to their works (a sense of myth different from any we have encountered before), means an expressive configuration. Frazer's individual pattern of thought is as expressive as Spengler's because both works are the articulation of the concern or anxiety shared by many people. The difference between their myths, according to Frye, is that Frazer's myth expresses an anxiety common to everybody from primitive times through the present, while Spengler's expresses a concern characteristic of *our* time.

Frazer can help us see why Frye names his story types after the four seasons, so that comedy is the "*mythos* of spring," romance the "*mythos* of summer," and so on.[4] Frazer says "the spectacle of the great changes which annually pass over the earth has powerfully impressed the minds of men in all ages."[5] The most striking event in what Frye calls "the world that nature presents to us" (*NFCL*, 116) is for Frazer "the annual death and revival of vegetation," a "conception" that "presents itself to men in every stage of savagery and civilization" (Frazer 1922, 392). The cycle of nature is a constant to which humans have continually sought to relate, reconcile, or accommodate themselves. There are three relationships which humans have had with nature. These he designates as the primitive age of magic, the later age of religion, and the present age of science.[6]

Frye dismisses Frazer's three-stage schema—his "historical framework" —and works instead through an adaptation of Spenglerian metahistory (*NFCL*, 92). Yet Frye's circle of story types retains its association with the rhythm of nature across the diameter of his circle of story types.[7] He associates the rhythm of nature with the plot line of romance. The elementary themes of all four story types unfold like seeds from core elements within romance. His assumption that the four seasons are "the mythical backbone of all literature" is the assumption, hypothesis, or "myth" which he inherits from both Frazer and Spengler. Their organic rhythms are related in the *Anatomy*. The process of dying into and growing out of a natural landscape is integral to both Frazer and Spengler. Their individual versions are deliberately conflated in the *Anatomy*.

A. C. Hamilton suggests that Frye's circle of story types is the "turning wheel in a Spenglerian cycle of birth, growth, maturity, and death" (Hamilton 1990, 135). His observation applies to the circle as a whole. To it can be added Frye's remark, applicable to the hub of his circle, about Spengler's "central symbol" for Western culture, which Frye applies to Western literature and places at the center of his circle (*SM*, 183). Our culture is presented by Spengler through the spatial metaphor of "a center with radiating points"; "infinite expansion," or movement from the center outwards, is its predominant characteristic (*RW*, 324).

Though Spengler thinks of the temporally successive Classical, Magian, and Western cultures as autonomous, Frye does not. He views them in a developmental relationship: they die into and rise out of one another. The progression is that Christian culture becomes "at once the coffin of the old classical culture and the womb" from which Western culture emerges (*NFCL*, 79).

Frye conceives of these three cultures as interpenetrating or existing within a synchronic relationship; at the same time, the cultures also developed into or out of one another. He incorporates three features of Spengler's thought in his atemporal perspective. There is, first, Spengler's conception of the mythopoetic foundational stage or "springtime," (*Decline*, I, 399). This conception is displayed in the *Anatomy*'s perception of Classical and Christian myth as continually influencing Western literature. There is, perhaps, a relationship between Spengler's view of Magian culture as a "fairy tale" or romance world (with the Bible and the Arabian *The Thousand and One Nights* its representative works or symbols) and Frye's view of romance (II, 237; I, 248).

Within the "cycle of nature," Frye says, "the world of romance," at least initially, occupies the entire upper half of what becomes his circle of story types (*AC*, 162). Frye inscribes a line across his circle, which is the plot line of romance, and embedded within it are the seed-ideas, or archetypal themes, of all four story types in their embryonic form. Developmentally, all four of these embryonic forms exist as four elements or episodes within romance; synchronically, they are concentrated in the "seed-plot of literature" at the center of Frye's circle and within romance (*AC*, 122). They do not remain there, however; they become and (this is the third conception Frye adapts from Spengler) the "center with radiating points," which, though initially gathered or concentrated at the hub of Frye's circle, are capable of expansion outward.

Though Frye tends to link Spengler and Frazer, they make an unlikely couple. James Frazer (1854-1941) was born long before Spengler (1880-1936). Early in the century, Frazer was at the very center of social anthropology, somewhat as Frye was the cynosure of literary studies just after mid-century. Spengler never accepted an academic post. He was despised by most historians.[8]

Despite these and many other differences, Frye interrelates them as persons, often relative to what he perceives as their shared negative attributes. He calls them "rather stupid men and often slovenly scholars" (*C&R*, 8). Both were "extraordinarily limited and benighted in general intelligence and awareness of their world" (*SM*, 111). Though Frazer is merely a "vague" and "sentimental sort of Victorian liberal," Spengler is "the most stupid bastard I ever picked up" to read, because of his "muzzy, right-wing, Teutonic, folkish" mind (*NFCL*, 91; *NFN* 3 [Winter 1990-91], 6).

Since Spengler's *Decline* has already been introduced, Frazer's *Golden Bough* can be discussed briefly.[9] A compact overview of the book occurs in the prospectus he sent to his publisher just prior to its first edition in 1890. His comparative project focuses upon "the legend of *The Golden Bough*," as given by Servius, a fourth-century, late Roman commentator on Vergil's *Aeneid*:

> According to Servius the *Golden Bough* grew on a certain tree [the mistletoe] in the sacred grove of [the Roman goddess] Diana at Aricia [a dozen miles southeast of Rome], and the priesthood of the grove was held by a man who succeeded in breaking off the *Golden Bough* and then slaying the priest in single combat. (Fraser 1990a, 52)

Frazer says that he can show that "the priest represented the god of the grove ... and that his slaughter was regarded" by the local society "as the death of the god" (Fraser 1990a, 52). This ritual slaying is scarcely unique. Through his "Comparative Method," Frazer tells his publisher, he will relate this ritual to Druidical practices of human sacrifice and to the Balder legend in Norse mythology. Moreover, there is a "striking" likeness between these "savage customs and ideas" and "the fundamental doctrines of Christianity," i.e., the crucifixion and resurrection of Christ (Fraser 1990a, 53).

Frazer eventually wove Christianity into his cross-cultural narrative, which includes the Roman, Druidical, and Norse legends just mentioned. Together, these provide a precedent for the *Anatomy's* mythic mode, which brings together "Christian, late classical, Celtic, or Teutonic myths" (*AC*, 34). However, the central myths which *The Golden Bough* treats are those Mediterranean stories about Adonis, Attis, and Osiris.[10] Frazer straightforwardly recounts recorded stories of these gods. "Myths" are god-stories.[11] "The peoples" of the Mediterranean regions commonly "represented the yearly decay and revival of life, especially of vegetable life," in rites which "personified" the natural process "as a god who annually died and rose again from the dead" (Frazer 1922, 378).[12] Osiris, for instance, was a "king of Egypt, who suffered a violent death and was henceforth worshipped as a deity" (Frazer 1922, 426). He suffered, he died, and he rose: this is the plot line of the myths, or god-stories, Frazer selects for treatment.

This Frazerian plot line is relatable to Spengler's view of all major historical cultures as mortal. "Civilization" is the terminal phase of what had been a sequence of growing, cultivated epochs. Civilization marks the down and out, the decline and death stage that all historical cultures eventually experienced and that the West is now experiencing. The tragic winter-death of the West is the common destiny humans, in their various cultures, go through.

The individual gods Frazer selects for treatment—notably Adonis, Attis, Osiris, Dionysus, Demeter and Persephone, and Christ—are all dying gods. Their dying is but an episode in their total myths. Their common myth, according to Frazer scholar Robert Ackerman, tells the story of "how the god suffered a wound as the result of combat, ... died and was buried in the earth to the accompaniment of universal mourning," and then "revives to show himself" in "the rebirth of green and growing things" (Ackerman 1991, 62). The final act of the

myth, the rebirth, is for Frazer tragic, in contrast to the Christian perception of the resurrection as a "comic," or upward, movement.

What Spengler and Frazer share is the perspective of an organic
process: the dying into and growing out of the natural landscape.[13] For
both men, the process is tragic.[14] Frye calls the tragic shape that
Spengler gives to our history a "myth" because the *Decline* expresses
something within us. It crystallizes and gives form to a cluster of our
assumptions about the situation of the West. "Myth" in this sense
means a climate of contemporary opinion. Spengler, Frye says, gave
"complete expression" in the *Decline* "to a myth which had been
widely accepted for a century" (*FI*, 224). The cluster of assumptions
are these: (1) our Western culture is now "old, not young"; (2) in the
Middle Ages our mythic, religious, and social fabric was fully embroi-
dered—all of a piece—while the fabric of our present-day life is
mythically threadbare, with the little that is left fast unraveling; (3) the
Roman Empire went through the same decline and fall that we are now
experiencing; (4) and our decline began at some point early in the last
century—roughly "around Napoleon's time" (*RW*, 323; *SM*, 187).
Frye thus sees Spenglerian metahistory as an imaginative, synthetic
expression of Western man's cluster of beliefs about the ways things
now are for us. Everything in any culture's history moves along the
same organic plot line; Spengler, viewing our culture from the metaphor of decline, has a uniformly tragic perspective.

Earlier, we noticed that Frye's early response to the volume of *The
Golden Bough* on the dying god, was to designate its dying and rising
god pattern as "the very life-blood" and the "historical basis of art"
(Ayre, 106). That "repetitive rhythmic pattern," according to Ackerman, "constitutes" the "myth" which is "at the heart" of the entire
work (Ackerman 1991, 63). Moreover, because of its "recurrence,"
Ackerman deems it "tragic" (Ackerman 1991, 63). A god who dies
annually lives tragically. Frazer's pattern displays gods moving
through constant or annual rotation within external nature. For Frye,
"constant rotation within the order of nature is demonic" (*AC*, 162).

The Golden Bough is as expressionistic as the *Decline* for Frye.
While for him the *Decline* articulates the present-day beliefs we have
about our culture, *The Golden Bough* is "about what the human imagination does" in trying "to express itself about the [perennial] mysteries

of life and death and afterlife" (*NFCL*, 89). Frazer's ostensible concern is with "what people did in a remote and savage past," according to Frye (*NFCL*, 89). Frazer says that among the "great achievements of the nineteenth century" was its "discovery" of a "substantial identity everywhere" among people: "the dull, the weak, the ignorant, and the superstitious," who constitute, unfortunately, the "vast majority of mankind" (Frazer 1922, 64). All such people share "a belief in the efficacy of magic," which merely has been driven underground by the advent of civilization (Frazer 1922, 64). Prior to civilization, there was a "solid layer of savagery" (Frazer 1922, 64) everywhere, an age of magic, when everyone "attempted to force the great powers of nature to do their pleasure" by acts of magic (Frazer 1922, 63). These acts are simple. They directly affect nature. Surveying "spring and harvest customs," Frazer summarizes the characteristics of "primitive ritual": they involve no priests, no temples, and no gods (Frazer 1922, 476-77). Myths, which are stories about gods, are later developments of primitive man and involve a group of stereotypical agents such as the "Corn-Mother" and the "Old Woman." For example, primitive rituals consist of such practices as

> throwing the Corn-Mother into the river in order to secure rain ...
> for the crops; by making the Old Woman heavy in order to get a
> heavy crop next year; by strewing grain from the last sheaf
> amongst the young crops in spring; and by giving the last sheaf to
> the cattle to make them thrive. (Frazer 1922, 477)

The Golden Bough is characteristic of nineteenth-century thought in that it provides a developmental framework: ages of magic, religion, and science. Frazer compares the customs of European peasants, who belong to historical times and to a seemingly civilized culture, with primitives all around the globe. Spengler regularly compares Western with Classical culture. For both thinkers, similarities count more than differences.

There is a still more important resemblance between the two. Spenglerian metahistory gains its intensity from its point of view. Spengler's chief subject is Western culture, which comes into focus by his constant comparing of it with other cultures but most of all by his presenting it through the metaphor of decline.[15] The metaphor through which he presents Western culture is for Frye the "myth" of his book.

"Myth" does not even exist, according to Frazer, in the age of magic. Instead, it comes later, in the age of religion. Frye says that Frazer defines "myth as mistaken notions of natural phenomena" and that Max Mjller refers to "mythology as a disease of language" (*C&R*, 7). According to Frye, mythology for both is a form of "primitive science." For Frye, mythology has nothing to do with science or "making direct statements about nature." It is, instead, "the embryo of literature and the arts" (*C&R*, 7).[16]

The real interest of Frazer for Frye does not reside in what Frazer says about myth, about the age of magic, or about the age of religion. It is in that combined, unnamed stage, just after religion, which synthesizes magical practice with religious belief—in short, "works" with "faith."[17] Robert Segal observes that "for all of Frazer's rigid differentiation of his three stages, the bulk of *The Golden Bough*, especially the second and third editions, ironically deals with the unnamed stage, or semistage, that comes between religion and science and that constitutes a fusion of supposed opposites: magic and religion."[18]

This reconciliation unites force with fraud.[19] Magical acts "attempted to force the great powers of nature" to do as men wish; religious beliefs express the substance of things men hope for (Frazer 1922, 63). The focal point of *The Golden Bough* is upon a point in time when magic had already begun "to fuse and amalgamate with religion," which it does "in many ages and in many lands" (Frazer 1922, 62). "The old magical theory of the seasons was displaced, or rather supplemented, by a religious theory," which projected "the annual cycle of change" in external nature upon "corresponding changes in their deities" (Frazer 1922, 377). Frazer is concerned with these different "theories" as they have "blended" into one another: "the combination is familiar in history," he says, and it is even more common throughout *The Golden Bough* (377). Frazer adopts this point of view throughout his telling of god-stories.[20] It is also his focal point for the work as a whole, and for the event to which he recurrently returns: the priest-king ritual.[21]

Frazer relates ritual and myth.[22] They are brought together in the ritualistic enactment of the myths of dying and rising gods and in the story of the ritualistic killing of the king, though myth and ritual are initially separated in his historical framework. A difference between Frazer and Frye is that, while Frazer is much concerned to demonstrate that ritual regicide actually occurred, Frye thinks it unnecessary "to Frazer's argument to assume this grisly rite ever had anything more than sporadic historical existence" (*NFCL*, 99). Frye says flatly that it "does not matter two pins" whether the ritual ever had "any historical existence" (*AC*, 109).

A second difference between them emerges in Frye's insistence that he can "logically, not chronologically, derive" from Frazer's dying god or the king must die pattern a nuclear core of dramatic principles (*AC*, 109). Frazer works chronologically, like most nineteenth-century thinkers, and his goal is to uncover the source, or origin, of myth. Frye works "logically" in the same way that many twentieth-century theorists have done, for he wishes to see something as an integrally related array of parts exclusive of temporal factors. *The Golden Bough*, for Frye, is "an essay on the ritual content of naïve drama," which crystallizes the elemental actions at the core of all drama and helps literary criticism extract the "structural and generic principles of drama" that apply even to later, sophisticated works (*AC*, 109).

Frye is also unlike Frazer because he has little interest in any particular ritual. Among his notebook entries is the sardonic statement that he does not "care what the Fatass tribes in New Breakwind believe about the proper time for planting yams" (*NFN* 5 [Summer 1993], 14). Frazer's work eventually extended to some four thousand pages because he kept adding particular examples, but Frye attends only to the classes into which the rituals are fitted, and even more, to the "archetypal ritual" which he thinks Frazer devises to explain these types of ritual.

The kinds of rituals that Frye emphasizes are, first, the "scapegoat" ritual, in which someone is banished or killed in the hope of renewing communal life. Then there is the "carrying out death" ritual, in which, as Frye says, "some figure or symbol identified with death is driven away or killed" in the hope that death can be avoided. Third is the custom of appointing a temporary ruler, or mock king, of the carnival, who substitutes for the real one.[23]

Though each of the three kinds is relatable to the "archetypal," or "hypothetical," ritual that Frye thinks Frazer constructs out of them and others, Frye designates only what he calls the "hypothetical" ritual as Frazer's "mythical structure" (*WP*, 256). Frye's point is comparable to what he said about "Spengler's book," namely that the *Decline* "outlines one of the mythical shapes in which history reaches everybody except professional historians" (*SM*, 187). Frazer's "structure" is "mythical" because it expresses humanity's anxiety about its own survival of death; this anxiety goes back at least to the time of the erection of the "pyramids," which Frye mentions because those immense mausoleums symbolize it. Frazer's chief significance as a thinker is to have identified and articulated a pattern of anxiety latent in all minds, modern and primitive alike.

If Frazer's "hypothetical ritual" is a "mythical structure" which expresses what otherwise would remain a latent anxiety, the various classes of this ritual are "types of myth" (*WP*, 256, 264). Here Frye implies that the ritual of the killing of the god is the antitype, the complete expression, the fulfillment of the different "types" of ritual that Frazer presents. It is "hypothetical" in the sense that it is the representative or expressive form they take. It is the "symbolic key" that unlocks them (*NFCL*, 99). It is Frazer's "one tremendous intuition" (*NFCL*, 91, 99), his "central idea" (*NFCL*, 89), as well as the working "hypothesis" that he uses to explain them (*AC*, 109).

What connection might there be between the myths Frye thinks *The Decline* and *The Golden Bough* express and the myth the *Anatomy* articulates? This chapter began with two possibilities. Perhaps Frye's myth consists of his assumption that the reader has the capacity to become the center of an intertextual cosmos. Then again, it might be his supposition that the cycle of external nature somehow undergirds all of literature.

To start with the latter possibility: Frye relies on Spengler and Frazer for his hypothesis that the structure of literature is relatable to the cycle of external nature. Commentators have sometimes suggested that Frye fails to show how his four story types represent the four seasons, but could he have done so without drawing more explicitly upon these thinkers in the *Anatomy*?[24]

As to the other possibility, that the questing reader who has the capacity to become the center of a cosmos in which everything is literary,[25] Frye expresses his indebtedness to this "key idea" of the *Decline*, which he says has always preoccupied or obsessed him.[26] The goal of integrating one's literary experiences is the myth of the *Anatomy* in the sense that much of that book is directed toward helping the reader to do so. The recurring comparative devices, the modal tables and circular diagrams, provide a playing field upon which readers are invited to situate their reading experiences.

If the circle of story types is like a literary chessboard, then it may be possible to suggest how Spengler and Frazer help Frye construct it. Frye's playing field is like a three-dimensional chessboard. Its middle level is the plane upon which secular literary works belong. The circle of stories is conceived in accordance with the natural cycle. Yet even in the theory of myths (*AC*, 163-329) he takes us off that central plane. The rules of his game involve us in vertical moves which take us above or below it (*AC*, 185, 203-6, 223, 239). His top level is one to which we move up (*AC*, 185); his bottom level is one we move down upon (*AC*, 223, 243).[27] The central playing field of Western secular literature is continually affected by the "Christian myth" of the death and resurrection of Christ (*AC*, 185) and its opposite, "the ritual of the killing of the divine king in Frazer" (*AC*, 148). For Frye, Biblical and Classical myth are not just productions lying inertly at the beginning of our civilization. They actively animate any and all the literary eras to which a writer or reader may belong.

Spengler and Frazer were the "twin culture heroes" of Frye's student days" in the 1930s (*SM*, 111). When, some forty years later, Frye adds that "their conceptions seemed to get into and inform everything I worked on," the implication is that he interwove them into his books. They inform, for one thing, the diameter of the *Anatomy*'s circle of story types, where his organic rhythm is a conflation of those of Spengler and Frazer. The vertical axis of his circle is affected by Frazer, whose divine king ritual hovers just below the circle and affects the adjoining story types of tragedy and satire. In Frazer, both Jesus and dying and reviving gods such as Dionysus are entirely confined to dying into the cycle of nature and rising from it. In Frye, by contrast, Frazer's dying god figure is positioned below Frazer's cycle and Frye's

41

circle; this figure is set in antithesis to or is the demonic counterpart of the god of the Christian resurrection. While Jesus is the same as Frazer's other dying god figures, He is their polar opposite in Frye. They stand, for Frye, in the relationship of Christ and Antichrist. What Frye had said of a recent book can well be said of his own circle of story types, which is "hitched onto an Antichrist figure."[28] The third essay of the *Anatomy* begins with the figure of Christ (*AC*, 141) and closes with "the devil," as seen upside down "in the same attitude in which he was hurled down from heaven" into hell (*AC*, 239). To the notion that satire supplies a corrective vision, Frye joins an apocalyptic perspective. The "constant rotation within the order of nature" may be tragic for Frazer and demonic for Frye, but there is also in Frye an apocalyptic perspective that governs these and other relatively limited ones. Frye takes Frazer as his Vergilian guide to the lower reaches. Nevertheless, just as he disagrees with Spengler that modern literature has arrived at a down and out stage, so he leaves Frazer behind when presenting his levels.

Our comparison of Frye with Frazer and Spengler elicits some likenesses; so will later chapters with Ernst Cassirer and Carl Jung. Still, though we can find him saying what their "myth" is, that will not tell us what his "central myth" might be. In fact, our study of these myth theorists will not disprove the assumption of many in Frye studies that he takes everything from Blake, but it may make that single source theory less appealing.

Perhaps Kermode provides a third possibility as to what Frye's myth is. Frye thinks the reader has the capacity to become a center of an intertextual universe; Frye as well asserts that the cycle of external nature is the backbone or backdrop of a universe of texts. In attempting to follow a writer of enormous imaginative scope such as Frye, it is better to avoid discarding either of these choices as this third one is considered. As Kermode presents it, Frye's myth is that the world is like a book or that the Bible is a world.

For Kermode, Frye "may in the end be associated with" a "speculative tradition, as Blake had been before him" (Kermode 1989, 77). "Speculative" designates the aftermath of what had been a more organic tradition through most of the Middle Ages. What became an organic tradition starting with Origen in the third century tended to become more "speculative" and, apparently, remains the refuge of idiosyncratic writers ever since. Alternatively, Frye's Biblical and literary criticism may both stem from his entrance into what had constituted the central interpretative tradition of the Middle Ages. Frye helps us resurrect an imaginative landscape in our time by suggesting how writers have continuously re-created a Biblical, mythopoeic world.

CHAPTER FIVE

CHRISTIANITY AND CLASSICAL CULTURE

Frazer, Spengler, and Frye inherited competing nineteenth-century interpretations of Classical culture. An idealistic view of it was later rivaled by a revisionist theory. Moreover, these competing views of Classical culture have their counterparts in views of Christian culture. Frazer and Spengler affected our twentieth-century perceptions of both cultures directly through their works and indirectly through their influence upon other imaginative writers.[1]

Frazer altered the way we think of both by suggesting that primitive and brutal elements are at the core of their religions. By contrast, Spengler severs the foundational stage of a culture from primitive times. His innovation was to subordinate the role religion plays, within this foundational stage to the same plane, within his comparative framework, as other cultural activities—among them the arts. Frye's accomplishment, as a literary critic, has been to set religious myth on the same plane as literature. He aligns Classical with Christian myth by placing both in the *Anatomy*'s initial category: "mythopoeic literature" (*AC*, 188).[2]

The rival outlooks upon Classical culture that Frazer and Spengler inherited from the nineteenth century are epitomized by the contrasting attitudes toward it held by Goethe and Nietzsche. Goethe and others, such as Matthew Arnold, take Greek culture as the model for their own age. They typically characterize Greek culture by attributing to it the things they admire most or think exemplary for our culture. The values they argue are most needed in their age include proportion, serenity, and reserve or self-restraint.

Later nineteenth-century thinkers share Nietzsche's perception of an intense irrationality, a Dionysian feature, permeating otherwise Apollonian culture. This is the view of Frazer, who initially thought of himself as a Classical scholar like Nietzsche.[3] Frazer and some of the English classicists who followed him, such as Gilbert Murray at Oxford and the Cambridge Ritualists, argue for an initially Dionysian under-side that continued to run throughout Greek culture.[4]

Spengler makes a place for both Goethe's and Nietzsche's view-points. He adopts the name, familiarized by Nietzsche, "Apollonian," for Classical culture as a whole in the same way that he takes over Go-ethe's name for Western culture, the "Faustian" (*Decline*, I, 183). Spengler's initial spring stage of Classical culture is an organic whole which is then supplanted by a second stage that arises as an internal, populist "Dionysian" reformation against the "Apollonian." The two exist, in this temporal succession, as medieval or universal Catholicism later did vis-a-vis the Protestant Reformation.

It might seem, at first sight, that Frye is the follower only of Spengler, since neither of them is much concerned with the usual point of departure of the revisionists: the development of Greek or Roman culture out of primitive beginnings.[5] In actuality, Frye adopts and unites the views of Frazer and Spengler alike.[6] Frye sets Frazer's death and revival pattern within Western culture or at least literary history. The "death-and-rebirth rhythm of *The Golden Bough*" is an "essential part" of the organic "structure" of history; Spengler is "quite wrong in ignoring it" (*NFCL*, 81).[7] Yet Frye's starting point is still Spenglerian: The "mythopoetic" (*Decline*, I, 399) or "mythopoeic" (*AC*, 88). Where, however, Spengler compartmentalizes his cultures for him Classical and Western culture are not just distinct, as he says all major cultures are, but opposed—Frye deems their relationship one of death and rebirth.[8]

Nietzsche and the revisionists often assume that the Dionysian pre-cedes the more rational Apollonian. Frazer's "comparative approach," according to Ackerman, "emphasized how much the great [cultural] achievement of Greece had been overlaid on the darkness of the old brutal pre-Olympian religion" (Ackerman 1991, 64). Spengler places the Apollonian first. Frye, as little interested in chronology as in ori-gin, places both Apollonian and Dionysian across the grid of his mythic mode. They stand together in a synchronic rather than developmental relationship. On the one side his tragic class of myths are "Dionysiac … stories of dying gods"; on the other his "Apollonian" stories of rising or ascending gods tell how a hero became "accepted by" or rose into a "society of gods" (*AC*, 36, 43). Between these two classes of myths he sets "the central Christian myth" of the death, resurrection, and assumption of Christ. (Resurrection means that Jesus is raised from the dead to our world; Assumption means that He is raised from our world to His Father's world.) Classical and Christian myths are, to the extent that he follows Frazer, "interlocking" and, to the extent that he follows Spengler, "interpenetrating."[9] In either case, he has a synchronic starting point from which to trace the development of different forms of literature. From the perspective of historical scholarship, it probably seems strange to interrelate cultures that belong to different places, develop in different ways, and have separate origins.[10] Yet Frye's primary interest is not in any of these things but in the effective history that Classical and Christian myth had upon the body of Western literature "during the last fifteen centuries" (*AC*, 34). Given this interest, he takes the point of view Hans-Georg Gadamer happens to express: "the basis of the art and literature" of Europe is "the reconciliation of the Christian tradition and classical culture" (Gadamer 1991, 79).

It is easy enough to follow Frye's developmental portrayal of the forms of literature out of the main mythic fountainhead of our literature, the Bible.[11] After pertinent portions of the *Anatomy* have briefly been surveyed, we shall be able to see how he deploys Frazer and Spengler. The Bible is a literary and cultural guidebook, which Frye, as a literary critic, treats as the genetic code informing and continually affecting literary genres and conventions.[12] There is for him a central mythopoetic tradition which descends from the Bible. It belongs to his mythic mode and most directly affects encyclopedic and epic forms of literature throughout the other modes. His discussion, in the *Anatomy*, of "Specific Encyclopedic Forms" (315-26) deploys Spengler's medieval to modern historical schema of Western culture. With its help, he seeks to present the recreation of Biblical myth in the "works of Dante" in the medieval period ("romantic mode"), in Milton at the end of the Renaissance ("high mimetic mode"), in the more ambitious works of Victor Hugo ("low mimetic mode"), and finally in Joyce ("ironic mode"; *SER*, 5 and *AC*, 317-24).[13]

Frye's treatment of the story type of romance (*AC*, 286-306) over-
laps with that of the Bible and encyclopedic and epic forms (*AC*, 315-
26). He explicitly links the sections when he observes that "the stages
and symbols" of "the heroic quest of the central figure" of the Bible—
the Messiah—have "been dealt with under the *mythos* of romance"
(*AC*, 316). There he presents the developmental "stages" in his sequence of six "phases" that together "form a cyclical sequence in a
romantic hero's life" (*AC*, 198-203). What follows these phases is his
treatment of the "symbols" of the quest—his "points of epiphany"
(*AC*, 203-6).

Frye's discussion of these points of epiphany can be related both to
Spengler and to C. G. Jung.[14] Their conceptions help him to conceive
what for him is the synchronic beginning (Spengler) and conclusion
(Jung) of a dynamic developmental process. Our present concern,
however, is with his developmental canvas of literary forms. That canvas includes both encyclopedic and epic forms. It also includes romance, which encompasses both legend and folk-tale. The encyclopedic and epic writers work directly from the Bible, which occupies a
"central canonical position" in that every writing or reading culture
assigns cultural importance to it, while marginalizing romance (*AC*,
188). Only the encyclopedic and epic forms, in his developmental
framework, descend from the central Christian myth. Romance and its
auxiliary forms do not.

There is no direct relationship between romance and the mythic
mode, where Classical tragic myth, Christian myth, and Classical
comic myth reside. The reason for the disassociation is that the mythic
mode is reserved for gods only, where romance treats human heroes.
Nevertheless, tragic and comic forms descend directly from Classical
myth. If, then, romance does share the "stages" and "symbols" of the
Biblical hero myth—"the Messianic myth" or "heroic quest" of
Christ—romance presumably ought to share the same middle ground in
the developmental framework Frye positions under the Christian myth
and in which are situated the encyclopedic and epic forms (*AC*, 316-
17). The mythopoetic writing culture begins by drawing a distinction.
Classical myth becomes apocryphal or untrue myth, in contrast to Biblical myth. Later cultures consistently maintain the view of encyclopedic and epic forms as the serious ones, while dismissing or displacing

romance, legend, and folk-tale as forms for their own entertainment. Nevertheless, the Messianic myth and romance stories are structurally the same. "Mythical meaning" in both is condensed or concentrated (*AC*, 188). "Tradition," throughout Frye's modes, centralizes Christian myth and encyclopedic and epic forms, while simultaneously, throughout cultural history, marginalizing romance (*AC*, 188).

The relationship that the story type of satire has to romance is perhaps revealing for what it suggests about the relationship of myth to romance. Although it has no fixed position on Frye's complete canvas of story types, he views it vis-à-vis romance. Satire occupies a place underneath (spatially) or after (temporally) romance. Analogously, romance is underneath and the romantic mode follows the mythic mode. Satire follows romance because it feeds upon romance. While mythic and romance structures are similar, the structure of satire is, initially, a romantic structure, which satire proceeds to tear apart. In a satire, a romance structure is present only to be deconstructed. "As a structure, the central principle of ironic myth is best approached" by the literary critic "as a parody of romance" (*AC*, 223).

The relationship of satire to myth stands in contrast to that of tragedy and myth. These story types differ in the direction and movement that Frye assigns them. Tragedy moves downward to a point below the circle of story types and "into a hell of narrowing circles" (*AC*, 239). Satire ultimately takes us up from a "dead center," figuratively the south pole at the bottom or just below his circle of story types, all the way up the axis running through it to his north pole, where he situates "Christian myth" (*AC*, 185). As it was in the beginning of the development of literature out of myth, so it continues to be in the relationship of satire to romance. Biblical myth became true for what had been the Roman culture, and when it did, that culture, as it were, pushed Classical myth from its position at the center of Roman culture. At that point in time "Biblical myths were true and Classical ones false" (*WP*, 145). "The only way to account for the resemblances" between Classical and Christian myths "was to call" Classical myths "demonic parodies of Biblical ones"—an assumption which "lurked at the bottom of the Christian view for centuries" (*WP*, 145). Satire continues to do the same. It treats a romance pattern as if it were an untrue myth. Satirists continually erect a romance pattern so as to feed upon and

48

undermine it by showing it to be inadequate in the face of the complexities and ambiguities of actual human experience.

Finally, in his opening presentation of tragic and comic forms of literature, Frye is completely Frazerian. Christ is here just another dying and reviving god. "Stories of dying gods" are classed as "Dionysiac" but include "Christ dying on the cross" (*AC*, 36). Equally interlocking are stories in the Apollonian class: "stories of how a hero is accepted" into a divine society, which in the Bible is the story of Christ's "assumption" and in later "Christian literature" is present in the "theme of salvation" (*AC*, 43).

Frazer is helpful to Frye not only because he "treats myths," or god-stories, "as interlocking story patterns" but also because "his center of cultural interest is close" to Frye's (*GC*, 35). That center is a focus upon Classical culture *and* Christianity.[15] Frazer's view of both is revisionist. Like other revisionists of the idealistic view of Judaism and Christianity, he rejects the traditional assumption that their religions differ in kind from the bloody, sacrificial practices of, say, the Canaanites or the adherents of Mithraism. For Frazer, both Judaism and Christianity have the same kind of bloody fertility rites as other religions.[16] Canaanite, Hebrew, Celtic, Roman, and the Christian religions tout figures who suffer, die, and rise to ensure the crops. Like his counterparts, Jesus is a young man at the height of his powers. His body and blood are associated with bread and wine and with the harvesting of crops in general. His life story moves through the same cyclical rhythm of suffering, death, and rebirth.

Frazer and Spengler treat the Bible differently. Frye says that Frazer looks at it "centrifugally" (*GC*, 92), that for Frazer there is nothing in the Bible that cannot be found in some parallel form outside it." Given this comparativistic viewpoint, Frye thinks Frazer's procedure is then to set about "collecting analogies" on Biblical themes from surrounding cultures (*GC*, 92). For Spengler, the Bible belongs to Magian culture in accordance with his geographical literalism: early Christianity is its spring era, Augustine its summer reformation, and Mohammed its Enlightenment, while Islam is the winter-death. Frye, by contrast to both Frazer and Spengler, thinks that "a study of Western culture" should begin with the Bible; the study of any historical culture begins with its sacred text (*WP*, xx). Unlike Frazer, he finds that the Bible "deliberately subordinates its referential or centrifugal meaning" to its own, inner "centripetal meaning" (*GC*, 77). Its "two testaments form a double mirror, each reflecting the other but neither the world outside" (*GC*, 78). Frye's theory of symbolism seems an anti-mimetic vision until we encounter this Scriptural mirror. His attempt to elicit the "structural principles of Western literature in the context of its Classical and Christian heritage" begins with the Bible as it becomes a "canonical unity," a process that is completed by the end of the fourth century (*AC*, 133; *WP*, xx). In the penultimate section of the *Anatomy*, Christianity's "Messianic myth" shapes encyclopedic and epic forms of Western literature; from his book's beginning, Christian and Classical myth enter into and effect a sequence of different writing and reading cultures (*AC*, 317). Though Gadamer uses the terms differently, one might borrow them and say that, for Frye, the study of Western literature necessarily involves us with the "effective history" of Biblical and Classical myth as these a sequence of periods each having its own "horizon."

In the first essay the *Anatomy* lays before us a continuous landscape of literary history. Gradually this landscape, in the course of the book, can be seen as Frye's version of what a Classical education produced, the "study of a completed civilization" (*OE*, 32). "Classical training in the eighteenth and nineteenth centuries" involved the study of one culture by people participating in another (*OE*, 107). At the time he wrote the *Anatomy*, Frye, like others in his field, blithely assumed that "English studies are now clearly what Classical studies used to be, the clearing house of the humanities" (*OE*, 23). Spengler thinks Western cultural history had begun its decline around 1800 (I, 353), and that it has become as moribund as the Classical culture that preceded it. Frye lays Western literary history before us *as if* it had come to an end. Spengler surveys the whole pattern of the development of Western culture because he assumes it is depleted and can be grasped as a whole. Frye surveys "European" secular literature "during the last fifteen centuries," as they are informed by a synthesis of Classical and Christian culture (*AC*, 34). The shared effort of Spengler and Frye is to make cultural traditions of the past speak into the present in the form of traditions—to recreate within us, as Scruton says of Spengler, "the historical consciousness of the cultivated man" (Scruton, 21); Frye's educated imagination starts with the Bible, then Classical mythology, and then Western secular literature (*EI*, 110-14).

The second essay of the *Anatomy* starts with Dante's version of medieval hermeneutics, which was then part of around a thousand-year-old set of traditions for interpreting the Bible and which Frye adapts to Western literature. Among the first attempts to provide a systematic set of rules for reading Scripture, is Origen's *First Principles*, Book IV. Origen and Frye share the notion that the entire narrative of the Bible is a total verbal structure with a sequence of "forms and types of hidden" meaning; that by dying to the literal surface meaning, the possibility of making contact with deeper meanings opens, and that the reader sets out in a quest for spiritual or imaginative apprehension which is indeterminate and uncompletable because every reader is finite and the meaning embedded in texts infinite. There is no evidence that Frye ever read Origen. As his interpreter, however, I think that part of Frye's importance can be seen as a new beginning: after the extended muteness of Origen's text throughout the eras of Reformation's broadsides against the literal, plain sense of Scripture and the Enlightenment's obliviousness to it, his text gains renewed power in the version Frye proposes during our era of the conflict of interpretations. As Origen is the beginning source of several traditions of interpretation, so Frye reopens these imaginative means of responding to whatever texts from the past may speak to, and through, and beyond us. "Myth," for Gadamer is "the form in which religious texts speak." In Frye's third essay, myth becomes the form through which literary texts speak through their own traditions.

CHAPTER SIX

THE RHYTHM OF ROMANCE

The pattern that Frazer finds in the religions of the world is the same pattern Spengler portrays moving through all of the world's cultures. For Frye, Frazer's plot line of myth applies to the god-stories which religion and literature share.[1] Spengler's plot line of history applies equally well, for Frye, to the development of Western literature out of Classical and Christian myth. Frye's rhythm of romance unites the organic rhythms of Frazer and Spengler.[2] Across the circle of story types in the *Anatomy*, Frye inscribes the plot line of romance.[3]

"In poetry, as in Spengler," Frye says, "civilized life is frequently assimilated to the organic cycle of growth, maturity, decline, death, and rebirth in another individual form" (*AC*, 160). This is a flagrant misreading of Spengler. Had Frye stopped after "growth, maturity, decline, and death," he would have accurately represented Spengler's historical stages, which terminate in a winter-death stage. But when Frye adds "rebirth in another individual form," he is going beyond Spengler. He is in fact supplementing Spengler with Frazer.

Consider the place both their organic rhythms have within the list of cyclical patterns in the *Anatomy* (158-60). There are seven such patterns (some with variations). Two of them are metacyclical patterns: the one stemming from Frazer affects the others in religion; the one relatable to Spengler affects the others in literature. The one Frazer contributes pertains to god-stories (which are usually placed in religious categories). The one that Spengler provides bears upon "civilized life" as depicted by "poets" (160). These two patterns stand out from the other five because they inform the others.[4]

Frazer's pattern comes first in Frye's list. The "god of vegetation, dying in autumn," he says, revives "in spring" (159).[5] Frye finds it a "regular feature" of this pattern of cyclical movement for "the dying god" to be "reborn as the same person" (159). This is a "pattern of identical recurrence" since "the continuum of identity in the individual life from birth to death is extended from death to rebirth" (159). The principle of identity is lodged in this cyclical pattern, yet it informs the others: "to this pattern of identical recurrence, the death and revival of the same individual, all other cyclical patterns are as a rule assimilated" (159). What he calls a "rule" is a guideline for reading or interpreting his list. By his rule or interpretation of it as "the mythical or abstract structural principle," he distinguishes it from the rest of the patterns (159).

His other metacyclical pattern, attributed by him to Spengler, is followed by an interpretation of it.[6] To juxtapose Spengler and Frazer for Frye:

> In Spengler, civilized life is frequently assimilated [he just said Frazer's rhythm was the one "all other patterns are as a rule assimilated"] to the organic cycle of growth, maturity, decline, death and rebirth in another individual form. (*AC*, 160)

> [In Frazer, the individual life of a god] is extended from death to rebirth. (*AC*, 159)

For Frye, Spengler and Frazer are complementary. Spengler provides the pattern through which cultures or societies move and Frazer the pattern through which individuals move.[7] Both patterns are tragic. Every culture for Spengler ends in winter-death. Every god for Frazer dies. The fact that the Frazerian dying god dies into and then rises out of external nature only to die again means that he goes through "a constant rotation within the order of nature" (162). While Frazer construed this pattern as tragic, Frye deems it "demonic" (162). The word "tragic," he says, has to do with lives "cut off violently by accident, sacrifice, ferocity, or some overriding need," while "continuity which flows on after the tragic act" belongs to "something other than [human or animal] life itself": to an apocalyptic or demonic dimension beyond us (160).

In Frazer, the ritual of the killing of the divine king occupies the landscape of external nature. What this corresponds to in Frye is the rhythm of romance. This organic rhythm runs right across the middle of the whole body of secular literature. Since Frye presents that body as a circle of story types, the rhythm of romance is in effect the equatorial line across the map of Western literature. The combined rhythm taken from Spengler and Frazer is embodied in romance.[8]

The account of romance in the *Anatomy* (186-206) arrives quickly at Frazer's pattern: "the three-day rhythm of death, disappearance, and revival which is found in the myth of Attis and other dying gods" —the god stories Frazer retells (187). Frye is not content to accept Frazer's pattern. He modifies it by adding something to it that is not in Frazer. Frazer's threefold structure becomes a four-part structure in Frye.[9]

Basic to romance is adventure, he argues. The adventure of the hero in romance involves conflict, which enters into each of the three parts of romance.[10] These three parts -- death, disappearance, and revival -- operate along a cyclical, or horizontal, line. Conflict, which constitutes the additional fourth part of the structure of romance, introduces a "dialectical," or vertical, dimension (187). This vertical dimension, however, is never fully disclosed in secular quest romance. It becomes fully visible only in myth. In the central Christian myth, Jesus is "the mythical Messiah or deliverer who comes from an upper world, and his enemy" represents "the demonic powers of a lower world" (187). Frye's comparative study of romance, set within four story types, is confined to "secular quest romances" (192). "Conflict" in romances "concerns our [human] world," which is characterized by the cyclical movement of [external] nature" (187).

With help from the Frazerian classicist Gilbert Murray, Frye expands Frazer's threefold version of the pattern so that it becomes a fourfold pattern starting with conflict. Frye adopts many of Murray's phrases:[11]

Frazer	Murray	Frye
Combat	Contest or conflict between god and enemy	Conflict between hero and enemy
Death	Death and disaster which often is in the form of a tearing-in-pieces	Death-struggle Disappearance of hero which often takes the form of tearing to pieces
Revival	Discovery or recognition	Discovery: the recognition of the hero

Frye's use of Murray to expand Frazer's pattern allows him to analyze not just romance but all secular literature. The stages in romance of conflict, death, disappearance, and revival become the "building blocks" of literature as a whole (*SS*, 5). Conflict is elemental in romance. The three other elements found in romance are embedded in the other story types: death in tragedy; the tearing to pieces or disappearance of the heroic in satire; and the revival, reappearance, recognition, or return of the hero in comedy.

The four stages of the romance hero's quest, conceived of as a synchronic whole, constitute secular literature's "central unifying myth" (*AC*, 192). These terms are flexible. "Myth" may mean the plot line of romance that stretches across his circle of story types. It can also mean the secular quest-myth. Does it also mean, more subjectively, Frye's hypothesis that all of secular literature does form a whole? He uses the spatial metaphor "central" to suggest that the plot line of romance has been situated by him between the Christian myth above his circle of story types and the ironic, counter-myth below. Yet romance's plot line is also "central" because he locates it in the middle of his synchronic circle. "Unifying" means that the four elements constituting romance are the core elements in literature. It also implies that the plot line of romance has a force of its own, a centrifugal force working itself out or radiating from that center.

The rhythm of romance can be seen as a single, still point in the turning world of secular story instead of as a plot line.[12] This point is at the center of the natural, human cycle of actions. It is the stasis between death (the terminal phase of culture in Spengler) and rebirth (an element that Frye adds to Spengler's organic rhythm on the basis of his understanding of Frazer). Frye calls this point "a place of seed, into which everything subject to the cyclical order of nature enters at death and proceeds from at birth" (*AC*, 205). The notion of a "seed-plot" from which, out of the infinite variety of actual human experiences, "a few [seeds] grow up" or germinate and mature is shared by Spengler and poets such as Spenser (*AC*, 205).[13] From the "seed-plot of literature," romance, tragedy, satire, and comedy eventually emerge (*AC*, 122).[14]

In Frye's metaphoric language, the soil is human experience. The seeds become, in the third essay of the *Anatomy*, the points of the story types, or their archetypal themes. "Culture is born out of its mother-landscape," according to Spengler (*Decline* I, 174). This "soil" is not just the natural or geographical setting but the primitive or pre-cultural human landscape from which mythic and religious ideas suddenly and inexplicably exfoliate. They unfold, as Karl Jaspers says, "out of the mass of vegetating mankind like plants springing from the soil" (Jaspers, 97). In fact, the seeds are not "like plants"; instead, the prime symbol *is*, metaphorically, a plant, since the culture receives its very identity from the prime symbol it has. Spengler takes his assumption about the identity of a culture with seeds from Goethe.[15] When the seed-idea, or prime symbol, does emerge, it becomes a creative, shaping *a priori* form through which the members within the culture look out upon the landscape of their lives. It becomes as well the key that opens other peoples' cultures to us by having deciphered the prime symbol containing the identity of a major culture.

Frye thinks that the prime symbol which Spengler assigns to Western culture is "that of a center with radiating points" (*SM*, 183). Frye does not think that the landscape of literature exists in the same way that, say, the planet Mars does. He assumes that his four forms of story exist within the reader's mind as they grow, gradually, out of the experiences of reading. And, as they do, they provide the reader with the means "to see through what" the reader is "experiencing," as if viewing that landscape through "field glasses" (*WGS*, 198). His ideal reader looks out upon what he experiences in the same way that for Spengler people look out upon the landscape of their shared cultural lives. Spengler's point of departure is from the moment the transformation of a natural into a humanly significant or cultural landscape has already occurred. Frye's is from a point at which "the gradual transformation of mythology into literature" has begun (*DV*, 62).

The "archetypal themes" are "symbols of the heroic quest" (*AC*, 316). Spengler's prime symbol is for Frye the "central symbol" of any one culture, while "the central symbol for the Western culture," and for his own vision of Western literature as a whole, is a "center with radiating points" (*SM*, 183). An archetypal theme in Frye is relatable to a Spenglerian prime symbol in that both are primal or primary: they are radical, root principles. Conversely, if the center is that from which these root themes emerge and then radiate outwards, his archetypal themes resemble primary symbols in that both are "central" themes or still points. The central archetypal themes for Frye or the central symbol for Spengler does not remain stationary at the center since there is movement outwards towards a circumference.

Frye presents his archetypal themes within a discussion of the plot line of romance. These themes are gathered from a perspective that typically, like Spengler's, looks at a process that has already come to an end. They are abstracted from Frye's comparative study of the resolutions the four forms of story have. An archetypal theme is the endpoint an elemental kind of story typically has. A recurrent line of action ends as a single point. An archetypal theme is embedded within the rhythm of the typical plot as a whole. The point running through romance is "conflict" (*AC*, 186, 187). Comedy typically displays a movement from an older to a younger, more desirable society, but "the point of resolution in the action" is the "comic discovery" or recognition (*AC*, 163). He presents similar "points" for tragedy and satire.

His discussion of romance closes with what he calls the "point of epiphany" (*AC*, 203). All four story types have "analogous forms of the point of epiphany" (*AC*, 205). Each of them, except for romance, is a "symbolic presentation of the point at which the undisplaced" or mythical worlds above and below his circle of story types "come into alignment" with one or another of the archetypal themes his story types have (*AC*, 203). Frye is suggesting the places, in his synchronic presentation of the circle of story types, itself confined to "the cyclical world of nature," at which that world intersects with the mythic worlds above and below it. There are three such places: one at the apex, another at the nadir, and the third at the center.

The point of epiphany of romance is set in the midst of the natural, human cycle. He contrasts the points of epiphany of comedy and romance by saying that in romance "there is no apocalyptic vision," as there can be in comedy, "but simply a sense of arriving at the summit of experience in nature" (*AC*, 203). Comedy, tragedy, and satire take us up or down to the vision just outside the natural, human cycle of stories. Yet these three are similar to the epiphany of romance, at the hub of the circle of story types, in that each is a point of stasis. Here the idea, which goes back to Aristotle and Boethius, is that the hub is stationary even though everything else within the circumference of the circle is in motion. The central point of the epiphany of romance is the quiet, motionless center, a place of gestation in the midst of the moving circle, a caesura that Frye introduces between Spengler's cycle terminating in and including death and Frazerian rebirth.

The point of epiphany of comedy takes us just beyond the top of the circle and into another world: "the undisplaced apocalyptic world" above ours (*AC*, 185). Secular comedy presents only "the human comedy," which Balzac's novels explore. Beyond it is the divine comedy, as in "the undisplaced *Commedia*," which is "the vision of Dante's *Paradiso*" (*AC*, 185). The vision bestowed upon the questing Dante in that work crosses the boundary between secular and sacred literature. Dante presents an "imitation" of the "Messianic myth" in the Bible (*AC*, 317). When normal human comedy is juxtaposed to the Christian myth, we notice a pattern: the more popular and formulaic the comedy, the more it "has much the same structure" as that myth, which has a "son appeasing the wrath of a father" and renewing a society (*AC*, 185). The Christian myth of the redeemer helps the archetypal critic detect the structure which runs through secular comedies but which would remain invisible if our view were confined to them since they are displacements from the myth.

At the bottom of the circle of story types are the points of epiphany of both tragedy and satire. If we follow Frye's spatial metaphor of the circle, we enter into his representation of a vertical axis descending from just above its upper polar region, then intersecting with the rhythm of romance at its diameter, and arriving at a point just below the bottom of the circle. Tragedy eventually leads us into "a point of demonic epiphany, where we see or glimpse the undisplaced demonic vision, the vision of the *Inferno*" (*AC*, 223). Here we encounter "sacrificial symbolism" which is Frazerian, an area of "demonic ritual" (*AC*, 223). Satire, too, ends in "the point of demonic epiphany" (*AC*, 238). The difference between tragedy and satire is that the point of epiphany of satire begins only where that of tragedy ends. While tragedy takes us out from the nadir of the circle to something beneath it and allows us to see "evil in personal form," satire ultimately reverses the perspective and direction of tragedy. "The *mythos* of irony and satire" turns the tragic vision of evil upside down (*AC*, 239).

The final sentence, in the theory of myths, indicates the reversal of the ultimate perspective of tragedy. Frye says that "we shall pass a dead center and finally see" things from a point of view like that of the traditional Christian perspective, except that ours will be an entirely imaginative vision (*AC*, 239). With this sentence, Frye traverses his entire vertical axis, the line running from the bottom to the top of his circle of story types. There is first the vision of tragedy at the bottom, then a "dead center" in the middle of the circle—what can be seen as the "dead center" between Spenglerian death and Frazerian rebirth—and finally the Christian vision as an imaginative outlook. At the dead center of the circle of story types, then, lies the horizontal Spenglerian rhythm that Frye inscribes across his circle, the "cycle of growth, maturity, decline, death," which Frye completes with the Frazerian notion of "rebirth in another individual form" (*AC*, 160).

For Frye, the writings of thinkers such as Spengler, Frazer, Darwin, Marx, and Freud "are complex and difficult and require years of study. Yet the central themes of their work are of massive simplicity" (*RW*, 323). Similarly, he says that the *Anatomy*, his "most difficult book," has "a very simple center" (*WGS*, 197). The circle of story types has the rhythm of romance inscribed across it; the plot line of romance contains, in their embryonic form, the seeds that become the four forms of story. Spengler and Frazer, in this chapter, have been brought to bear upon our understanding of Frye's organic rhythm of romance. The *Anatomy* continually and flexibly adjusts their organic rhythms to his literary contexts. Literary history in his book is as simplified as cultural history in Spengler, and for the same expressionistic purpose. In Spengler, "history, like art, becomes an expression, to be understood" by us relative to "the spirit that is embodied in it," the prime symbol a culture has, when as a whole (Scruton, 21). Frye's adaptation of Spenglerian cultural history helps him display "Western literature in the context of its Classical and Christian heritage," especially Classical and Christian myth. Frye wants us to re-member our heritage just as his contemporaries, Gadamer and Ricoeur, wish us to do. Spengler "builds a theory on something that exists (and perhaps ought to exist) without theory: the historical consciousness of cultivated" men and women (Scruton, 21). Frye's "theories" have their ground in the thing he is trying to build up in us, the educated imagination cultivated by reading literary and religious works. His theory of reading, as will be seen, is developmental in that our experiences of literature gradually grow within us, but the end of the theory, and the aim of the *Anatomy*, is to impel us toward the same kind of synchronic experiences he himself had, in part thanks to Spengler: the perception "that literature is not just an aggregate of texts but a total structure"; reading individual texts aids our own expressionistic endeavors in "articulating a total vision of reality" (*NFN* 1 [Spring 1989], 26).

CHAPTER SEVEN

MYTH AND CULTURE

Frye came to his reading of philosopher Ernst Cassirer (1874-1945) after he had assimilated the works of Frazer, Spengler, Freud, and Jung. His reading of Cassirer was probably concurrent with his writing of the *Anatomy*. Cassirer's ideas had a more immediate effect upon the *Anatomy* than those of any of the other theorists, as will be seen in this and the several chapters that follow.

Cassirer's project of writing a philosophy of symbolic forms occurred to him when he was nearly as old as Frye was when he produced the *Anatomy*, for he conceived it in 1917 when in his early forties. While stepping into a Berlin street car on his way home, "the conception of the symbolic forms flashed upon him; a few minutes later, when he reached home, the whole plan of his voluminous work was already in his mind."[1] Whatever the whole of the plan he initially envisioned may have been, he published, between 1923 and 1931, the *Philosophy of Symbolic Forms* in three volumes: *Language*, *Mythical Thought*, and *The Phenomenology of Knowledge*.[2] Language and myth are for him primitive cultural forms from which other forms of culture, such as science or art, develop. Philosophy is not itself a symbolic form. Instead, it has the task of interpreting the meaning these forms have in the Western cultural tradition. As Paul Ricoeur suggests, the task of a philosophy of symbolic forms "is to analyze ... the ways of a world-making proper to each kind of version" of it (Ricoeur 1991, 207).

Ernst Alfred Cassirer was born in what was then Germany (though now within Poland) in 1874. He was a contemporary of Jung, who was born a year later, and of Spengler, who was born in 1880. Like them both, he studied at various universities, as was common. Like them, his interests changed: he began with jurisprudence, switched to German literature, and ended in philosophical studies. When he decided upon philosophy, he necessarily focused upon Kant, the study of whom was the doorway to an academic career in it. As he says, "no one could enter the field of philosophy" then without studying "the work of Kant."[3]

Cassirer taught at Hamburg while writing his three-volume work. He was elected Rector of the University in 1930. Since he was Jewish, the advent of Hitler severely disrupted his career. After Hitler came to power in 1933, Cassirer left Germany. He lived and taught at Oxford for several years, then in Sweden between 1935 and 1941, and finally in New York City until his death in 1945.

Three of the books that he wrote or had translated into English during those final years in America were the works through which he became known to North American literary scholars such as Frye. *The Myth of the State* (1946) depicts the devastating rise of the Nazis as the latest display of the destructive power of myth. *Language and Myth* (translated into English by Susanne K. Langer in 1946) begins with the view that myth was in place, as a cultural force, long before Greek philosophy emerged from it. Though a primitive or archaic form of thought, myth continually affects other cultural forms. It acts as both a destructive and creative force in and upon human culture. *An Essay on Man: An Introduction to a Philosophy of Human Culture* (1944) is both an introduction of his thought to an English-speaking audience (the title is from Alexander Pope's poem) and a re-thinking of his philosophy of symbolic forms. The symbolic forms which he treats are myth, language, religion, art, history, and science. There is no world of which these forms are different versions, since symbolic forms grow out of each other in a process that begins with a pair: language and myth.[4]

The effect of these books upon North American literary scholars during the 1940s and 1950s is suggested by the discussion of Cassirer by Cleanth Brooks in their *Literary Criticism*, which was published, like the *Anatomy*, in 1957.[5] They make four brief points, each pertinent to our understanding of Frye. First, there is Cassirer's expressionist definition of the symbol as that which unites a perceiving subject with an external object; a symbol creates or expresses an identity between them (699). Besides this epistemological sense of "symbolic form," there is, second, the larger sense of that term as an autonomous form of culture. Art presents an integrated vision of the world and not just a copy of it. Art becomes one of the major ways of world making by presenting the inner landscape of human life as it is experienced, in contrast to the outer, external world approached by science (702). Third, there is the relationship between art and other symbolic or cultural forms: in particular, the "relation of poetry to myth" (703, 708). The relationship of myth to literature is among Frye's major preoccupations as a thinker. Finally, and this point is the only one I will pursue at present, there is his treatment of "the laws that govern the development of primitive ritual and myth" (700).

Myth forever remains a generative symbolic form for Cassirer. His first law of myth pertains to the way in which other cultural forms develop from it. In *Literature and Myth*, he deems it a "law" because it "holds equally for all symbolic forms and bears essentially on their evolution. None of them arise initially as separate, independently recognizable forms." Instead, Cassirer adds, "every one of them must first be emancipated from the common matrix of myth" (44). "Mythology," according to Frye, "is the matrix of literature" (*FI*, 33). "Myths" for Frye are emancipated from or "liberated by literature" (*NFMC*, 143). Frye adopts Cassirer's first law: myth provides the material, the cultural "matrix" out of which other cultural forms arise, though he limits himself in scope.

Frye's focus is upon the study of the direct development of myth in or by literature. "The theory in [the] *Anatomy*, he says, "rested on the continuity and identity of mythology and literature" (*WP*, xvii) His assumption of the continuity between them is relatable to Cassirer's first law of myth. While Cassirer thinks that all the forms of culture grow out of and then outgrow or "emancipate" themselves from myth, Frye restricts himself to this process as it affects literature. While the philosopher suggests that every symbolic form outgrows myth, the literary critic stipulates that literature alone is mythology's "direct descendent in culture" (*SM*, 72). Or again, "the direct descendent of mythology is literature" (*GC*, 34). While Cassirer thinks that "art" is only one among many cultural forms to develop out of the mythic matrix—and means by "art" painting, literature, and so on—Frye insists that "literature" is "the only one of these arts" that has a "direct connection with myth" (*NFCL*, 69).[6]

Cassirer's second law of myth distinguishes other symbolic forms from myth even as his first law relates every other cultural form to myth. "If there is any characteristic and outstanding feature of the mythical world, any law by which it is governed," he says, "it is ... metamorphosis" (Cassirer 1944, 108). Everything in myth's world changes; conversely, "nothing," in the world of myth, has a "static shape," since "everything may be turned into everything" (108).

Cassirer's second law is that "everything may be turned into everything" in the world of myth (108). "Everything is potentially identical with everything else" in the world of literature, according to Frye (*AC*, 124). It might seem, then, that just as Frye appears to follow Cassirer's first law (that myth provides the cultural matrix out of which other symbolic forms develop), so he concurs with the second law of myth. It is helpful to recall, however, that Frye says that it was Spengler who "showed how" the notion that "everything is everywhere at once" operated in [cultural] history" (*NFN* 3 [Winter 1990-91], 6).[7] The implication seems to be that it was Spengler, whose schema of cultural history Frye adapts to his own framework of literary history, with whom Frye is in agreement.

Frye differs from Cassirer and agrees with Spengler that myth is situated within the beginning of an historical culture. Cassirer assumes that mythical thinking is primitive thinking. The difference between Cassirer and Spengler has to do with when culture begins. For Cassirer, primitives, like animals, occupy the physical landscape, but humans, with their development of the activities of myth and language, begin to insulate themselves from external nature by creating the landscape of culture (Cassirer 1944, 43). The difficulty is that, in the world of myth in primitive times, everything seen by men is subject to constant change. Primitives, insofar as they differ from animals, universally share a capacity to fill their world, their mythical world, with humanly expressive shapes. "Myth appears at first sight to be a mere chaos," Cassirer acknowledges, "a chaos of undeveloped imagery," which would be close to Spengler's observation that there is only "a chaos of undeveloped imagery" prior to any of his historical cultures (Cassirer 1994, 97; Spengler, I, 399). However, Cassirer thinks there is an underlying and characteristic way of living and acting in the mythical world. For primitives, everything in the world is animate. Their landscape is informed by the "*solidarity of life*": "the consanguinity of all forms of life seems to be a general presupposition of mythical thought" (Cassirer 1944, 109).[8] There is no sense of an external nature set apart from man, no inanimate objects, no habit of accounting for change through causation. The mythical world is a dramatic world in which "every shape can metamorphose into another: anything can come from anything" (Cassirer 1961, 94). For Cassirer, the world of myth—and later of the humanities in general and art in particular—is the antithesis of the external world studied by the sciences. The difference resides in the elemental modes of perception: the root principle of mythical thinking is the "perception of expression." All the objects of man's perception appear animate, in motion; they are experienced through the expressive qualities with which they are imbued by primitives. For the sciences, by contrast, the phenomena of the world are inanimate, fixed images or sense data from which we are detached (Krois 86, 124).

In Spengler, too, a synchronous living relationship exists between man and his environs. Humans share a capacity to fill their "world with shapes" they themselves impose upon what they perceive (I, 399). Yet Spengler adds that this capacity "belongs most decidedly not to the world-age of the primitives but exclusively to the springtimes" of his major cultures.[9] Frye follows Spengler, according to A. C. Hamilton, in assuming that a foundational or springtime stage of culture provides a "unifying or mythical shape" to "everything, for everything in culture—especially the arts—expresses its essential nature"; everything is "part of a synchronous totality" (Hamilton 1990, 56).

Spengler, like some other myth theorists, defines his conceptions relative to Kant.[10] Cassirer is usually called a neo-Kantian. Some of his starting points can be related to Kant, but they are often points of departure from him.[11] Both he and Spengler start from Kant's *a priori*: the notion, new with Kant, that the human mind makes the form of the world it perceives. Philosophy before Kant assumed that there was a real world, an external reality, perhaps a world that external nature presents to us or a reality behind or above the appearances of things. Human knowledge or truth depended upon a passive relationship to external reality. For Kant, though, human understanding does not derive truths from an external world. It imposes certain categories, concepts, or rules upon the world we see. We constitute reality. We make the form of the world we see. Space and time are among the categories that the mind supplies. As Cassirer, agreeing with Kant, says, "space and time are the framework in which all reality is concerned" (Cassirer 1944, 62). For Kant, there is a single set of principles that make knowledge possible. Ricoeur calls them the "set of Kant's categories of relation"; Cassirer, though, dissolves "substance into function," which serves to complete the dissolution of the assumption that there is a single external world (Ricoeur 1991, 201).

Frye says that "Cassirer's major effort" as a thinker is to have "abandoned the search for a systematic or rational unity in human consciousness," and to have focused instead upon a "'functional unity' of human work in the world" (*NFCL*, 70, 68). Both Cassirer and Frye think that Kant's view of reason is relatively static. They suggest that feeling and imagination are active partners with reason.[12] Kant's association of reason with scientific knowledge tends to devalue other forms of knowledge. For Cassirer, as we have seen, there are several forms of perception, some appropriate to the sciences and some to the humanities. In Spengler, there are "systematic" approaches, which bring into view an objective knowledge appropriate to the sciences, and a subjective, "morphological" knowledge that elicits the inner and underlying forms, the living forms of history.

Frye is the inheritor of a line of thought coming from Kant through the revision of him by the German Romantic philosophers, and, through them, of Coleridge and the English poets. He is also, of course, the exponent of Blake's thought. This line of thought differs from Kant in its emphasis upon the creative role of the imagination. What for Kant is our constitution of a common world becomes for them the creation, through the individual imagination, of a world on the analogy of an artist creating a work. Yet Cassirer and Frye alike assume that there is no external world, a world of external nature, that serves as the original. For both, our visions or versions of the world are not copies of a neutral prior world of external nature. For Cassirer, symbolic forms of the world grow out of other symbolic forms, and all begin with man's expressive activities in myth and language. For Frye, the world of literature is not at all constructed out of nature. Rather, "poetry can only be made out of other poems; novels out of other novels. Literature shapes itself, and is not shaped externally: the *forms* of literature" belong to an autonomous literary world (*AC*, 97).

With the onset of myth and language, Cassirer assumes, men begin the process of creating the landscape of culture, which insulates them from external nature. Since then, humans "no longer" live in a "merely physical universe" but now reside within a "symbolic universe" (Cassirer 1994, 43). If human life, for him, is contained within a symbolic universe, Frye places it within a "mythological universe" (*SM*, ix). Cassirer says that symbolic activities interpose between humans and external nature a "symbolic net" in which men are "enveloped" and thus set apart from the animals, which remain upon a natural landscape. Similarly, Frye says that "man does not live directly and nakedly in nature like the animals, but within an envelope that he has constructed out of nature" (*C&R*, 5). "The envelope," he adds, is usually called "culture" by others; despite this, he prefers to call it "mythology."

In 1954, three years prior to the publication of the *Anatomy*, Frye reviewed one of Cassirer's books. The review seems to have been occasioned by the English translation, the year before, of the first of the three volumes of *Philosophy of Symbolic Forms*, the one entitled *Language*. Though he makes some comments on it, he suggests that "the real contemporary importance of Cassirer's thought is displayed not in this book, but in the later *An Essay on Man*," which appeared in paperback in 1953 nearly a decade after the hardbound edition (*NFCL*, 67). His review is significant because it is our main source for considering his relationship to the philosopher. Furthermore, he later spliced together different parts of the *Anatomy* from it.[13] Entitled "*Myth as Information*," he distinguishes his review, in the acknowledgments in the *Anatomy*, from the many he had by then written by according only it a place there (*AC*, viii). It differs from even the many articles he had incorporated into the book. While they tend, with varying degrees of revision, to be set within one or another of the book's four essays, ideas from or portions of his Cassirer review are distributed across the entire book.

Frye's review of *An Essay on Man: An Introduction to a Philosophy of Human Culture* begins with an exposition of Cassirer's philosophy of the symbolic forms of culture (*NFCL*, 67-69). The rest of it delineates Frye's solution to a problem that he thinks the philosopher left unresolved (*NFCL*, 69-75). Frye wants to see if he can "discover" for himself what "the relation of myth actually is to language on the one hand and to literature" on the other (*NFCL*, 69).

Consider the procedure Frye uses to work out that problem. He proceeds, he says, "on the basis of Cassirer's general conception of symbolic form" (*NFCL*, 69). What he means is that he chooses to start by retaining the narrower, more epistemological sense of Cassirer's conception of it as a form of making; he sets aside, for a time, the other sense he gives it in his exposition, which is that of an autonomous field of cultural activity. Only at the conclusion of the review does he return to the question of cultural forms.

Frye begins with Cassirer's assumption that art, myth, and language can be thought of together as a symbolic form in which subject and object are united by the intermediate area.[14] Frye agrees with Langer and departs from Cassirer in replacing the general term "art" with particular arts—in Frye's case, literature.[15]

Having set up the problem that he thinks Cassirer left unresolved in this way, Frye offers a solution that involves the shifting from the epistemological to the cultural sense of a symbolic form. As forms of making, Frye groups myth, literature (or literary myth), and language together synchronically, so that they become a symbolic form in the more epistemological sense. Literature, the intermediate term, is subject to the same principle that "reappears" in each of the arts, for there is in them all "an inseparable unity of a mental constructive principle and a reproductive natural content" (*NFCL*, 73). What distinguishes literature from the other arts is that fictions have myths as their "formal or constructive principle." Literary myth contains, as its units of language, metaphors, which are brought into literary works *from* external nature, yet these basic linguistic structures are contained within the work (*NFCL*, 74-75). Myth and metaphor, when they enter into a literary work, become "hypothetical" (*NFCL*, 74). Myth in literature and metaphor in literary language are for Frye equally hypothetical. Myth in literature becomes cut off from whatever existential ties it may have had as a form of religious thinking, since a myth in a literary story is purely imaginative. A metaphor is a hypothetical equation of two things that in the world have nothing to do with each other but which, in imaginative or literary language, are structurally fused.

All this is Frye's answer to the problem of the relationship of literature, myth, and language on the basis of Cassirer's epistemological sense of symbolic form. Yet Frye wants as well to see these three not just as forms of making, but as cultural forms. Paul Ricoeur suggests that "in the *Philosophy of Symbolic Forms*, linguistic forms, mythical and aesthetical forms, and scientific forms were indeed held as irreducible (in a cultural rather than transcendental sense of the term 'form,'" Ricoeur 1991, 201). In *Language and Myth* Cassirer says, "myth, language, and art begin as a concrete, undivided unity," and thereafter other cultural forms develop from and emancipate themselves from myth (98). Frye is close to Cassirer's assumption that art is the "one intellectual [or cultural] realm in which the word [the mythic word of power] preserves its original creative power," though he substitutes the more specific term "literature" for what the philosopher thinks of as art (98).

There is another Cassirean assumption from which Frye diverges. Here the question is not of the development of art or literature from myth at some point close to the beginnings of human culture. The question is instead what cultural form emerges toward the end of this process of the development out of myth. Cassirer's assumption here is not a departure from Kant but is in keeping with him. For Cassirer, as with Frazer, the entire developmental grid, the historical framework, has its climax in the relatively objective manner of apprehending reality by science. As Ricoeur says, Cassirer assumes, in his philosophy of symbolic forms as a whole, "a teleological development ruled by the mind's thrust towards objectivity, i.e., scientific knowledge" (Ricoeur 1991, 201). For Frye, however, literary criticism is the latest symbolic form to have developed out myth. If, as Cassirer thinks, every cultural form develops out of myth, what would it mean if there was a cultural form that specialized in the study of myth as it affects its objects of study? These objects, in literary studies, are literary works. Throughout Western literary history, fictions "retain the same structural outlines," because myth continually informs them (*NFCL*, 74). Literary criticism, as it emerges in Frye's version of it, is the study of the *informing* role, the informing power of myth in literary works. Hence the title of his essay on Cassirer: "Myth as Information" about literary works. "The word *myth* ... in literary criticism" is now coming "to mean the formal or constructive" or informing "principle in literature" itself (*NFCL*, 74). This perception of the role of myth in literature differs radically from the more usual view of Classical and Christian myth as the mere content found in some literary works, as mere allusions to ornament a work. Pursued in literary criticism, this approach would involve no more than the noting or classifying of myths in an objective or scientific manner—in other words, approaching myth as mere information. That is the other, ironic, sense of Frye's title.

Finally, Cassirer's vision of the task of philosophy can be compared with Frye's vision of the task of literary studies. Cassirer invites whoever would follow his philosophy of symbolic forms to enter into fields other than philosophy. As Ricoeur says, the task of philosophy "is to analyze with great precision the ways of world making [epistemological sense of a symbolic form] proper to each version of the world" (symbolic form in its sense of a cultural area, 1991, 207). One obvious reason that he has had few followers is that he asks philosophers to assimilate not only their own tradition or body of knowledge but other fields of knowledge as well.

For Cassirer, myth and language are primitive cultural forms and so can be classed as pre-logical, while art is extra-logical. Frye says that Cassirer divides his cultural forms into a "logical group and another group which is either pre- or extra-logical" (*NFCL*, 69). He observes that, for Cassirer, mathematics informs the natural sciences in that it provides the elemental symbols they have in common—numbers. By analogy, Frye suggests, the relationship of mathematics to the sciences resembles the relationship of literature to most of the social sciences and the humanities:

> Literature resembles mathematics and differs from other structures in words in that its data are hypothetical: mathematician and poet alike say, not 'this is so,' but 'let this be.' Mathematics appears to be a kind of informing or constructive principle in the natural sciences: it continually gives shape and coherence to them without being involved in any kind of external proof or evidence. (*NFCL*, 74)

Mathematics, then, is to the quantifiable sciences as "literary myth" is to:

> a constructive [or expressive and informing] principle in the social or qualitative sciences, giving shape and coherence to psychology, anthropology, theology, history, and political theory without losing in any one of them its own autonomy of hypothesis. (*NFCL*, 74-75)

Mathematics thus shares its symbols—numbers—with the natural sciences and with those portions of other disciplines that are readily quantifiable. It differs from them in regarding numbers hypothetically. Frye's analogical perception is that literary studies share myth along with all the disciplines in the other major group of them. It is distinguishable from them in apprehending myth as an entirely imaginative or hypothetical form. In the other disciplines, myth tends to be submerged: it becomes the hypothesis that organizes, at least for a while, a particular field of study. Or it serves to organize a particular thinker's ideas: that is the sense in which, as has been seen, Frye applies "myth" to other myth theorists. He applies that sense of myth to each of the other myth theorists with whom we are concerned except Cassirer. Myth tends to become anchored in particular concepts within an individual thinker's work or within a field of study. Frye designates the entire process by which myth tends to be employed in fields other than his own as "conceptual myth" (*NFCL*, 74). His stock example is Freud's use of the Oedipus myth. Sophocles' *Oedipus Tyrannos*, he says, is a literary or "dramatic myth" that "informed and gave coherence to Freud's psychology" (*NFCL*, 75). He means that the play provided Freud with not only a concept but also a point of departure, a plot, a means of organizing his thought at a certain time in his career.

However that may be, the argument of the next chapter is that Cassirer's construction, "symbolic form," as well as his several laws pertaining to myth, helped Frye to organize the thought of the *Anatomy*. Portions of the Cassirer essay and of Cassirean ideas appear in the introduction, the four essays, and the conclusion of Frye's book. The *Anatomy* starts with the premise that literary criticism is the latest symbolic form to appear on the horizon of knowledge; it ends by repeating his speculation on the reconfiguration of neighboring disciplines that the emergence of literary criticism as the newest symbolic form occasions. The purpose of my extended tracking of Frye's relationship to Cassirer, as with the other myth theorists, is not to reduce Frye's thought to a study of others' ideas. It is to suggest that, like any great thinker, like Ricoeur or Hans-Georg Gadamer, Frye thinks through and expresses himself with the help of those who have preceded him. As myth theorists, Cassirer, Frazer, Freud, Jung, and Spengler are the Vergilian guides of the most significant literary critical classic of our century. Though he works through these "myth theorists," he is also endeavoring to resurrect the foundational ideas of our heritage.

CHAPTER EIGHT

CASSIRER AND THE *ANATOMY*

The most obvious place to look in the *Anatomy* for the influence of
the philosopher of symbolic forms is in the essay on symbolism. Frank
Kermode says in his review of the book that Frye's theory is "the adaptation of an Aristotelian scheme to a Symbolist view of literature"
(Kermode 1959, 320). In particular, he adds, it is an adaptation of
Aristotle to "the latest manifestation of Symbolist aesthetics, the neo-
Kantianism of Cassirer's Symbolic Forms."[1] Perhaps, however, it is
the other way round. The essay on symbolism may be an adaptation of
a Cassirean "scheme" to Aristotle's *Poetics*. For the word "scheme"
substitute "containing form." Cassirer provides Frye with the containing form of the second essay, just as Spengler provides Frye with
"the containing form of historical criticism" in the first essay (*AC*,
343).

The relationship of the second essay to the others, as well as the
sense in which any of them has a "containing form," becomes apparent when the reader considers the strategy Frye uses in the introduction
to the *Anatomy*. There he initially divides all literary criticism into
"scientific criticism and meaningless criticism" (18). This sweeping
bifurcation is followed by a "second division," which involves literature, not literary criticism (20). Only with this second division does
Frye begin adopting Cassirer, who says that "we are in the habit of
dividing our life into the two spheres of practical and theoretical activity" (Cassirer 1944, 109). This distinction, as used by Frye, comes
with an added Cassirean expression: every "form of mental construction" has a "theory and a practice" (*AC*, 20). The expression "mental
construction" is applied to Cassirer's philosophy in Frye's review of
An Essay on Man. The philosopher, he says, "starts by looking at the
variety of mental constructions in human life" (*NFCL*, 68).

Cassirer continues by disparaging our "habit" of dividing any or all of our activities into a theory and a practice, for "in this division we [moderns] are prone to forget that there is a lower stratum [in life] beneath them both" (Cassirer 1944, 109). "Primitive man," by contrast to us in our late state of historical culture, does not split life into theory and practice since life for him "is still embedded in this lower original stratum," which knows no distinction between them (109). Beneath theory and practice, and uniting the two, is myth; if we moderns neglect this "lower," and unitive force, Cassirer warns, we will "miss" the very "approach" leading into the "mythical world" (109).[2]

When the reader of the *Anatomy* takes Frye's Cassirean starting point into account—a mythical substratum which bridges theory and practice—Frye's strategy throughout the *Anatomy* becomes clear and distinctive. The relation between theory and practice is the same in each of the four essays of the *Anatomy*. Frye applies an expressive shaping form to an existing area of literary critical practice. On the one hand, there is a theory, a subjective theory; on the other, there is a relatively objective area of current practice. In the "theory of modes" he organizes literary "historical criticism." In his second essay, the "theory of symbolism" is applied to what he calls "ethical criticism." His "theory of myths" is an historicizing and systematizing of "archetypal criticism." Finally, his "theory of genres" encompasses "rhetorical criticism," or New Criticism.

Consider the middle area between theory and practice in the *Anatomy*. This area is especially important because the various myth theorists enter here. Just as a symbolic form has flanking areas that are unified by an intermediate area, so Frye organizes his essays with the help of a containing form that he takes from a metahistorian or myth theorist. Not only does he advance a theory so as to organize an area of literary studies, but there is also an intermediate area by means of which he hopes to contain the particular area of sub-field of studies. Frye says of the first essay on historical criticism that its "containing form" has already been "postulated" by various "philosophical historians" or metahistorians "of our time, most explicitly by Spengler" (*AC*, 343).

The present chapter merely extends what Frye says of his first essay—that it has a containing form—to the second essay. He begins his second essay with the suggestion that there are a "finite number of valid critical methods" presently being practiced in literary studies (*AC*, 72). Since the number is limited, he thinks that "they can all be contained in a single theory," his theory of symbolism (*AC*, 72).[3] The various methods being practiced he distinguishes by the unit of symbolism each tends to employ.

Frye shares with Cassirer the view of the symbol as a unit. Symbols are the units of literary expression for Frye, just as symbolic forms are the units of cultural expression for Cassirer. Frye's theory of symbolism starts with the symbol as a "unit of poetic expression" (*GC*, 224). He contrasts his view of the symbol to that held by philosophers such as Hegel, who "would most naturally start ... with the concept" instead of a symbol (*GC*, 224). Cassirer, however, is a philosopher whose units are not concepts but symbols. As Frye says in his review of Cassirer, each of his symbolic forms is "built out of units called symbols" (*NFCL*, 68). Frye's theory, too, treats "symbols as isolated units" of expression (*AC*, 122).

There are five kinds of symbol that Frye finds employed in literary studies: motif, sign, image, archetype, and monad. "Literary meaning," as it occurs throughout his gamut of symbols, is continuously "hypothetical" or "imaginative" (*AC*, 74).[4] From the outset (with "literal" meaning), he drives a wedge between the real and the imaginative, as Cassirer does in his "law" for art. For Cassirer, the salient feature of art is that "the image" is "recognized purely *as such*," as a purely imaginative structure (Cassirer 1955, 261).[5] Frye's initial phase of symbolism, the "literal," involves discerning that the literary work is self-constituted. Each literary work "constitutes" what Frye calls a hypothetical verbal structure.[6] With the middle, or "formal," phase of symbolism, it becomes easier to track Frye's linkage to Cassirer. In his review of Cassirer he says that "we seem to have missed something. The content of a poem ... is translatable. What about the form, which is usually the complementary term to content?" (*NFCL*, 73). He revises this passage a bit in the *Anatomy*: "Surely, it will be said, we have overlooked the essential unity, in works of literature, expressed by the commonest of all critical terms, the word form" (*AC*, 82).

The review continues with his definition of Cassirer's symbolic form, which Frye says is "neither subjective nor objective: it is intermediate, taking its structure from the mind and its content from the phenomenal world" (*NFCL*, 73). On the basis of Cassirer's symbolic form, the *Anatomy* proceeds to interrelate Frye's first three phases of symbolism. The formal phase resolves the tension between the literal on one side and the descriptive phase on the other by uniting them. In the Cassirer review, content and form are "complementary" terms; in the *Anatomy*, they are also designated by that word: the formal phase joins form and content into a symbolic form (*NFCL*, 73; *AC*, 82).

Another connection with Cassirer involves Frye's final kind of symbol. For Frye, "the symbol is a monad" (*AC*, 121). According to Cassirer, modern philosophy, beginning with Leibniz, brings in a "new view of the symbol" which goes beyond both primitive man's mythical thinking and Dante's medieval religious thinking (1955, 258). Leibniz regards the symbol, or "monad," as an "entirely independent and self-contained unit"; at the same time, because of its "particularity and independence," the monad is itself a miniature "living 'mirror of the universe,'" which it expresses, each monad according to its own perspective" (1955, 258). To Cassirer's account of the monad Frye adds the reader:[7]

> The center of the literary universe is whatever poem we happen to be reading. [The poem is here a monad.] One step further, and the poem appears as microcosm of all literature, an individual manifestation of the total order of words. (*AC*, 121)

The poem or work has become the living mirror within the reader through which he looks out upon a literary universe constructed from his extended experiences of reading. For Frye, the monad is a window through which the individual reader, looking into a poem or work, sees reflected in and through it his entire imaginative experience of literary works. The particular is the individual poem; the universal is poetry seen synchronically.

The theory of symbolism, then, "start[s] with a 'symbol' ... and end[s] with a verbal universe in which the symbol has become a monad" (*GC*, 224). It starts with a "unit of poetic expression" and ends with what for Cassirer is a symbolic and for Frye a literary universe (*GC*, 224). Cassirer reaches a purely symbolic universe by eclipsing imitation—the copying of the real world by the re-presentation of it—

so as to have a self-constituted realm altogether different from the real one. Every one of his symbolic forms begins in a mimetic, or representational, stage and ends in a purely symbolic stage. For Cassirer, art is "like all other symbolic forms" in presenting something other than "the mere reproduction of a ready-made, given reality"; art is "not an imitation but a discovery of reality" (1944, 183). Cassirer's "masterstroke," according to Susanne Langer, is to "accentuate the constitutive character of symbolic renderings in the making of 'experience.'" [8] He cuts off the self-constituted realm of art from the imitation or representation of the real world.

By the same stroke, Frye arrives at his entirely imaginative literary universe. He severs the Gordian knot between *mimesis* and myth by producing his "anti-mimetic theory of literature." [9] Life in the real world and the literary landscape the reader constructs out of imaginative experiences are distinct. "Literature" is self-constituted: an author inevitably turns to the work of his predecessors because his work "can only be made out of" earlier works of literature (*AC*, 97). The real hero of Frye's story is the imaginative reader, who as will be seen in a later chapter, creates an imaginative cosmos out of the library of all that he has read. [10]

So far, however, our account of the relationship between Cassirer and Frye has merely inspected the beginning of Frye's theory in the "literal" and its end in the "monad." Now the manner in which Cassirer is helpful to him in providing the containing form of the theory of symbolism will be considered. When this containing form has been grasped, it becomes easier to perceive the simplicity and elegance of his theory.

In his review of Cassirer, Frye distinguishes a more epistemological sense of symbolic form, from the sense in which it is a cultural form of human creative activity. The same distinction occurs in the theory of symbolism. Frye grounds himself in Aristotle by taking from him a set of terms. Aristotle's three terms are "*mythos*," "*ethos*," and "*dianoia*." Twentieth-century literary criticism conventionally designates "*mythos*" as "plot," "*ethos*" as "character," and "*dianoia*" as "theme." Frye, however, clasps Aristotle's terms into a triad with the help of Cassirer's more epistemological kind of symbolic form. Starting from the list in the *Poetics* of six elements of poetry, Frye divides them into two distinct groups of terms (*AC*, 244). Only the first group (plot, character, and thought) is under consideration in his theory of symbolism (*AC*, 73). While most literary critics focus on thematic matters, Frye is among the minority more concerned with plot. In the *Anatomy*, *mythos,* or plot, becomes the subject in the latter half of his theory of myths. It is *ethos*, or character, that becomes the secret agent of his theory of symbolism. This Aristotelian term, moreover, is given not only a symbolist expansion but also the same function as Cassirer gives to a symbolic form. That is to say, it unifies several things on either side of it—in this case, *mythos* and *dianoia*, plot and theme. Retrospectively describing his last three phases of symbolism, Frye says that he has

> portrayed the poetic symbol as intermediate between event and idea [in the formal phase], ... ritual and dream [in the mythical phase], and [that he has] finally displayed it as Aristotle's *ethos*: [now defined as] human nature and the human situation [in the anagogic or final phase of the symbol]. (*AC*, 243)

As noted, Frye designates Cassirer's symbolic form as "intermediate." The symbol in the anagogic or universal phase— Cassirer, too, takes the word "anagogic" from Dante—as in the stages before it, is portrayed in this intermediate area: it is neither subjective nor objective but instead the union or unity that fuses them into a whole. In the passage above, for example, Aristotle's *ethos* is a picture of human identity in the cosmos, man's nature relative to his destiny, or "human nature" in the light of the "human situation," or, in short, *ethos* is self plus setting.

Frye's notion of *ethos*, through the last three phases of symbolism, moves from a latent to a manifest position. *Ethos*, in this progression, applies to Cassirer as well as Aristotle. In fact, the several allusions to Cassirer are points in his delineation of *ethos*. Frye's presentation of his formal phase plays off the language that Cassirer employs. In his last paragraph on the formal phase, Frye says that "the work of imagination presents us with a vision ... of something impersonal" —namely, "the vision ... of the recreation of man" (*AC*, 94). Here he echoes Cassirer's view of the recreation of the "original creative power" of mythic language in art:

> The regeneration is achieved as language becomes an avenue of
> artistic expression. Here [in art] it [language] recovers the fullness
> of life [in mythic or primitive thought]; but it [art's mythic lan-
> guage] is no longer a life mythically bound, but an aesthetically
> liberated life. (Cassirer 1946a, 98)

According to Cassirer, Schiller (his source for this view) thinks that
"aesthetic contemplation or reflection is the first liberal attitude of man
toward the universe" (1944, 211). Frye says that in the reader's study
of literature "the vision of something liberated from experience,"
which is "the center of a liberal education," necessarily involves "the
liberation of something" within the reader (*AC*, 93). What it gives the
reader, perhaps, is the meditational space, the place for contemplation
of the model of action which the literary work proposes, a theater of
exposure to the impenetrable—or, as Ricoeur likes to say, a world that
the reader may inhabit.

Frye clasps his phases of symbolism together by employing the tri-
adic structure of a Cassirean symbolic form. Cassirer's construction
organizes his entire theory. He constructs not one but two symbolic
forms. The first ends at the point of *mimesis* and the second at the
point of myth—the myth of a self-constituted, sheerly symbolic, or
literary, universe. This second symbolic form begins with the
"imaginative revolution" in the formal phase and with the shift there
from a reflection of external nature" to what becomes an entirely self-
constituted cosmos. It begins as well with the movement of the latent
to manifest structuration of Aristotelian *ethos* in a symbolist direction.

Frye unifies his first three phases of symbolism by presenting them
as a symbolic form in which several adjacent phases are united by the
formal phase. Now the second of his symbolic forms, with his final,
anagogic phase also performing the role of uniting adjoining phase, has
the same structure. Both symbolic forms can be represented as follows:

	Subjective Shaping Form	Symbolic Form	Objective Content
1st group of phases:	literal	formal	descriptive
2nd group of phases:	mythic	anagogic	formal

This elaborate structure is the containing form of the theory of symbolism. Frye's theory is necessarily a dual vision, for its structure is dual. The exposition of this structure comes in his recurring comparativistic passages, especially in the recapitulations in his sections upon the formal and upon the anagogic phases.

Frye does not swallow whole anything he takes from other myth theorists. He adapts whatever he adopts. The theory of symbolism is considerably influenced by Cassirer's view that all symbolic forms develop through mimetic, analogical, and symbolic phases of understanding.[11] Frye's second group of phases is presented in the same order. His "formal phase" of the symbol is the pivot upon which his theory turns. Frye finds in "Aristotle's word *mimesis*" what he calls a "clear reference to two orders of nature" (*NFCL*, 116). What his two groups of phases, his two symbolic forms, delineate is his view that there are "two orders of nature," or "two orders of reality": the "world that [external] nature presents to us, and the world that human society constructs out of it, the world of art, science, religion [and] culture" (*NFCL*, 116). These are all autonomous symbolic forms for Cassirer, except "culture," which is the unity they comprise. The formal phase has a place in both symbolic forms because it completes the attempts of art or literature to represent the external world—"the world that nature presents to us"—and because the formal phase initiates the discovery of human reality. This effort is carried to completion by the mythic and anagogical phases.

Frye presents his formal, mythic and anagogic phases developmentally and, as he arrives at his conclusion, presents them synchronically, all of which repeats the process he had employed with his first three phases. Every one of his phases is embodied in the practice of literary critics and the poetic thought both of previous times and of what for Frye was the present time. All have functions within the study of literature, just as Cassirer's symbolic forms have their functions within the understanding of human culture. Yet Frye emphasizes the role found within his last three phases. Literary criticism has "a beginning in the text studied" (*AC*, 342). The study of the meaning of individual texts is supplemented by archetypal criticism, which is concerned with the relationships among texts. Yet archetypal criticism would remain ungrounded without the idea that literary "criticism has an end," or purposive goal, in establishing "the structure of literature as a total form" (*AC*, 342). The study of a text alone produces merely isolated commentary on it. Archetypal criticism by itself intuits isolated connections among works. Anagogic criticism by itself consists "chiefly" of "the more uninhibited" or oracular "utterances of poets themselves" (*AC*, 122). Each of the myth theorists with whom we are concerned has some vision of his discipline as a revolutionary enterprise that will either supplement or replace the field of study he inhabits. Cassirer is soft-spoken about his proposal, Spengler is shrill, and Frye is merely suggestive. He later abandons what in the *Anatomy* he proposes as a reformation of literary criticism. Such a reformulation of literary studies is nowhere in sight today. If Frye's theory of symbolism has a future, it may be as part of an effort to resurrect Biblical and medieval hermeneutics. Frye's essay may acquire new life when set within the concerns of a Biblical and literary hermeneutics.

CHAPTER NINE

DISPLACEMENT AND CONDENSATION

This chapter treats the presentation in the *Anatomy* of the "displacement" and "condensation" of mythic and metaphoric elements of literature.[1] The starting point is Cassirer, whom, as has been seen, Frye both follows and departs from on the topic of myth. The influence of Freud, who uses the terms "displacement" and "condensation" in *The Interpretation of Dreams*, will be considered. Frye's initial discovery of the process the *Anatomy* designates as "displacement" seems to have occurred during the Cassirer review he wrote three years earlier.

The first of the many descriptions Frye was to produce over the years on the development of literary structures out of myth occurs in his 1954 review of *An Essay on Man*:

> In primitive periods ... fictions are myths in the sense of being anonymous stories about gods; in later ages they become legends and folk tales; then they gradually become more 'realistic,' that is, adapted to popular demand [by an audience or by readers] for plausibility, though they retain much the same structural outlines. (*NFCL*, 74)

The outlines of myth show through structurally over time, despite changes in the content of stories. In the review, however, he offers no explanation of how or by what mechanisms the outlines of myth are retained in the stories that writers produce throughout the history of literature.

The passage quoted enters into the *Anatomy* with one modification. Since it occurs in the first essay, in which his context is the exposition of the tragic and comic classes of fictional modes, he gives those forms a place in this developmental framework:

> Myths of gods merge into legends of heroes; legends of heroes
> merge into plots of tragedies and comedies; plot of tragedies and
> comedies merge into plots of more or less realistic fiction. (*AC*,
> 51)

As can be seen from the following juxtaposition of the two passages, the difference consists of the addition of "tragedies and comedies" to the account of the development of myth in literary history:

Review of Cassirer	*Anatomy*
myths or stories of gods	myths of gods
legends and folktales	legends of heroes
realistic fiction	tragedies and comedies
	realistic fiction

After the *Anatomy*, Frye alters his account a little each time he presents it.[2] Our concern, however, is with his complications or expansions of it in the subsequent discussions within the *Anatomy* on myth's
development in literature. It is by surveying them that we arrive at his
full view of the topic. As in the works of Frazer, Freud, and Spengler,
the *Anatomy* distributes an argument across many pages.

Frye's earlier account of the development of myth itself, taken from
the Cassirer review, provides the point of departure for the third essay
of the *Anatomy*. Complication enters the hitherto straightforward account with the flurry of spatial metaphors in this passage:

> Myth, then, is one extreme of literary design; naturalism is the
> other, and in between lies the whole area of romance, using that
> term to mean, not the historical mode of the first essay, but the ten-
> dency noted later in the first essay [*AC*, 51-52], to displace myth in
> a human direction and yet, in contrast to 'realism,' to convention-
> alize content in an idealized direction. (*AC*, 136-37)

Here are two extremes between a middle area as well as a pair of
directions struggling against one another. The reader seems in need of
a compass to get some bearings. Is one to conceive of myth, romance,
and naturalism occupying successive areas within an horizontal framework, or do they occupy a sequence of positions in a vertically layered
framework (as in the lists compared a moment ago)? Whichever way it

is, the reader has then to imagine the "human direction" and the "idealized direction" as if they were transposed upon the line leading from the extreme of myth to that of naturalism.

The easiest way of apprehending Frye's schema is to think of it as a symbolic form, a threefold structure united by its middle term—in this case, romance. In any romance, myth supplies the form of the story and the content comes in through its realistic elements. Opposing processes are at work in the romance. Myth, in a romance, is displaced: whatever pertains to a god in myth is transferred to the human hero. At the same time, there is at work in romance the process of conventionalizing content in an idealized direction. So far, then, Frye says that romance "displace[s] myth" and simultaneously idealizes what otherwise would be a strictly naturalistic story, as in Emile Zola's novels, by encapsulating a story's natural content in literary conventions. The notion of conventionalizing content is close to John Reed's remark about Victorian fiction.[3] It is, he says, thoroughly informed by "conventional" literary "patterns and stylized characters or scenes" (Reed, 3). Frye had earlier in the *Anatomy* (52) spoken of "displaced myths" and he now speaks of the "principle of displacement" (137). Observe that he widens his discussion to include metaphor in literary language while defining this principle: "what can be metaphorically identified in a myth can only be linked in romance by some form of simile" (137). He then implicitly links different forms of literary language to four of his five modes. Mythic language is metaphoric. The three middle modes all use some form, increasingly displaced, of simile. The difference between these three modes is that analogy is characteristic of his romantic mode, significant association is implicitly aligned with his high mimetic mode, and writers in the period extending through naturalism use incidental imagery.

Fifty pages later in the third essay, he resumes his argument. It is now set within a discussion of romance as an elemental kind of story. In the third essay's introduction, he had presented a variety of examples displaying the relation of Classical myth to literature; now he broadens his scope by turning to Biblical myth. As in the last passage, his argument includes metaphor as well as literary myth. Finally, while in the several previous passages, he has only said that the dual patterns are at work in literature, he now starts by viewing them within literary criticism (188). For the literary critic, looking at the whole area of romance, "myth is normally the metaphorical key to the displacements of romance" (188). He seems to mean that, when the literary critic recognizes or identifies a particular myth, he holds a "key" to a romance story, but why is it a "metaphorical key?" Perhaps because the critic, by scrutinizing the degree to which the story's language has departed from metaphor and become simile, significant association, or merely accompanying imagery, can assess the degree of the particular romance's displacement from myth.

Having surveyed the *Anatomy* passages that bear upon Frye's argument about the development of myth in literature, let us return to our point of departure. His Cassirer essay presented his answer to the problem he thought the philosopher left unresolved: the relationship myth has to literary myth on one side of his "general conception of symbolic form" and to language on the other (*NFCL*, 69). We will then be able to place his several principles within the schema that he had advanced in the review. As can be seen in the chart below, the different forms of myth correspond to the different forms of literary language. The headings are from the review. The various terms in the columns beneath them are either from it or from the argument of the *Anatomy*:

Literary Myth	Myth	Literary Language
Myth	Undisplaced	Metaphor
Romance (displaced myth)	Displacement	Simile (displaced metaphor)
Ironic myth (condensed myth)	Condensation	Literal metaphor (condensed metaphor)

Observe that "Myth" is the central term in the layer of headings and "Displacement" the middle term in the column beneath it. One of the principles of the *Anatomy*, as mentioned, is that "the central principle of displacement is that what can be metaphorically identified in myth can be linked in romance only by some form of simile" (*AC*, 137). With the help of the schema above, we can see that by "central" Frye may mean that displacement itself is his central principle, for it accounts for the various forms not only of myth in literature but also of literary language. Romance is as displaced from myth as simile is from metaphor. On his scale of language, simile comes in between metaphor and the modernist technique of working through literal or condensed metaphor. In this case, Frye may mean that simile is "central" among the vertically aligned columns of terms relating to language.

Another feature of the schema, and something that Frye continually does in the *Anatomy*, is the yoking together of the synchronic and the developmental. The headings are synchronically arranged. Frye thinks the central category, Myth, unites the categories which flank it. The layer of terms underneath Myth is also cast in a symbolic form, but is diachronic. Just as he does with the development of myth in literature, so he develops a rough historical account of the pattern of the poetic use of language over time. Different forms of metaphor tend to be prominent within different writing cultures. A metaphor might identify a god with the sun by saying the god is the sun. A simile might liken some character to the sun or, in a more displaced form, name the character Esther Summerson. Ironic, literal, or condensed metaphor might use the hyphenated expression "sun-god."

His uniting of the synchronic and the developmental is more characteristic of Spengler, Jung, and Cassirer than of Frazer and Freud, both of whom are entirely developmental thinkers.[4] Frye closes his Cassirer review with his solution to Cassirer's problem: myth relates to both literature and language because it provides the elemental structures of both. Stories down through time "retain the same structural outlines" of myth; "the basis of myth," in literary language, "is the metaphor" or "statement of identity" (*NFCL*, 74-75). The *Anatomy* suggests that many literary critics since Aristotle have assumed that the metaphor is the basic unit of language: it is "the testimony of critics from Aristotle on" (*AC*, 123). One might add that it has sometimes been the testimony of philosophers and that it is the philosopher Cassirer who specifies that "the basic principle of mythic metaphor" is "concentration" or "condensation" (Cassirer 1946a, 95, 34).

If we consider the lowest layer in our chart, at the three sets of terms (Ironic or condensed myth / Condensation / Literal or condensed metaphor), then we notice another symbolic form with "Condensation" as the unifying term. In condensed myth, a fresh form of story unites two earlier forms within itself: a myth and a displaced myth. The literal metaphor is a complex or union of images.

The *Anatomy* segregates its one extended piece on poetic language (122-24) from the sequence of discussions on the writer's production of myth in literature. As we have seen, however, his basic framework is the same for both: an overarching view of myth in literature and in language. When we focus upon the brief section on poetic language, the presence of Cassirer and not Freud is discernible.

His section on language, toward the end of the essay on symbolism, has verbal allusions to Cassirer which come from the end of his essay on Cassirer. There, Frye endeavors to distinguish literary criticism, which studies myth in its imaginative form, from other disciplines, which study myth in its conceptual forms. As earlier seen, Frye's view of "the literary universe" as one "in which everything is potentially identical with everything else" echoes Cassirer's "law of metamorphosis" that "everything may be turned into everything" (*AC*, 124; Cassirer 1944, 108). For Cassirer, the law applies to a purely expressive "mythical world" (Cassirer 1944, 108). For Frye, his or Cassirer's principle applies to the purely expressive possibilities that language has, when seen as if there were a purely literary realm—something no one before the romantic poets had ever conceived (Cassirer 1944, 108).

Frye echoes Cassirer again when he suggests that there is not only a "structure of poetry" but a "structure of [literary] criticism as well," for he says that "the universe of poetry ... reveals [itself] only on its own terms and in its own forms: it does not describe or represent a separate content of revelation" (*AC*, 125). Here he echoes Cassirer's final sentence in *Language and Myth*: the human mind tends to discard "the sensuous forms of word and image" prevailing in the world of myth, yet the arts perpetuate these forms "and recognizes them for what they really are: forms of its [the human mind's] self-revelation" (99). For Cassirer, "the world of poetry" is a "world of illusion and fantasy," which yet is indispensable, since it allows the mind to recognize what it projects. For Frye, the world of poetry is as imaginative as the real world is imaginary, a view that derives from Blake and other poets, but he extends Cassirer's philosophy of symbolic forms by thinking of literary criticism as the latest of them to emerge. Its chief vehicles are the study of myth and metaphor.

In the third essay, Frye suggests that "mythopoeic literature" features a "greater degree of metaphorical identification" than secular literature does (188). This pattern furnishes his "literary criticism" with the principle, mentioned earlier, that "the myth is normally the metaphorical key to the displacements of romance" from "the quest-myth" of the Bible as well as "legend and folk-tale" (188). His assumption of a "greater degree of metaphorical identification" in "myth" or the "great concentration of" it found in "mythical meaning" resembles Cassirer's statement that "the work of art implies an act of condensation or concentration" (1944, 183). "An impulse toward concentration," defined as the "focusing of all forces on a single point," Cassirer says, "is the prerequisite for all mythical thinking" as well as of the "mythical formulation" that occurs in art (1946a, 33).

The notion that "condensation" occurs in mythical formulation provides a link between Cassirer and Freud since "condensation" is an aspect of the formation of dreams in Freud. Their common use of the word is not just incidental. Susanne Langer, in an essay Frye very probably read, observes that there is a "close and vital" resemblance to what Freud called the "dream work" of the unconscious mind and what Cassirer designates as the "mythic mode" (1946a, 62, 32) of primitive or mythic religious thinking (Schilpp, 395). What for Cassirer is "the *morphology*" or structure "of the 'mythic mode,'" she says, is quite the same as "'unconscious' ideation" in Freud (Schilpp, 398). Freud "discovered and described" what Langer calls "this nondiscursive mode of thought," and explored it in "dream, fantasy, infantile thinking" as well as in unconscious ideation (Schilpp, 398).

Others since Langer have drawn attention to the remarkable similarity between what Freud thought of as the "primary process" of dream formation (in contrast to his "secondary process" that applies to dream's interpretation by analysts) and "Cassirer's distinction between mythical thought and the representational thinking inherent in discursive language" (Krois, 82). It is apparently the case that Cassirer was more affected by Freud than he acknowledged publicly or perhaps was aware of himself. While this relationship complicates the problem of Frye's relationship to the two, it is still possible to distinguish between what Frye owes to each.

Frye summarizes some of the ideas literary critics find useful in Freud's *Interpretation of Dreams*. The sentence which follows reads like a distillation of the points the *Anatomy* takes over from Freud's book. Therein Freud treated dream:

> as a construct of wish fulfillment made by the repressed uncon-scious, and the fact that the wishes are often forbidden in ordinary experiences made it [the dream] an oblique symbolic construct, subject to certain mechanisms called "condensation" and "displacement," which enabled it to get past the socially disap-proving attitude in the mind called "censor." (*HH*, 204)

In Freud's theory of the libido, according to Frye, "the libido cre-ates dreams," which are themselves the products of wish fulfillment (*RW*, 36). In Frye's theory of story types "romance is the nearest of all literary forms to the wish-fulfillment dream" (*AC*, 186). The role of the libido in Freud and myth in Frye is similar, for in myth the story is about characters who can "do what they like—which means in practice what the story-teller likes" ("M&P," 227). Yet in romance humans replace the gods of myth and so live under some degree of constraint. Myths are "stories told without adjustment to demands for realism, plausibility, logical motivation, or the conditions of limited power," but with romance some of the complications of human social life enter ("M&P," 227). Frye begins with a hypothetical storyteller's paradise which is then subjected to the fall of displacement even with romance when writers begin to recreate earlier mythic stories. The imitation is part of the fall in Frye: the writer both imitates someone else's earlier mythic action and, at the same time, imitates life as it is for the writer and the writer's audience. Frye's account in the *Anatomy* is that:

> Imitation of nature in fiction produces, not truth or reality, but plausibility, and plausibility varies in weight from a mere perfunc-tory concession in a myth or folk tale to a kind of censor principle in a naturalistic novel. (*AC*, 52)

Strictly speaking, if myths are "stories told without [any] adjust-ment to demands" for "plausibility," then Frye ought to say romance and not myth ("M&P," 227). In any case, displacement begins with his three middle modes, which start with the romantic mode:

> Reading forward in [literary] history, therefore, we may think of
> our romantic, high mimetic, and low mimetic modes as a series of
> displaced myths, *mythoi* or plot-formulas progressively moving
> over towards the opposite pole of verisimilitude, and then, with
> irony, beginning to move back. (*AC*, 52)

These modes are the ones subject to displacement, which increases
progressively, so that the "censor principle" virtually takes over in the
late nineteenth-century naturalistic novel. The area of conflict is in the
three modes, or eras, of literary history. It is between the writer's desire to express what he wishes and the increasing demands made upon
him for plausibility.

In Freud, the primary process applies to the dreamer's experience
of the dream; the secondary process applies to the meaning or interpretation of the language of dream as it is recounted to an analyst. The
latter process includes a variety of interpretive, or symbolic, devices
used by analysts in making sense of dream language, and which have
also been helpful to literary critics in making use of poetic language.
Nevertheless, Frye, insofar as he follows Freud in the *Anatomy*, ex-
plores only the analogy he finds between the writer's production of
myth and Freud's primary process. Though displacement and condensation are two among a variety of the interpretative devices that Freud
uses to elicit the meaning of dreams, Frye does not use them to track
what a poem might mean. He follows Freud's' use of those terms only
within the primary process to account for how myth appears in different forms in literature. Therefore the area for comparison is the landscape of dream as experienced by the dreamer and myth as produced
by a writer. Here is the place to suggest that the attempt to relate Frye
to the area covered in Freud's secondary process will result in a blind
alley. The *Anatomy* follows Freud on the writer's production of myth;
it follows C. G. Jung on the reader's assimilation of archetypes. This
point will be delineated in subsequent chapters. The remainder of this
chapter compares Frye with Freud on the primary process.

For Freud, dream is the projection of an internal process. For Frye,
myth "begins in a projected form" ("L&M," 38). Freud says, in *Interpretation of Dreams*, chapter six, that "dream-displacement" and
"dream-condensation" are "the two craftsmen" mainly responsible for
the structure of dream. Frye may have become interested in these two

techniques for their potential bearing upon T. S. Eliot's understanding of "tradition," defined by Frye as a "creative and informing power operating on the poet specifically as a craftsman" (*CP*, 23). Eliot, according to him, offers no account "of what it is that makes possible the creation of new works of literature out of old ones" (*CP*, 23). Frye turns to Freud for these factors: the displacement and condensation of mythic stories. Still, his starting assumption that there is a body of mythic stories from which literature develops is to be found not in Freud or Eliot but in Spengler and Cassirer. Remember that it is Spengler who suggests that myth starts when a culture does: "myth-forming power," an "ability of a soul [Frye would say writer] to fill its world [Frye would say a fictional world] with shapes, traits, and symbols ... belongs ... to the springtimes of great Cultures" (I, 399). And remember that it is Cassirer who suggests that myth is a cultural world from which other symbolic forms develop; that symbolic forms develop out of each other, just as Frye says literary works do; and that expressive worlds all have a beginning in myth, as literary works do in Frye.

Myth for Frye can be traced through Western literature as a whole. He delineates three forms that myths take over time. It is undisplaced and projected at first, then displaced, and finally condensed or contained. In its initial form, it is projected. A myth is a god-story told by a human in which human qualities are attributed to or projected upon divine characters.

In undisplaced myth, for instance, there is the story of Proserpine, a divine character. Frye abstracts a mythic action, that of "death and revival," from her story (*AC*, 138). The simple fictional design of her story is that she "disappears into the underworld for six months of every year" and then returns from it (*AC*, 138). Among his favorite examples of a displaced form of this mythic pattern is the story of Hermione in Shakespeare's *Winter's Tale*. Hermione displays "the mythical outline of a Proserpine figure," for one thing, because the outline of the action Hermione goes through is the same plot line of death and revival the goddess goes through. Frye focuses upon the way Proserpine's pattern of action shows through in Hermione's. He also selects the word "outline" to indicate the specific character outline, something like the silhouette, by which Hermione is recognizably like Proserpine. The difference between their stories is that Shake-speare's is somewhat more plausible. Hermione's death is only an apparent death. "The final scene" of the play, during which "a statue comes to life, is displaced with a more plausible explanation that there is no statue and that Hermione has simply been hidden away for fifteen years, practicing standing still [as the statue] at intervals" (*WP*, 249). Works after Shakespeare down to the nineteenth century tend to become more displaced, more concerned with plausibility. The mythic action of the story of Proserpine recurs in Dickens' *Bleak House*, for example. He presents his heroine, Esther Summerson, through a heavily realistic filter. She nearly dies of a common disease, smallpox, but recovers though retaining some of the marks of the disease upon her face.

The third and last form of myth is "ironic myth" (*AC*, 42). Myth is contained within an unprojected, entirely hypothetical story structure, which exists alongside a realistic story. Ironic myth is myth present in neither an undisplaced nor a displaced, concealed, or latent form. It is instead condensed myth. In *Outline of Psycho-analysis*, chapter five, Freud says that "dream-condensation" means "an inclination to form fresh unities out of elements which in our waking minds we should certainly have kept separate." For Frye, mythic and naturalistic stories are brought together in ironic juxtaposition and contained within a condensed structure. Fresh unities are formed out of things usually kept separate in Freud, and ironic myth is for Frye a fresh story form in which two previous forms of myth are united.

The mythic outline or character is no longer concealed but instead revealed by the writer in this new form of myth. In contrast to displaced myth, ironic myth is not latent but manifest. A writer may even identify a mythic or legendary character before the story begins by naming him in the title, as with James Joyce's *Ulysses* or *Finnegans Wake* (where "Wake" means both death and revival).

For Frye, then, myth, after being increasingly disguised by writers through the technique of displacement, is revealed, by modernists such as Joyce, through the technique of condensation. In Freud, insofar as these terms affect the dreamer, not the analyst's work with the dream recounted to him, displacement calls attention away from a dream symbol, while condensation calls attention to it. Similarly in Frye, displacement offers a writer the means of calling attention away from the myth he re-presents by disguising it as an unmediated vision of the life of his times. For Frye, though, the representation of the kind of reality affecting both author and reader applies to the content or surface of the story. Underneath an apparently realistic story is a mythic outline that directs the form the story takes. Myth, in this form, is submerged to varying degrees, and so requires the literary critic to elicit the myth, somewhat as the analyst helps the dreamer make sense of a dream. Condensation, by contrast, is the technique by which the writer calls attention to the myth he is re-presenting. The myth is, to apply another pair of Freud's terms, "latent" in its displaced form and "manifest" in its condensed form.

CHAPTER TEN

THE FORCES OF CONVENTION

Initially the third essay in the *Anatomy* (131-239) resembles other streamlined products of its time. Like a 1957 Cadillac with rising tail-fins, dual exhausts, and so on, the essay, the longest of the book, has an elegant structure. Almost everything about it seems dual. It has a pair of introductions (131-40; 158-62), matching Aristotelian terms (*dianoia*, or thought; *mythos*, or narrative), a bifurcated title ("Archetypal Criticism: Theory of Myths"), alternating perspectives (archetypal, which looks for recurrence; anagogic, or universal), two parts (a survey of imagery; a study of story types), with each part neatly hinging upon a polarity (apocalyptic and demonic imagery; Christian myth and a demonic counterpart), two comparative frame-works (classification table for imagery; circular diagram for story types), and two means of proceeding (the developmental and synchronic species of comparativism inherited from the myth theorists). Despite these dualistic features, Frye's third essay has the same simplicity of structure as those before it.[1] It is helpful to perceive his organization of the entire essay before entering into a discussion of its several parts.

Like the second essay, the third can be visualized as the presentation of two sets of relationships obtaining within a pair of symbolic forms. In the first symbolic form, "apocalyptic" and "demonic" imagery affect "analogical" imagery which is displaced from one or the other of them. Their effect is to give the analogical imagery, which would otherwise be inchoate complexes or clusters of images, a structured form. Frye presents the three kinds of imagery with the help of the modal table he adapted from Spengler. The second part of his essay has, as its shaping forms, the polar worlds of Christian myth and its demonic counterpart. These worlds affect the mythic structures within the cyclical world of story types. The containing forms consist of all three of these worlds. The structure of the third essay, then, has much the same elegant simplicity as the second, as can be seen.

	Shaping Form	Containing Form	Structured Content
(first part)	apocalyptic and demonic imagery	table of three kinds of imagery	Analogical imagery or metaphoric structures
(second part)	world of Christian myth and its demonic counterpart	three worlds: the poetic world of the circle of story types and above and below it	mythic structures within a cyclical world of story types

This chart helps us confront the chief problem that the essay poses: how its several parts interrelate. A rule by which the chart may be read applies to both parts. Apocalyptic and demonic imagery, in the first part, act upon, but remain unaffected by, analogical imagery; similarly, the worlds of Christian myth and its demonic counterpart shape the structures they work upon without being influenced by them. The shaping forms bring the Bible's metaphoric language and the world of Christian myth to bear upon the imagery and the story types of Western secular literature.[2]

The containing forms of the several parts of the essay consist of three kinds of imagery and three worlds. The same rule applies: apocalyptic and demonic imagery remain unaffected by analogical imagery; the high and lower worlds remain unaffected by our cyclical world.[3]

In the third column, the analogical imagery and the circle of story types both belong entirely to our cyclical world of nature. The complexes of imagery and the story types belong to Western literature as it has developed from medieval times to the present.[4] The purpose of the entire table of five modal spectrums of imagery and his circle of four story types, as these metaphoric and mythic structures have been employed by writers, is to elucidate them for readers.

The twin topics of his essay are literary conventions (141-58) and genres (163-239), both of which are treated in a thoroughly unconventional way. Conventions, for him, are forces acting upon and within secular literature as a whole. His super-genres of romance, tragedy, satire, and comedy are informing forces running through secular literature as a whole. Conventions and genres are brought together, in the third essay, because conventions for Frye are structures of imagery and genres are narrative structures to which or by which that imagery is assimilated. For him, the structures of imagery in secular literature are metaphoric structures, and the structures of narrative are, or can be seen as, mythic structures. Frye usually assumes that "nobody can catch literature in the act of originating" (*NFMC*, 140). Nevertheless, his archetypal literary criticism views literature's recurring "structural elements," convention and genre, in the light of their constitution by, primarily, the Bible: by the radically metaphoric language of its final book, Revelation, and Biblical myth. Frye brackets the questions of the origin and historical development both of the language and myth of the Bible and of secular literature. He addresses, instead, on the basis of its metaphoric and mythic structures, what he calls secular literature's archetypes of imagery and its "archetypes of genres" (*FI*, 12). Both together, for him, constitute the forces of literary tradition. Separately, the archetypes of imagery are the forces of literary convention, where the archetypes of genres are the forces acting upon them, or the "pregeneric elements of literature" (*AC*, 162).

Frye's project, in the first part of the essay, was unconventional in literary criticism, but quite in keeping with the projects of other myth theorists. Robert Graves' *The White Goddess: A Historical Grammar of Poetic Myth*, "outlines the imagery of the cyclical earth-goddess cult as he reconstructs it from Classical sources," according to Frye (*WP*, 219). Jung's *Psychology and Alchemy* is for Frye another "grammar of literary symbolism" (*NFCL*, 129). Graves treats ancient Welsh poets and Jung treats the imagery of medieval and Renaissance alchemists, but they display the influence of, respectively, Classical and Christian myth.[5] Frye's project begins with the "grammar" that Revelation provides (*AC*, 141). He is assisted, in treating the demonic dimension of the imagery of Revelation by Frazer, whose *Golden Bough* is a "grammar of the human imagination" (*NFCL*, 89). With the help of Frazer, whose book he finds indispensable in both halves of his essay, he can cross over from the demonic imagery of Revelation to demonic imagery, as in images of human torture and mutilation, in secular literature; later on, he moves from "the ritual of the divine king in Frazer" to "the demonic or undisplaced radical form" he situates just beneath the "tragic and ironic structures" of secular literature, or the several story types, tragedy and satire or irony, in the lower half of his circle of story types (*AC*, 148). Frye's project, then, in the earlier part, is to survey the structures of poetic imagery and secular literature as these have been shaped by our "Classical and Christian heritage" (*AC*, 133).[6]

The earlier part of his essay (141-58) constructs a comparative table. It contains different kinds of theopoetic and poetic imagery that writers from Revelation to the present have used. The table is intended to help us relate the imagery of any particular work we read to the overall classification of imagery. Frye recognizes three main classes of imagery: "apocalyptic," "demonic," and "analogical," a kind displaced from the first two. Apocalyptic and demonic are Biblio-poetic imagery; analogical imagery is the kind characteristic of most secular poetic writing. Frye expands his class, analogical imagery, into three distinguishable species of it. It becomes easy to see that his various classes are arranged by his adaptation of Spenglerian metahistory. His classification table of imagery relates his five modes to the several classes of imagery, with the analogical imagery divided into three species.

Mythic Mode	Apocalyptic Imagery	Biblio-poetic
romance mode	Romance structures of imagery	poetic
high mimetic mode	High mimetic structures	poetic
low mimetic mode	Low mimetic structures	poetic
Ironic mode	Demonic imagery	Biblio-poetic

The three "structures" of imagery, in the middle of this table, are associated with the modes to their left. Frye situates almost the whole of Western secular literature relative to two classes of radically metaphoric language contained in the "the book explicitly called the Apocalypse or Revelation" (*AC*, 141). He thinks that Revelation is not only "designed to form an undisplaced mythical conclusion to the Bible as a whole," but serves, also, as a repository of condensed metaphoric language (*AC*, 141). The main point in arranging the several classes of theopoetic imagery above and below the three species of analogical imagery is to encapsulate almost the whole of secular literature. The entire development of secular imagery, from the medieval era through the nineteenth century, is subjected to what a military strategist would call a "pincer movement."[7] Frye envelops secular, poetic, or "analogical" imagery when he suggests that all of it is more or less displaced from the apocalyptic or demonic.

Though opposed, apocalyptic and demonic imagery present imaginative worlds, "worlds of total metaphorical identification" (*AC*, 158). "Apocalyptic imagery in poetry is closely associated with a religious heaven" and its opposite with a hell or a world beneath ours (*AC*, 147). The "conception of a heaven above, [and] a hell beneath" our middle earth, itself an outgrowth of Biblical metaphoric language, provides a canvas of the cosmos upon which secular poets have modeled their imaginative worlds, though Romantic and modern poets have often drawn their own world pictures (*AC*, 161).[8] Though Frye thinks that "in its apocalyptic context" in the Bible, it functions as a "vision of plenitude," the Great Chain of Being, as it developed after the Bible, became a hierarchic structure (*GC*, 165).[9] The Great Chain extends vertically through the order of nature. The links in the Chain are distinguishable levels of existence. They extend from God through various levels or planes of existence, including human existence, down to matter, or an inorganic baseline. The Great Chain provided poets with a scaffold from which to organize their imagery. It provides Frye with another dimension for his classification table. His complete framework relates the various levels of imagery to the levels of the Chain, which he designates as "worlds" or "categories of reality" (*AC*, 141). Here again we encounter Frye bringing together the synchronic and the developmental. All the levels of the Great Chain, his various "worlds," exist simultaneously, while his levels of imagery descend through the entire span of literary history. Working in tandem, these dimensions disclose the landscapes of poets. Their imaginative worlds can portray a world entirely desirable to humans, a completely abhorrent world, or one somewhere in between these polar extremes.

Though Frye's classificational schema seems intolerably complicated, the good news is that there is but a single rule to remember. Any single "world," such as his "vegetable world," is joined by *ethos* (discussed later) to any single level of imagery. With that rule for reading in mind, let us look at his classification table.

Worlds	*Ethos* or Character	Levels of Imagery
heaven	a world fully desirable to humans	apocalyptic
human animal vegetable mineral	Human desire and work in a world	romantic high mimetic low mimetic or realistic
hell	a world fully abhorrent to humans	demonic

Let us select his "vegetable world" and relate it to his various levels of imagery one at a time. Starting at the top level of imagery, an apocalyptic vision of the vegetable world would be a prophetic or poetic depiction of a garden of the gods, or paradise. A garden of Eden, with human figures, is the vegetable world in a highly desirable form since it requires but modest cultivation. As Milton's Adam says, it is "not to irksome toil, but to delight" that he and Eve cultivate their garden (*PL*, IX, 242). Delight or recreation in the romantic mode becomes "the painful labor of the man with the hoe" in the realistic mode, as in Hardy. In between would be the formal gardens Alexander Pope prefers, with "nature to advantage dressed," cultivated by man with the cooperation of external nature. Hence a high mimetic garden, as depicted by Pope or by Jane Austen in *Mansfield Park* or at Pemberley in *Pride and Prejudice*, presents external nature as shaped by man, yet retaining its naturalness. The full sequence of Frye's modulations of the vegetable world starts with a paradise, then moves through a human garden or grove, a formal garden or park, and then, when realistic landscapes become the new convention in the nineteenth century, to a farm. Any wasteland or wilderness is the demonic counterpart of the paradise. I have merely inflected the category "vegetable world" through his five levels of imagery, but of course Frye takes us through the whole gamut of categories on the left-hand side of the chart and applies each of the "worlds" to each level of imagery. His is a tour de force of literary critical comparativism, or "archetypal criticism."

His classification table presents Biblio-poetic and sheerly literary landscapes in layers. The uniform characteristic of his analogical spectrums of imagery is that the are conventionalized. He assumes that all sheerly literary "art is equally conventionalized"; the "communism of convention" interrelates his three species of analogical imagery (*AC*,

96, 97). The force of convention marks them all, yet each has a recognizable convention of its own. The distinct conventions, like the discrete genres he presents later, are to be located within literature, which "shapes itself, and is not shaped externally" (*AC*, 97).

The purpose of his classification table is not just to catalog structures of imagery. It displays as well the operation of forces that act upon and constitute the imagery in secular literature. The *Anatomy* presents an "anti-mimetic theory of literature" (*NFN* 5 [Summer 1993], 34). The ingenuity of this part of the essay consists of his effort to show that nowhere along the development of the three modes of analogical imagery—romantic, high mimetic and low mimetic—does *mimesis* have as much effect as the several forces he isolates. All three levels do retain a relationship to non-literary experience. Imagery, in these levels, is "attached to" and draws its "sustenance from experience outside literature," as a mimetic view of it would suggest (*SM*, 123). Yet what actually shapes or constitutes the imagery is a pair of anti-mimetic forces. One of them stems from the mythopoetic and the other from within literary history. His three spectrums of imagery are "analogical" because they are reflective, not of nature, but of, first, "the adaptation of myth to nature" (*AC*, 158) and, second, of forces that he designates the "organizing ideas" of particular secular literary periods (*AC*, 153). The adaptation of myth to nature is accomplished through "the analogies of innocence and experience": they are analogous to the worlds religious myth projects, yet secular literature confines such imagery to our human middle-earth (*AC*, 158). The organizing ideas of a particular writing or reading culture inform the imagery the writers of that period deploy in their different works.

Here again we have advanced into another confusing welter of terms. The main thing is to grasp the relationships that Frye's "analogies" and his "organizing ideas" have to his levels of imagery. Like any such visual aid, the table below is an oversimplification. Yet it may help us perceive the several operations at work upon the levels of imagery.

In this table, the "analogies" differ according to the "world" (higher, lower, or our poetic middle-earth) they present, but they also help produce or constitute a sheerly literary world. Frye's "organizing ideas" are shaping forms that constitute what otherwise would be merely associative complexes, or loose clumps of imagery into intrinsically metaphoric structures.

Organizing Ideas	Relationship of Poetic to Another World	Level of Imagery
chastity and magic	analogy of human innocence to higher world	romantic
love and form	analogy of human reason and nature to our world	high mimetic
genesis and work	analogy of human experience to lower world	low mimetic or realistic

In this arrangement, any single level of analogical imagery (right-hand column) is structured by a set of organizing ideas (left-hand column). He seeks to identify, within literary history, the constitutive ideas of the period. A set of organizing ideas can be considered a force of convention since it modifies a convention coming out of the past, so that poets, within their era, adapt that prior convention to the writing and reading culture of their time.[10] The middle column indicates the relationship between the sheerly literary or poetic world that a secular writer invites us to "enter," a world we may imaginatively inhabit, and some other world: a higher world, a lower one or the world we live in (*AC*, 154). The writer's selection and adaptation of a world varies according to his era. Yet we, retrospectively considering the sequence of eras, with the help of Frye's comparative arrangement, can now see them as three conventional landscapes that secular literature has produced. His comparativism helps us think these landscapes relative to each other. From that perspective, the romantic is an idealized world, the high mimetic is a stylized world, and the low mimetic is a literary presentation of an unstylized world in that it depicts an ordinary world much like our own, at least as we perceive it during ordinary experience.

His comparativism also displays, for our inspection, the relation of these conventional literary landscapes to the mythic-religious worlds that also contribute to their constitution. "The mode of romance presents an idealized world" the imagery of which "presents a human counterpart" of the higher, divine world (*AC*, 151). The analogy of experience can be seen in the same purely formal way or from the comparative perspective. Here the "demonic world" has the same relationship to the conventional landscape which realism usually presents as the "apocalyptic world" does to the equally conventional landscape he calls the "romantic innocent world" (*AC*, 154). The developmental strand of Frye's comparativism consists of the "integrating or cohering ideas" poets share with each other within an era.[11] His synchronic comparativism is comprised of the threefold set of analogical or purely formal relationships that are constituted by his religio-mythic worlds. Those mythic worlds and the three established by them comprise, together, a system.

The several parts of the third essay both feature Frye engaged in the "practice of archetypal criticism" (*AC*, 112). We see him, so to speak, filling in the spaces in an enormous canvas of imagery and then constructing a comparative circle of story types. Thus far, however, I have overlooked the main principle upon which his classification table is based. He says that poetic language comes to us in "the form imposed by human work and desire," as in apocalyptic imagery; alternatively, poetic language can give us "the world that [human] desire totally rejects" (*AC*, 141, 147). His three kinds of analogical imagery fill up the space between his antithesis. The first part of the essay hinges upon a dichotomy: his "polarizing of the apocalyptic and demonic" (*NFN* 5 [Summer 1993] 4).[12] The form imposed by human desire and work upon a world is the principle upon which his individual metaphoric structures, his comparative units, are based. Yet he presents the principle, without explanation, at the beginning of the essay. So we start his third essay in the same position as the participants of the game, which was popular at the time, "Twenty Questions."[13]

His major literary critical categories, in the third essay as a whole, seem to be taken over directly from Aristotle.[14] *Dianoia* (thought or theme), in this part of his essay, and *mythos* (plot or narrative), in the later part, are the terms he uses. The central term, in what is for him a literary critical trinity of Aristotelian terms, is *ethos,* or character. As in the latter part of the second essay, *ethos* is the secret agent of the entire third essay. As we explore some of the meanings that the term has for Frye, much of what otherwise seems opaque comes into focus. One such meaning has to do with human "characters and setting" as these appear in literary works (*AC*, 52). In its universal sense, he says it means "human nature and the human situation" (*AC*, 243). Still another meaning, the most important to our present concerns, is that it applies to "the poet and the poet's readers—or, more broadly, to the "relation between the writer and the writer's society" (*AC*, 53, 52). All this has a bearing on the present part of the essay, but none of it is quite so significant as the fact that *ethos* here comes to us filtered through Frye's reading of Freud and Cassirer.

The single concept that Cassirer finds valuable, in the whole body of works which he otherwise found almost as distasteful as Spengler's, is Freud's notion of "the omnipotence of thoughts."[15] This notion consists of the universal human disposition to think that whatever is outside us in the world can be subjected to our own, individual desire. Omnipotence of thought is universal, since we seek to enact this principle as children, our dreams often seem to express it, and perhaps we even construct the landscapes of our myths on the basis of it.

Each of the metaphoric structures, the units of Frye's comparative table, is constituted by *ethos*, human desire and work in a world. A completely desirable world may be inhabited by divine beings, whose power of action can be fully exercised. They can *do* what they desire. Yet this world can only be divined by us. Perhaps we can divine such a world because we are at least initially impelled by desire, despite our incapacity to enact the heart's desire. What is uniquely human is omnipotence of thought. "Thought," after all, coincides with the Aristotelian term upon which Frye founds this part of his essay (*dianoia*). By "thought," however, he means the same thing Cassirer does by the expression "mythical thinking." Such thinking is not at all limited to discursive thought. Mythical thinking, which Cassirer at once situates in primitive times, yet finds continually perpetuated by the poets and artists, engages human feelings and intuitions. Though Frye chooses to anchor his comparativistic units, his "structures of imagery," in Aristotle's *dianoia*, what he means by "thought" can also be set within the context Cassirer and the other myth theorists provide. Every single one of them contrasts modern, discursive, logical thinking with some more expressive form of consciousness.[16]

Structures of imagery, even within the various kinds of analogical imagery, are metaphoric structures for Frye because they are not just clumps or complexes of imagery, based upon the "real" world, but have their place in an imaginative, constructed world. His metaphoric structures feature the interplay of human desire and work not on the real world but on religio-literary, poetic worlds. Now we can see how *ethos* furnishes the rule for reading his classification table. His units of analogical imagery are, in effect, miniature symbolic forms. They are constituted by *ethos*, by human desire and work.

The projective power of human desire perhaps stems from the way desire recreates whatever it perceives in either external nature or in the human, social world as something in its own image. The objective side of *ethos* is the work it accomplishes in fashioning and cultivating a world. Every unit of his analogical imagery has both of these subjective and objective features working in tandem, but each, united by *ethos*, can be thought of as a miniature symbolic form, since it is *ethos* that unites the two sides and contains the several features.

The various sets of organizing ideas (e.g., "chastity and magic") each have the dual features just mentioned, but it is *ethos* that unites and constitutes them. Chastity is expressive of the hero in the literary era extending from at least Dante through Milton; magic applies to the setting or landscape upon which the hero walks: *ethos* is the power at work in these poetic worlds. For instance, in Milton's *Comus*, the heroine's chastity reflects the innocence of her inner mental state and outlook, which is "associated with magic" (*AC*, 151).[17] The poetic world she inhabits is "the innocent world" which is "an animistic world," a world where spirits have some power of action (*AC*, 153).

High mimetic works, which extend through the eighteenth century, have love and form as their organizing ideas.[18] Imagery typically displays a stylized relationship between man and external nature; nature is incorporated into man's works, so that human love recreates ideal forms.[19] Low mimetic works extend through the nineteenth century when genesis and work become organizing ideas for writers (*AC* 154).[20] A. C. Hamilton says that "as an inner power," a low mimetic world "may be called genesis; and as an outward effort to change the ordinary world, it may be called work" (1990, 130). The element of *ethos*, which unites the two, Hamilton designates as the "poet's power to create" (130).

Frye's account of the high mimetic organizing ideas relates them to his analogy of reason and nature. The constituting ideas, or poetic mental constructions, have their effect upon "the field of high mimetic imagery" (*AC*, 153). There is, however, a difference between his organizing ideas and his analogies. The province of each set of organizing ideas is the writing and reading culture in which the writer lives. Frye's analogies, though they also bear upon the writing cultures, have at least as much to do with us as readers. Apocalyptic and demonic imagery both function by "pulling the reader toward the metaphorical and mythical undisplaced core of the work" (*AC*, 151). The key word is "toward," for we move toward that core and not into it. Frye places us in the position to move toward his essentially Biblio-poetic kinds of imagery; later in the essay, he again takes us toward the polar caps of his circle of story types. So, in this part of the essay, at least in the discussion of analogical imagery, he suggests that the reader is pulled toward an undisplaced core of metaphorical structures, while, later in the essay, the reader is pulled toward the undisplaced core of mythical structures.

Frye's organizing ideas are the forces of convention affecting writers in particular eras. His analogies are the force of convention affecting not only them but also us. The analogies, too, allow us to see the effect, upon the body of secular works we read, of Biblio-poetic imagery. The point of connection seems to be that, while the organizing ideas are the means through which writers adapt the convention they inherit from the past to the requirements and interests of their own writing and reading culture, the analogies are constructed by us. The analogies are what the various periods of secular literature look like, when seen through the lens of Biblio-poetic imagery. The analogies are spectrums of imagery, but we see them only through the prism of the mythico-poetic imagery of Revelation. What we see are no more and no less than the forces of convention, in the use of secular writers' imagery, that the Bible helped initiate.

CHAPTER ELEVEN

THE MYTH OF THE IDEAL READER

The theory of myths in the third essay of the *Anatomy* (163-239) is the main site of Frye's myth of the ideal reader.[1] By "myth," I mean an expressive configuration by which a thinker expresses what others in his time are also concerned with.[2] For Frye ours is "the age of the reader."[3] While I have focused upon the theory of myths, others have called attention to Frye's concern with reading in other parts of the *Anatomy* or throughout his works.[4] For example, Robert DeMaria, Jr. says that "Frye's Promethean reader is as creative and as heroic as any writer."[5] The real quest-myth of the *Anatomy*, I think, comes in the theory of myths. It consists of Frye's vision of an ideal reader who absorbs, assimilates, and internalizes the literary traditions of comedy, romance, tragedy, and satire so thoroughly that they can be brought to bear concurrently upon whatever texts he reads. This complete power of perception, attained at the end of the theory of myths, resembles the complete power of action in the mythic mode of the first essay.

Frye's theory of myths contains a theory of reading that has the same structure as his theory of the writer's production of myth. Both theories have five stages. Both have three developmental stages sand-wiched in between synchronically conceived points of departure and conclusion.[6] The displacement of myth, the topic of chapter nine of the present book, occurs in the romantic, high mimetic, and low mimetic modes. These stages are developmental since each of those modes is characterized by the increasing degree to which myth is displaced. The counterpart, in the theory of reading, to this developmental pattern is the reader's *increasing* degree in the assimilation of what ultimately can be called literary "archetypes," or story types—the "*mythoi*," or story types, of comedy, romance, tragedy, and satire. Frye thinks that writers initially produce myth in undisplaced form and they finally tend to produce ironic myth or myth in condensed form. While the writer juxtaposes a realistic story and a mythic one or holds them together in ironic relationship, Frye's reader exists, initially, in an ironic relationship to a text. The reader is, so to speak, outside the text and has only certain concepts with which to understand it. These concepts, of course, are *mythos*, *ethos*, and *dianoia* (plot, character, and theme). They are synchronically conceived since they are an interrelated set of terms: the conceptual framework that he has used throughout the first three essays. In order to follow Frye's theory of reading through its three developmental stages, we must track what becomes of this set of terms.

Below is an outline of his theory of reading. The three concepts on the left line become his symbols of the reading process.

	Developmental Stages			Synchronic
Concepts	First	Second	Third	Conclusion
plot	plot structure	genre	*mythoi*	archetypal narrative
character	character type	reader	point of epiphany	ideal reader
theme	thematic phase	convention	mythic world	archetypal theme

His three developmental stages take an archetypal perspective: they are concerned with recurring elements in a reader's experience of literary works. To use another word, Frye's focus is that of intertextuality.

Reader-imposed structuration of literary works comes so swiftly that it is easy to miss. The theory of myths has, as its starting point, symbols of reading and not concepts, though Frye relies upon us to recall his previous discussions of his conceptual framework (plot, character, and theme).[7] Symbols, in the context of the theory of reading, are units of the reader's apprehension that integrate elements within texts such as plots, characters, and themes over an extended period of reading. Latent reader-imposed structuration occurs in the first stage of reading. This structuration is signaled by the expression "plot structure." Frye writes of it, not of plot, so as to indicate the slightly projective aspect involved in reading. Character, too, is not just that—a person in a text—but something partly in the text but partly evoked by the reader. So Frye's expression, "character type," means something partly constituted by the reader on the basis of his experience with characters from other works. In the same way, Frye focuses upon the "thematic phase" to be discerned within a group of works by a reader over time instead of a theme in a work.

In this, Frye's first developmental stage of reading, he treats a typical pattern of action, which has recurring character types of its own and which is set within the midst of a sequence of thematic phases. As he says, his procedure is usually that of "abstracting a typical form"— namely, a plot structure—from the midst of his later sequence of thematic phases, "and discussing it first" (*AC*, 225). His next step is to identify the character types that recur within the typical plot structure.[8] The final step is the presentation of a sequence of five thematic phases.[9]

The names of the thematic phases for comedy are: "ironic," "quixotic," "*typical*," "green-world," and "Arcadian." The italicized middle term, the "typical" thematic phase, is the plot structure with which he begins his discussion of comedy. When he says that the third phase of comedy is "typical," he means that it is the kind with which readers usually or typically tend to identify comedy. Notice, too, that the colorful terms by which he names his thematic phases are scarcely intended to be conceptual. Their function resides in their expressionism. Terms such as "quixotic" are chosen because they exhibit the reader's response to literature.

The "typical" thematic phase of a form of story such as comedy is typical not only because readers tend to associate that phase with comedy but also because the "typical" thematic phase is an abstraction of the whole sequence of phases. As such, the typical phase is identical with the "plot structure." The difference, as Frye has said dozens of times, is that plot is the theme in movement; theme is the plot held in stasis: the dual vision is as that of the reader.[10]

Frye's discussion of the plot structure of comedy implicitly assumes different kinds of readers. He starts by saying that "the plot structure" running through the history of comedy is "less a form than a formula" (*AC*, 163). He ends with an erudite description of "the total *mythos* of comedy" (*AC*, 171). The difference between the boy gets girl formula with which he begins and the "ternary form" with which he ends is accounted for, to an extent, by the direction of his discussion. He begins with what Samuel Johnson and Virginia Woolf call "the common reader" and then shifts into what becomes an increasingly rarefied literary critical perspective.[11] The movement is from the naive or popular to the sophisticated.[12] He accepts the common reader's assumption that the "formula," or "simple pattern," of comedy is boy gets girl, and when he takes up romance, he even talks about comic strips (*AC*, 163, 186). As we shall see, he begins with the common reader, then distinguishes three stages of increasing literary critical sophistication, and ends with an ideal reader, who is the common reader transformed by his absorption, assimilation, and internalization of the traditions of literature.

With the second stage in the developmental account of reading, the structuration of literary experience by the reader increases. Unfortunately, this stage is not easy to isolate, for Frye has, in the theory of myths, only a single symbol for the reading process: "genre." He does not say very much even about it. Frye calls our attention to this difficulty when he introduces a distinction involving the genres he recognizes. "The distinction between an ironic comedy and a comic satire, or between a romantic comedy and a comic romance, is tenuous," he says, "but not quite a distinction without a difference" (*AC*, 177). Perhaps it can be said that, while the "difference" is more fluid than solid, more subjective than conceptual, such distinctions are often made by readers. Yet the reader who confined himself entirely to such distinctions would sound like Polonius in *Hamlet*. Since Frye does make these distinctions throughout the theory of myths, we are entitled to incorporate them as a stage in the theory of reading. When we do, the relationship of his generic terms can be outlined, as in the chart below:

Genres

ironic comedy	normal comedy	romantic comedy
romantic tragedy	normal tragedy	ironic tragedy
tragic romance	quest-romance	comic romance
comic satire	parody-romance	tragic irony

From left to right, the chart displays the genre in movement. For instance, the story type of comedy starts with ironic comedy and ends with romantic comedy. A "normal comedy" would be one that encapsulates or contains the features of both ironic and romantic comedy. Is "normal comedy" a genre, or does it consist of the conventions the reader brings to comedy on the basis of previous experience with this kind of story?

All that can be said is that Frye does not answer that question in the theory of myths. However, in later writings, he does provide some helpful comments. "A convention," he says, "is an aspect of the identity of a work of literature" (*MM*, 79). There are two aspects. A convention "is what makes" a work of literature "recognizable for what it is" by the reader; and it "invites the reader" to enter into the work (*MM*, 79). Then there is genre, the term used "when the convention is big enough to include the entire work" (*MM*, 79). While convention helps the reader recognize a work and invites him into it, genre goes a step further because it "establishes the identity" of the work (*MM*, 79). It does so in several ways: by suggesting "the context of the work" to the reader and "by placing it within a number of other works like it" (*MM*, 79).

Suppose, for instance, that someone picks up a book entitled *The Case of the Perjured Parrot*. By Frye's account, he would soon recognize that what he held in his hand was a detective story, and his experience would lead him to put the book down or to enter into it. Having chosen to read it, he now has a context for reading it, a context that involves comparativism. Frye begins his sections on each story type from the point of view of the common reader and with popular forms. He starts with comedy, which he regards as the most stable of the story types, and he presents only comedy, among them, on the basis of dramatic comedies, using fictional comedies "only incidentally" (*AC*, 163). This he does in spite of the fact that he has just said that "it would be silly to insist that comedy can refer only to a certain type of stage play, and must never be employed in connection," for instance, "with Chaucer or Jane Austen" (*AC*, 162). In fact, Frye's theory of myths dissolves such conventional generic categories as drama or novel. His theory of myths is an attempt to go beyond them and to establish, for literary criticism, "narrative categories of literature broader than, or logically prior to, the ordinary literary genres" (*AC*, 162). However, when he says that he has "answered the question" that there are indeed "four narrative pregeneric" forms of literature, it comes as a surprise because we had not been aware that the question had even been asked (AC, 162). Frye presents us with his conclusion before the theory of myths has even begun. The weakest area in the theory of myths is Frye's second stage, which comes between his plot structures and his story types. From one point of view, his story types are "pregeneric"; from another, they are "beyond genre" (*AC*, 162; *SM*, 123). Perhaps his remark that "the study of genres, or the differentiating factors in literary experience" by a reader "is not yet begun" in literary criticism can be taken as bearing upon this portion of the theory of myths (*SM*, 123).[13]

Frye begins with comedy, the most stable and continuous form of literature, and he ends with the form that he wrote about before any of the others—satire.[14] His work on satire reintroduced into literary criticism the form that had been largely overlooked by others, and so did his work on romance. The theory of myths assumes that all four forms can be seen as continuous literary traditions. It provides four contexts for reading a particular work, and these contexts allow his literary comparativism. What the theory of myths leaves out is what he calls the "discontinuous quality in the larger historical tradition" in which his four forms of story have a place (*MM*, 86). Speaking of conventions in writing, he suggests that they sometimes "disappeared for years or centuries," only to "suddenly reappear" or "materialize again" (*MM*, 86). If so, then it follows that the forms of structuration readers bring to and by which they place literary works are at least as unstable as the conventions and genres that writers work within.[15]

Despite all this, the reader is at the heart of the theory of myths. Compared with the first stage, in which reader response is relatively passive or conceptual, in this stage, he is both shaper and receptor. Relative to the third stage, he is not yet capable, as in it, of creating an expressive whole out of what he reads. Had this second stage been more adequately developed, Frye would probably have positioned the reader between convention and genre. However, the structuration the reader imposes through convention is assigned to the recognition of structures of imagery, the topic of the first half of the essay; the recognition of genres belongs to this half, the theory of myths, and he does indeed recurrently employ the generic terms that the last chart presented. Finally, as for the developmental theory as a whole, the reader is both the shaping principle, because he progressively shapes what he sees, and he is the containing principle, for he gradually absorbs, assimilates, and internalizes his literary experience.[16]

His third developmental stage employs this set of interrelated terms: "total *mythos*," "point of epiphany," and "mythic world." It is a stage because it grows out of those before it. "Total *mythos*," for instance, is an expansion of Aristotle's concept, "*mythos*," or plot," and, for Frye, it is a plot structure. Total *mythos* means an entire sequence of genres within a form of story such as comedy. While total *mythos* and mythic world are the inner and outer versions of the same thing, in relation to the reader, the "point of epiphany" is the hinge by which the reader internalizes some mythic world that is outside himself.

Frye's section on comedy (*AC*, 163-86) is entitled "The *Mythos* of Spring." Comedy is like spring because it has analogous form of renewal. Spring is characterized by the renewal of external nature and comedy by the regeneration of human society. Comedy receives its identity from spring, yet the *mythos*, the "total" *mythos*, relates to all four seasons. The entire movement of comedy, like the four seasons, involves movement through the complete cycle of nature.

Comedy's total *mythos* depends upon the reader since the very perception of comedy as a whole requires the reader's recognition of a pattern of movement in it. It is the reader who has the imaginative capacity to provide such structuration or the shaping of the whole. The total *mythos* relates to this subjective dimension of Frye's theory because it is not something objective, something to be encountered outside the reader, but belongs within the theater of the reader's memory. The total *mythos*, then, is the subjectively but imaginatively imposed element, which allows him to organize into a whole his experience of comedy or of some other story type.[17]

The term "mythic world" is the relatively objective counterpart to "total *mythoi*." Frye regularly uses the term "world" throughout his discussions of the thematic phases of the four story types. Some instances are the "green world" of comedy (*AC*, 182), an "innocent world" of romance (*AC*, 201), a "world of adult experience" in tragedy (*AC*, 222), and an "upside-down world" in satire (*AC*, 227). A "mythic world," though, is the sequence of five thematic phases when viewed by the reader from their end-point. For example, the reader's perception of a mythic world of comedy is "as a sequence of stages in the life of a redeemed society" (*AC*, 185). Frye then recapitulates his five thematic phases: "purely ironic comedy exhibits this society in its infancy, ... quixotic comedy [presents] adolescence, still too ignorant of the way of the world to impose itself," and so on until he arrives, "in the fifth" thematic phase, with a social world that has become a "settled order which has been there from the beginning" (*AC*, 185).[18] In other words, the mythic world of comedy depends upon a reader's following the birth, the building up, and the establishment of the comic society.[19]

"Point of epiphany" is the expression that Frye sets between total *mythoi* and mythic world. It can be related to Aristotelian *cognitio* or recognition, though for Aristotle the recognition occurs "between persons" in a work (*Poetics*, ch. eleven), and in Frye it is a recognition by a reader of the relations between a particular world of story and some other world. Perhaps, too, there is a contrast between the "surprise" that Aristotle says comes with the "change from ignorance to knowledge." For him, it is a "surprise" to a fictional character; for Frye, each of the points of epiphany is a synchronic surprise to the reader of a form of story. As Robert DeMaria says, Frye's reader, having moved into a particular kind of narrative, suddenly, "in a flash ... perceives [or recognizes] the total form of the narrative" (DeMaria, 469).[20] Another form of recognition, the epiphany, probably has its origins in the Christian rather than the Classical tradition and it has more to do with setting than with a person's recognition, as in the mountain-top visions in Exodus and the transfiguration scene in the Gospels.[21] In any case, Frye begins his discussion of the point of epiphany by discussing settings (*AC*, 203).

The point of epiphany is something that the individual reader "recognizes" or "realize[s]" (*AC*, 185), has "comprehended" (*AC*, 202), sees or glimpses (*AC*, 223), or can "finally see" (*AC*, 239).[22] It is an intuition by the reader into the way a world of story is and also a possible or imaginative world that he has come to inhabit on the basis of his literary experience. The point of epiphany comes to the reader who has integrated his experience of a form of story so that it has become a way of looking out at the world around him.

Beyond the three developmental stages lies what Frye, very sparingly, calls a "total quest-myth" (*AC*, 215), or "central unifying myth"

(*AC*, 192). A preparatory outline of the *Anatomy*, "The Archetypes of Literature," had boldly asserted that his project would have "the quest-myth" as its "first chapter," but in fact the *Anatomy* has only a few sentences, in the third essay, and they should be taken as the synchronic finale of his theory of reading (*FI*, 17). Frye's vision is of the reader as a heroic quester.[23]

As archetypal narratives, "romance, tragedy, irony [or satire] and comedy are all episodes in a total quest-myth" (*AC*, 215). As archetypal themes, "conflict is the basis ... of romance," "catastrophe" that of tragedy, a "tearing to pieces" or "disappearance of the hero" or even of any "effective [human] action" from the world that of satire, and "the reappearance and recognition of the hero" with a "newborn society" around him that of comedy (*AC*, 192).

Frye's points of epiphanies, as he says of archetypes in Jung, are "double-edged." (*NFCL*, 122)[24] He says that the heroic "quest" of the hero, in Jung's *Psychology of the Unconscious* and later in *Symbols of Transformation*, displays "the double-edged power of the archetypes" (*NFCL*, 122). Archetypal personages in Jung have powers "for good or evil" (*NFCL*, 122). Frye finds this to be true of romance characters. They often resemble the figures Jung describes, such as the "wise old man" and an "evil magician" or the "solicitous mother" and a "wicked stepmother" (*NFCL*, 122).

For Frye, though, the double-edged points of epiphany do not involve their moral ambiguity. Instead, they involve what is a symbolist expansion of Aristotelian reversal (*Poetics*, ch. eleven). Just as the recognition becomes a discovery made by the reader, so the reversal (Aristotle's *peripeteia*) is a turning point in the reader's perception. Perhaps the ambiguity Frye wishes us to notice is that, when something comes to an end and seems to be vanishing from our sight, the possibility of apprehending it imaginatively opens within us. What has vanished "out there" is recreated within us. One might say that the point of epiphany can be defined as an "archetype," in the sense defined by Harold Toliver: that for Frye "only an archetype ... has the full, undisplaced reality of primal myth and hence a total knowability" (Toliver, 150-51).[25] Alternatively, the point of epiphany is an archetype, in the sense that Frye says he borrowed from eighteenth-century poet James Beattie, who says archetypes are "forms of bright perfection" (*St. S*, 82; see also, *EAC*, 94). For Beattie, it is the poet who "learns to frame" the archetypes; for Frye, it is the reader who learns to frame them: "it is natural for a twentieth-century critic" or reader such as Frye "to think" of archetypes "as reflecting the same images in other poems." For Beattie, the poet learns by comparing the archetypes (they are "compared," he says). For Frye, there are "analogous forms of the point of epiphany," so that the point of epiphany of a story type can be compared with the others (*St. S*, 82; *AC*, 205). Frye compares their places within his circle of story types.

He starts with "the natural form of the point of epiphany" in romance, which is set at the center. It presents the reader with the "sense of arriving at the summit of [ideal human] experience in nature" (*AC*, 205). By contrast, the comic point is dual-edged: looking one way, the reader recognizes the total form of secular comedy; looking the other way, the reader recognizes an "undisplaced," divine comedy, as in "the vision of Dante's *Paradiso*," though this vision takes the reader "out of our circle of *mythoi* and into the apocalyptic or abstract mythical world above it." The "point of demonic epiphany" in tragedy is an "undisplaced demonic vision," which is the opposite of comedy's (*AC*, 223). Satire's "point of demonic epiphany" is, initially, quite the same as tragedy's (*AC*, 238).

However, it is with satire that Frye springs his reversal, which comes in the last sentence of the theory of myths. Hitherto, his ordering had begun with the comic point of epiphany at the apex of his circle. He had then placed the romance point of epiphany at the center and had arrived, with the points of epiphany of tragedy and then of satire at or just below the nadir of the circle. His last sentence reverses this pattern. With it, the reader travels all the way back through the pattern to arrive where he had begun, though he comes to a new or natural perspective rather than that of the traditional "Christian myth" (*AC*, 185). When the reader perseveres "with the *mythos* of irony and satire," he "shall pass a dead center," that still point in the turning world of story types occupied by romance's point of epiphany, and will "finally see" from the perspective at the top of the circle (*AC*, 239). The reader engages in "climbing out on the other side of the world" of story "to see the stars again" (*AC*, 239). This reversal takes the reader all the way back up the axis of Frye's circle of story types.

CHAPTER TWELVE

JUNG AND FRYE

I presented Frye's theory of reading from a sheerly literary perspective in the last chapter, but now compare it with C. G. Jung's theory of individuation. The theory of myths (*AC*, 163-239) has a developmental sequence of reading stages. At each of his three stages, Frye deploys a set of interrelated terms (his initial stage consists of the terms "plot structure," "character type," and "thematic phase," for instance). All such terms are comparative, since they recur through his successive discussions in the *Anatomy* of comedy (163-186), romance (186-206), tragedy, (206-223), and satire (223-239). The particular comparative terms serve as the units of his theory of reading. What makes these terms comparable to Jung is that they come in sets, and these sets have their place in an extended developmental process. The purpose of this chapter is to elicit the structural similarity between Jungian individuation and Frye's theory of reading. My procedure is straightforward. It compares Frye's interpretation of the individuation process, as presented in Jung's *Two Essays on Analytical Psychology*, with what he himself does in the theory of myths in the latter half of the third essay (163-239).[1] Jungian individuation is, to an extent, a developmental account of a person's attainment of maturity; insofar as it is a developmental process, individuation serves as a model for Frye's developmental account of a reader's assimilation of his reading experiences.[2]

Preliminary Stage

Just prior to the commencement of his stages of individuation, Jung begins from the standpoint of ordinary, rational consciousness. Frye's reading stages are preceded by an ordinary literary critical view of the text as an objective entity. Frye speaks of Jung's individuation process as a "journey" (*SM*, 116). He also likens it to a "drama," since it "does not take place entirely within" a person, but has to do with his recognizing various archetypes that come partly from outside him (*NFCL*, 119). The initial setting of this journey or drama is the "ego" as it exists in the ordinary world. At this preliminary stage, Jung shares Freud's view of the ego; thereafter, he parts company with Freud.[3]

The initial view of reading in the theory of myths is analogous to Jung's preliminary stage. The "prevailing assumption," in literary criticism, "is that the work of literature is an object set over against us" (*SM*, 119). The literary critic approaches a text in the way the rational ego approaches the world. He gazes at the work with clinical detachment. He examines it as if it were an objective structure. Frye's unideal reader or New Critic assumes the work ought to remain apart from him as an object to be scrutinized (*SM*, 119).

For Jung, the continued opposition of ego to unconscious leads to neurosis. For Frye the maintenance of the stance of critical objectivity blocks the path to literary understanding. Undeniably, one must *begin* with the work as an objective artifact. Frye shares this assumption with his chief enemy, the New Critic, much as Jung shares his with Freud. A New Critic looks at the work or poem as an objective structure, yet for Frye this view is not even the first stage of his theory of reading but an assumption preceding it. His first stage begins only when the critic or reader goes beyond this New Critical perspective. Frye's initial stage, then, begins in a departure from that perspective just as Jung's begins in a parting of company with Freud.

First Stage

According to Frye, the first stage in Jung's individuation process is that "the ego must come to terms with the shadow and recognize its essential continuity with it" (*NFCL*, 117). The shadow is the first of the psychological archetypes that the ego encounters. It comprises "one's suppressed or ignored desires" (*NFCL*, 117). When the ego does come to terms with the shadow, then "the center of the psyche ... shifts back from the ego to a balancing point between ego and shadow" (*NFCL*, 117). "The outer psyche now becomes a 'persona,' or social mask," Frye says, "and the inner one a 'soul,' or focus of love" (*NFCL*, 118).

In Frye's theory of myths, the first stage is that each of the relatively objective entities for analyzing a literary work becomes reader-informed. Frye takes his terms for these entities from chapter six of Aristotle's *Poetics*. He starts from the terms "plot," "character," and "theme" because these are among the established verbal tokens of literary critical discussion. Frye differs from many of the critics at the time in several ways. While others focused upon a particular literary work, he is interested in the relations between works. While others were primarily engaged in identifying the theme of a work, he begins his discussions of comedy, romance, tragedy, and satire by identifying the typical or normal plot structures of these story types, and then goes on to discuss their character types and their recurrent thematic phases. "Plot," "character," and "theme" are terms he shares with others, but the terms he uses, in the theory of myths, are "plot structure," not plot, "character type," not character, and "thematic phase," not theme.[4] What is the difference? It resides in the way relatively objective terms have already become imbued with meaning by the reader. Plot, character, and theme are "objective" in the sense that they are "in" a literary work, but that work depends upon a reader and Frye's reader has the capacity to recognize them as elements in his experience of literature. Hence, the first stage of Frye's theory of reading has already crossed over from the New Critic's "assumption," which is "that the work of literature is an object set over against us" (*SM*, 119). In Frye's first stage of reading, "plot structure," "character type," and "thematic phase" constitute a class of terms. The theory of myths, as we shall see, has three classes of terms. Together, these classes move from a latent-to-manifest pattern. These classes represent the increasing structuration of a reader's experience. Frye organizes his discussion with some help from Jung's *Two Essays*.[5] He works from Jung in presenting the development of the reader's experience of literature in the same way he works from Freud in presenting how writers, over time, displace and then condense myth.

The middle stage, in Jung, involves the surpassing of a second crisis. If the first consists of the tendency to consider the shadow as enemy, an alien outside the ego, then the second is for the newly established and emerging center of the developing self to avoid "being absorbed in either persona or anima" (*NFCL*, 118). These outer and inner aspects of the psyche are to be kept in balance if the newly established center is to be preserved.[6]

The same situation occurs in Frye. Balance between what he calls "genre" and "convention" is maintained by what is no less than the central personage of the theory of reading as a whole: the reader. It is the reader who needs to give both genre and convention an equal place within his reading. Genres are important because they are the "differentiating factors in literary experience" (*SM*, 123). Conventions have the function of allowing the reader to relate a work to its own time.

A third stage ensues when the emerging self has moved through that crisis.[7] "The natural result," Frye says, "is the release of two deeper powers from the unconscious" (*NFCL*, 118). In *Two Essays*, Jung calls these by such names as the "great mother" and the "magician" (228).[8] In Frye, the literary equivalent of these powers is a pair of factors that stem, not from the collective unconscious, but from literary tradition. The pair of factors is, in effect, reinforcements that come to and expand the study of genre and convention. He calls these two archetypes of literary experience the "total *mythos*" and the "mythic world."[9] They are the inner and outer aspects of the same thing: literary tradition. A "total *mythos*" is the inner aspect of tradition, for it involves a reader's experience of the particular form of literature.[10] A "mythic world" is the reader's outward apprehension of that form. It is his imaginative perception that there is, say, a world of romance. For example, the reader may take up the Joseph story in Genesis, a Greek, Latin, or Christian romance, or Spenser, Scott, Stevenson, or the latest piece of science fiction, and he recognizes the same "world" in them. The romance world is idealized: the leading character is brave, the heroine beautiful, and the villain villainous.[11]

Frye never fails to adapt what he adopts from another myth theorist. Relative to Jung, he observes that the "soul" within Jung's "system" of archetypal figures "is the anima" (*NFCL*, 120).[12] He objects to this, because it seems inconsistent to identify the "soul" (traditionally thought of as an immortal part of man) with the "anima," which is "a part of the undeveloped ego that is eventually dissolved into a function of an obviously mortal individual" (*NFCL*, 120). So, while the "soul" has a place in Jung's first stage of individuation, Frye does not think it belongs there. Hence, he corrects or revises Jung by placing the anima within the second stage of individuation.

This adaptation of Jung's "system" of archetypal figures is important for understanding his system of literary archetypes. "Plot" is one of them, and not merely one, but the first. The reason why is that he agrees with Aristotle that the plot is the "soul" of a story (*Poetics*, ch. six). Frye thus has plot, or rather "plot structure," as the very first thing he discusses in his comparative study of the story types. "Plot structure" is preeminent among his initial triad of terms (plot structure, character type, and thematic phase), a triad which provides the basis of his exposition.

From the point of view of his revision of Jung's system of archetypal figures, the anima is near the heart of that system. And, if the anima is near the heart of Jung's system, as revised by Frye, then it is the reader who is at the very heart of Frye's system. It is the reader who occupies the central place in Frye's developmental account of reading.

The centrality of the reader is indicated in the comparative chart below.[13] This visual aid helps us perceive the structural similarity between Jung's system of archetypes, as revised by Frye (*NFCL*, 117-118) and the literary archetypes he deploys in his theory of myths (*AC*, 163-239). All of the expressions, such as "balancing point" or "character type," are used by Frye.[14] The stages the chart compares are stages of the individuation process in Jung as revised by Frye and in his reading process.

		First Stage	
Jung:	soul	balancing point	shadow
Frye:	plot structure	character type	thematic phase

		Second Stage	
Jung:	anima	center	persona
Frye:	genre	reader	convention

		Third Stage	
Jung:	great mother	center of personality	magician
Frye:	total *mythos*	point of epiphany	mythic world

Among the three classes of terms assigned to Jung, the collective unconscious is the source of his psychological archetypes. The "reader" is the central term among Frye's entire constellation of terms. The reader is container of the other terms; he is the repository of the literary archetypes.

The stages, in Jung, are distinguishable, because one follows from another. The succession of archetypal personages occurs in a regular order. Jung's analytical treatment was based upon the assumption that the archetypal figures present themselves in a sequence.[15] A complete analytical treatment would move through a sequence of four archetypal figures: shadow, persona, anima, and counsellor (the last term stands for both the great mother and magician).[16] Even in *Two Essays*, Jung sometimes mentions other archetypes.[17] Similarly in Frye: even in the *Anatomy* he offers an almost infinitely elastic definition of an archetype, which can be whatever is "recognizable as an element" of an individual reader's "literary experience as a whole" (365).[18] Yet he does say that "the word archetype," which he uses "in Jung's sense of an aspect of personality capable of dramatic projection," refers to only four figures: "shadow," "persona," "anima," and "counsellor" (291).[19]

The chart above should not be construed as suggesting similarity between any particular archetype in Jung and Frye (e.g., between an anima in Jung and a genre in Frye). The purpose of the chart is to display the structural similarity between the developmental dimension of Jung's theory of individuation and a similar dimension in Frye's theory of reading. Frye draws upon Jung's theory in much the same way he works from Spengler in the first essay and Cassirer in the second. These theorists supply him with the scaffolding for his literary "theory of modes," "theory of symbols," and his "theory of myths." None of these theories can be said to be sheerly Spenglerian, or Cassirean, or Jungian, since Frye adapts what he adopts from all three men. Relative to the adoption of the developmental dimension of Jungian individuation, the most significant adaptation is his repositioning of the anima, so as to begin with what he regards as the Aristotelian insight that plot is the "soul" of a work. Finally, it is not just their stages of development that are similar. Jung and Frye begin and end in analogous ways. Jung begins, Frye says, with "the reasoning and sensational ego," and he ends with a "fully integrated human being" (*HH*, 255).[20] A person begins in the midst of ordinary experience and ends in something like creative fantasy or spiritual experience. Frye's contrast begins with a reader, in the midst of ordinary experience, confronting a text as if it were an enemy or as "an object set over against us" (*SM*, 119). He ends with an imaginative "way of reading literature, where, in Jungian terms, not the conscious ego but the superconscious individual directs" (*NFN* 5 [Summer 1993], 17, item 273).[21]

This "superconscious individual" is the ideal person in Jung and the fully imaginative reader in Frye. The developmental processes of both theorists issue into synchronic conclusions. Their synchronic portrayals of the self and the reader are the capstones of their three developmental stages. Thus far our procedure has been to track appropriate portions of Jung's *Two Essays* with the help of Frye's remarks about it in his review essay. Our track vanishes because, as Frye says, the synchronic capstone of the theory of individuation "comes somewhere in between" Jung's *Two Essays* (*NFCL*, 118).[22] In order to pick up the path along which the two men can be compared, we need a fresh start and a new chapter. Borrowing C. A. Meier's insight about Jungian individuation, we can suggest that the theory of myths "begins and ends with typology."[23]

CHAPTER THIRTEEN

CIRCLE OF STORY TYPES

Both Jung and Frye offer a goal towards which their respective developmental accounts of individuation and reading move. Both present their goals, their ideals, in synchronic fashion, through the symbol of a circle. Jung's circle presents an ideal "self" and Frye's an ideal reader. Four psychological types or functions are circumscribed within Jung's circle. Four story types are circumscribed within Frye's circle. Both circles consist of a set of four coordinated and simultaneously existing relationships, which the person or reader has brought to consciousness or internalized. Like a compass, both circles have four points of orientation. Both men present their ideals through a moving rather than stationary circle. Nevertheless, after examining these parallels, it is important to distinguish Frye's circle from Jung's. Often, Frye's points of departure from Jung can be observed with the help of the other myth theorists.

The circle below on the left represents the Jungian "self" as described by Frye.[1] Next to it is Frye's circle of story types.[2]

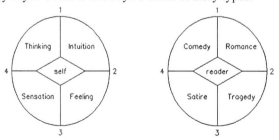

When the Jungian individuation process has been completed, according to Frye, "the self is now the center of a circle with four cardinal points" (*NFCL*, 119). Frye does not use the expression "cardinal points" in the theory of myths, though he does use it in several sections in the last essay of the *Anatomy*; he does, however, use a comparable expression: "points of epiphany" (*AC*, 203-06).[3]

Also comparable are the relationships between pairs of terms within their respective circles. In Jung's, for instance, "thinking" is the opposite of "feeling."[4] Frye's story types also "form two opposed pairs," since "tragedy and comedy contrast... and so do romance and irony" or satire (*AC*, 162). The self, in Jung, usually works with a pair of the opposing functions, as with "thinking" and feeling," yet has the capacity to bring all four functions into play simultaneously, in which case his portrayal of the self is entirely synchronic.

Frye says that the Jungian self has four interrelated "types of consciousness" (*MM*, 178). "There are," similarly, "four main types of mythical movement" in Frye's circle (*AC*, 162). He suggests that when selfhood has been attained, a person now "works with far more coordinated and schematic modes of perception" (*SM*, 116). By "modes of perception," he means Jung's four psychic functions, which Frye lists in this order: thinking, feeling, intuiting, and sensing.[5] Jung says that his "division" of the four types "entirely corresponds with experience"; Frye, too, appeals to "our experience," our reading experience (*AC*, 162).[6]

There is a contrast that Frye makes between the beginning and the end of Jung's theory of individuation:

> Structures of symbolism are seen as emanating from a collective unconscious through a consciousness that has accepted the Jungian shift from a rational ego, opposed to the unconscious [at the beginning of individuation] to an individuality [or self with which Jung ends his theory] in rapport with it. (*NFCL*, 95)

The contrast Frye says that Jung makes is in keeping with "one of the major cultural trends of our time," since the twentieth century has tended to contrast "our present form of consciousness, with its ego center" with a more desirable and constructive ideal of an expanded consciousness (*MM*, 74).[7] Within the context of his literary criticism, Frye's theory of reading begins with a literary critic appraising or evaluating a text or work "by what Jung calls the 'ego'" (*SM*, 119), and it ends with an expanded literary consciousness that has not only dissolved the ego-like work so that it "revives within" the reader, but which has that reader experiencing what he reads "with far more coordinated and schematic modes of perception" (*SM*, 116). That is to say, the reader eventually has the capacity to draw upon his accumulated experience of comedy, romance, tragedy, and satire, in the same way that Jung's individual draws upon all of his mental functions. The ideals of Jung and Frye assume that all four of these resources, functions, or types can be drawn upon synchronically in contrast to their initial ego-bound person or reader who has the random perceptions of ordinary life or literary experience available to him.[8]

Frye offers an interpretation of the "shifting" from the ego to the self that brings about individuation or transformation.

> The center of the personality has finally been *transferred* from the ego to a "self" which is the real center. The four "archetypes," or semi-autonomous personalities which the psyche has partly created and partly evoked, now *settle into* the four functions of psychic life: thought, feeling, intuition, and sensation. (At least I think they do, but this point comes somewhere between the two books, and Jung's argument here may be less symmetrical than my account of it.) The self is now the center of a circle with four cardinal points, and this fourfold circle appears everywhere in religion, art, and private dreams as the diagram called the "mandala." (*NFCL*, 118-19)

The several words I have italicized are verbs. To say that four archetypes "settle into" four psychological types or functions is an apt comment, since Frye seizes upon the word "settlement" in *Two Essays*; yet he avoids what makes this process dynamic, for Jung, the "transcendent function," which actively supervises or coordinates the four functions, and so flattens or makes static Jung's account: it is as though, by Frye's account, the restless archetypes somehow get poured into the molds of the psychological types or functions and so "settle" down.[9] In the same way, when he says that the center of the psyche "has finally been transferred," he adopts the passive voice. The passage above presents Jung in outline. It is nearly caricature, though: it is like the outline of a person that remains after he has been flattened by a steamroller. Nevertheless, I think he brings together what com-

mentators on Jung usually segregate.[10] He helps us to see that individuation ends with typology.[11]

When Frye says that four archetypes "settle into" four psychological types or functions, he implies that there is an end to their movement; when he says that the psychic center "has finally been transferred from the ego to the self," the shift from one to the other involves
movement. Reading Jung with Frye's help, one can say that
"transformation" has to do with what the archetypal figure, that had
been symbols of the libido along the way towards individuation, have
become: they have become dissolved into the four functions of the
mind. By contrast, "individuation" is applicable to a situation in
which the four forms of perception are no longer discrete or divided,
but an indivisible and synchronically functioning whole: a self-
expressive mode of apprehension that has gathered together four types
of consciousness into a unified outlook.[12]

Jung often draws upon religious or philosophical terms. When, for
instance, he speaks of "the revelation of the essential man," he wishes
to evoke the transformed perspective the completed process of individuation has elicited (*Two Essays*, 110). Frye's version of this process
draws instead upon several of the most traditional of literary terms.
"Recognition" and "reversal" are taken over by him from Aristotle.[13]
As we shall see, though, he virtually reverses the meanings they have
in Aristotle; alternatively, they are almost transformed beyond recognition. Frye, to say it more temperately, expands the terms he takes
from Aristotle by making them more expressionistic: they have to do
with the ways in which a reader, not a writer, expresses inner, subjective elements of his literary experience.[14]

Another difference between the two thinkers is this. Jung's circular
diagram stands for the self. Turn this picture of the self over and the
verso or reverse side is an integrally related picture of what he calls the
archetype of God.[15] For him, the recognition of the self simultaneously
involves the recognition of God and vice-versa. Frye's circular diagram ultimately represents an ideal reader, yet he begins by referring
neither to God or man, but to "the natural cycle" (*AC*, 162). He depicts the "cyclical movement within the order of [external] nature" and
not, as in Jung, "the revelation of the essential man" or human nature.[16] Frazer is more productively compared to Frye relative to this

natural cycle. The "order of nature," conceived as a whole by Frazer, is a "great cycle"; also, as a sequence of four seasons contained by this cycle, nature consists of "regularly recurrent events," which is, per- haps, like the view of Frye's archetypal critic whose focus is upon regularly recurring elements of his literary experience (1922, 162).

Jung's circle should be conceived as "vividly rotating," and so should Frye's (Meier, 257). Yet Frye's circle has a precedent in Frazer's cycle as seen from a Spenglerian point of view. To borrow again from Hamilton's insightful observation, Frye's circle is "a turning wheel in a Spenglerian cycle of birth, growth, maturity, and death" (135). In Frye's seasonal movement, the hero is born or emerges as the "mysterious" comic hero, the "life" of this figure is the focus of ro- mance, and his death the focus of tragedy; with satire, the hero whom the reader had recognized is seen from a reversed perspective: the very notion of the humanly heroic is increasingly removed from the natural landscape (*AC*, 192, 198).[17]

The most helpful perspective of Frye's circle of story types ought to relate that construction to *all* the myth theorists. Jung is most relatable to Frye's account of romance, but even the section on romance relates Jung to Freud and both of them to Frazer. "Quest romance," relative to Jung, "is the search of the libido or desiring self for a fulfillment that will deliver" the "self," but it does so through the assimilation of the various figures the self encounters: these include not only Jung's ar- chetypal personages, but equivalent figures in Freud (*AC*, 193). Rela- tive to Frazer, "the quest-romance is the victory of fertility over the waste land" (*AC*, 193). This view of the self and the natural landscape should be related to a central line of thought that starts with Frazer and reaches its culmination not only in Jung, but also in Cassirer. The natural landscape can be related to a central line of thought that starts with Frazer, is extended by Freud, and reaches its culmination not only in Jung, but Cassirer.

Frazer says that primitive man projects upon the landscape of ex- ternal nature "the fulfillments of his hopes or the accomplishments of his fears" (1922, 162). Freud follows right behind Frazer (and others) both in suggesting that man initially projected his desires and fears upon the natural landscape, and in assuming three stages of human development. These stages are the "animistic (or mythological), religious," and the "scientific."[18] Something Freud contributes to this discussion is his suggestion that "the field of art" is the "single field" in which the initial "primitive mode of thinking" (*Totem and Taboo*, 90) continues down through the present (*Totem and Taboo*, 86). Cassirer iterates Freud's point when he says that "there is one intellectual realm in which the world not only preserves its creative power, but is ever renewing it" (*L&M*, 98). Art, he agrees with Freud, returns to primitive thinking; yet a great advance (in his view, though not Freud's) is made: the human mind has internalized mythic word and image. They are no longer forces or powers outside the mind in external nature, but have become the "organs" of human perception (*L&M*, 99). They are the expressive forms through which the mind looks out upon reality. They are, in Cassirer's great phrase, "forms" of the mind's "self-revelation" (*L&M*, 99). The Jungian "self," with its "revelation of the essential man" is virtually identical with this, the closing sentence of *Language and Myth*.[19] It would appear, then, that Frye's view can, with equal plausibility, be compared with either Cassirer or Jung. Perhaps he works from Cassirer, in which case the assumption would be that the "forms" of the mind's "self-revelation" are four story types, which are the organized or most complete forms human experience ever takes. Or, perhaps, he works from Jung in assuming that there "gradually emerge," for the reader, "four fundamental types of imaginative experience in literature," which, when they have gradually been internalized through extensive reading experiences, have become "coordinated and schematic modes of perception" within him, like the modes of apprehension through which the self finds expression in Jung (*OE*, 117; *SM*, 116).

The theory of myths has a discussion of "points of epiphany" at its center (*AC*, 203-06) and each of the theory's sections concludes with a treatment of the point of epiphany of the individual story types (*AC*, 185, 205 223, and 237-39). Frye assumes that there are "analogous forms of the point of epiphany," which suggests the possibility of comparing the points of epiphany of the four story types (*AC*, 205). I shall approach his treatment of them with the help of Jung and Spengler. My thesis is that his comparative treatment of the points of epiphany is both developmental and synchronic, and that the developmental treatment is relatable to Jung and the synchronic treatment is relatable to Spengler.

The four points of epiphany can be situated within the context Frye's discussion of Jung provides. Remember that these points of epiphany have their context, in his developmental account of reading, between a *mythos* and its corresponding mythic world. We recall that Jung's archetypes of the great mother and the wise old man, in the final developmental phase of individuation, according to Frye, present the emerging self with a Scylla and Charybdis situation. The journey to individuation will be wrecked unless this potential self passes between these archetypes. As Frye says, the journey is only completed "if the psyche successfully navigates" its way between them (*NFCL*, 118). The situation is similar in Frye's final developmental phase of reading. The quest of reading is completed only when a tension is maintained between the potentially self-expressive *mythos* and an external mythic world. It is a point of epiphany that takes the reader through and beyond this incipient impasse.

Frye's version of the drama of the reader's individuation is helpfully marked with the stage direction "Enter Spengler." Recall that he says that "the central symbol for the Western culture," for Spengler, "seems," to Frye, "to be that of a center with radiating points" (*SM*, 183). These points start at the center, but are characterized, Frye says, by their "drive into infinite distance" (*SM*, 183). The difference between Frye's view of Jung's cardinal points and Spengler's radiating points is that he conceives of the former as stationary, like compass points, while Spengler's move outward from the center and "into infinite distance." In other words, Jung's cardinal points are points of orientation for the self at the center, and, if so, they act as a centripetal force that impels the four elements of the self inward toward a center of rotation. Spengler's radiating points are parts of a centrifugal force that move outward from a center of rotation. However this may be, it is in keeping with the notion that Jung's circle is, as mentioned, vividly rotating, and Frye's circle is, as Hamilton said, "moving," or a "turning wheel in a Spenglerian cycle of birth, growth, maturity, and death" (135). Frye's points of epiphany, insofar as they are relatable to the myth theorists, mediate between or reconcile the several views he attributes to Jung and Frazer.

However, the literary categories of recognition and reversal provide the appropriate context for Frye. His comparative treatment of the points of epiphany of the four story types is both synchronic and developmental. The individual points of epiphany are "analogous forms," because they each lead the reader into a synchronic recognition of the structure of a story type; they are analogous, as well, since he presents them as parts in a development: a development that hinges on a reversal.

As mentioned above, each point helps the reader to move beyond the either-or dilemma of choosing between a *mythos* and a mythic world. The movement beyond can be related to him or his ideal reader. Frye offers a conclusion about a story type at the end of the section devoted to it. These conclusions, though, involve his ideal reader in a movement: a movement in perception, in all four cases, is a moment of awareness. What these have in common is that they are momentary since they consist of no more than an intuition or a synchronic recognition.

We, as readers, enter into "the vision" of Dante's *Paradiso*, and "we realize" something about comedy—secular comedy—as a whole (*AC*, 185); then we "arrive at the summit of experience" that romance finally presents (*AC*, 205); then "we reach" the "point" of tragedy, which offers a contrasting "vision" to that of comedy, in that "we see or glimpse" the undisplaced demonic vision" (*AC*, 223); finally, with satire, the "point of view" is reversed (*AC*, 239). Frye's reversal takes us back through the three previous points of epiphany. What we "finally see," assuming that "we persevere" as readers "with the *mythos* of irony and satire" is, first of all, the same perspective as tragedy, for both story types see human experience "with the point of epiphany closed up" in the sense that we are at the nadir of the circle of story types, and yet confined within it (*AC*, 237). With satire, though, we cross from the nadir down beneath it: we are now "on the other side of this blasted [human] world of repulsiveness and idiocy" (*AC*, 239). The difference between the points of epiphany of tragedy and satire is that the reader is brought into confrontation with an inferno world without being in it, as with tragedy; in satire, the reader is brought across that boundary, initially. Thereafter, a reversal of directions occurs. This movement is to the "dead center" of Frye's circle, a center he discusses relative to the point of epiphany of romance (*AC*, 205), and then, "going up" still further, we return to the place from which his treatments of the four points begin: the point of recognition comedy offers. Notice the difference, though: the traditional Christian perspective he associates with comedy has given way to a sheerly imaginative perspective. The supernaturalism associated with comedy by Frye has become more like the naturalism of Jung's transformation by which the self claims its identity with "anything": "kinship with beasts and gods, with crystals and with stars" (*Two Essays*, 237). "To see the stars again," as Frye says, is to emphasize that we have been to this perspective before, as in comedy, but the "again" comes at the end of a development which allows a dual vision (*AC*, 239). Reversal, then, is three-fold: satire takes us beyond the point of epiphany of tragedy, past that of romance, and it offers a corrective vision or an alternative perspective to that of comedy. Comedy eventually "takes on an increasingly religious cast and seems to be drawing away from human experience altogether"(*AC*, 185); satire does not draw away from human experience, it draws upon the literary experience of each of the recognitions Frye's ideal reader has previously had.

CHAPTER FOURTEEN

RICOEUR AND FRYE ON MYTH

For my purpose of setting Frye in conversation Paul Ricoeur, I have chosen a few recurrent topics that twentieth-century writers on myth treat. Some of the topics come from a list of the salient features of myth in Percy S. Cohen's "Theories of Myth."[1] His list, based upon his survey of theorists in our century, is helpful because it tends to represent what has been called "the social science cartel" or the area from which most theorizing on myth has come.[2] It seems possible to distinguish between three different but successive approaches to myth in this century. At the beginning of it are theorists, such as Freud, whose treatment of myth is reductive. From such a viewpoint, myth is nothing but whatever the theorist is primarily interested in. Some later writers on myth, among them Jung, Eliade, and Campbell, tend to seek the recovery of myth for our time. For Ricoeur, the "restoration" of myth is an aim. The Frye of the *Anatomy* assumes writers in our time are engaged in a return. In *The Secular Scripture* the recovery of myth is envisioned, while the Bible and literature books seem to outline the possible "recreation" of myth. Both Ricoeur and Frye enter into earlier writers on myth and both endeavor to go beyond them. If they go beyond them, it is only after entering into their predecessors' works.

1. Writers at the beginning of the century often focus, according to Cohen, on "the events and objects which occur in myth, but which are not found in our world." Myth is implausible. The content of a primitive or ancient myth has elements that a twentieth-century myth theorist, an observing subject, finds incredible, as he scrutinizes mythic "objects." The attitude here is one of suspicion as the theorist seeks to "explain something about the phenomena." Cohen's assumption displays the depersonalization that entirely neutral inquiry requires, since only "events" or "objects," rather than persons or characters are on display. The relationship between the observing myth theorist and hi

mythic object is as direct as it is detached. Early social scientific explanatory projects also assume they are bringing primitive myth directly into the space of our world.

For Ricoeur, though, "myths are not the unchanging and unchanged antiques" or objects "which are simply delivered out of the past in some naked, original state" (1991, 486). Though social scientists can say that they have "explained the myth," such explanations, alone, are reductive (1991, 44). He who studies myth entirely in detachment has withdrawn from it. Ricoeur does make allowance for explanations, while Frye is closer to Hans-Georg Gadamer in disallowing them.

For Frye, "two new forms of allegorical interpretation" are those of Freud and Frazer around 1900 ("Allegory," 14). "The allegorization of myth is hampered by the assumption," he says, "that the explanation 'is' what the myth 'means'" (*AC*, 341). Instead of myths being "stories told as explanations" of "natural phenomena," he suggests, "myths are stories told in connection with them" ("L&M," 29).

Early twentieth-century theorizing tended to assume it was in the process of producing final explanations of whatever they studied including myth. For Ricoeur, our quests for final explanations tend to result in an unresolvable conflict of interpretations. For Frye it results in a "confused and claustrophobic battle of methodologies" (*MM*, 19). It is possible for observers of myth, Ricoeur suggests, to remain entrapped within the "literal dimension in myth," which surveys what it perceives as though gazing in sullen detachment, but it is better to become responsive to the symbolic dimension of myth (1991, 487). For Frye, "the old subject-object paradigm of experience" is no longer productive, whether for students of myth or literature, because "the reader is not a simple subject" and "the text he is reading is not a simple object" (*TLS*, 52).

2. Theorists often think of myth, Cohen asserts, as a "narrative of events." Ricoeur and Frye often start with Aristotle's designation of myth as plot. They both expand the term "myth" to the broader term "narrative." Just as they both depart from the limitation of myth to events, so they choose to speak of actions, which is a broader category than a narrative of events. Yet neither thinks that myth and actions are directly connected. It is through the interpreter's entry "into the

movement of the narrative," Ricoeur says, "that character comes into relationship with plot"; with this entry of the interpreter, "the event loses its impersonal neutrality" (1992, 142). For Frye, the propelling force that keeps the reader turning the pages of a story is "the line between personality and events" (*GC*, 31).

3. History and story are interrelated for both men. Earlier myth theorists may conceive of myth as a "narrative of events," but the events are assumed to be history-like events. Ricoeur and Frye invert an old-fashioned assumption about the relationship of history and literature. They think histories and fictions belong to the class that consists of narrations of actions. Novelists up through the era of realism, Fielding for example, or Thackeray, regarded their fictions as histories, and even Henry James got upset with Thackeray for calling attention to the fictional status of his "history." The assumption was that the capacity of readers to follow their stories hinges upon the necessity of telling a story that really happened. When the reader follows the narrative, he does so to get as close as possible to the past as it really was. Hence, literature was to be taken seriously to the extent that it presents itself as history. "Serious Victorian fiction writers," are serious to the extent that they are "realistic" in contrast to the "romancers" (*St. S*, 218).

Ricoeur and Frye assume, to the contrary, that history's ability to tell a story depends upon giving that story a narrative. The reader's ability to track events, whether in historical or literary narrative, for Ricoeur depends upon the pre-narrative capacities human understanding intrinsically has and that readers bring to narrative in the first place. To make actions in the world intelligible, humans turn to narratives because narrative "lifts itself above the opaque depths" of life and provides a possibility for "acting" (1984, I, 53). Frye thinks there are four rhythms of human action or mega-narratives. Each is a distinct way by which human experience can be organized. Both writers and historians typically organize their materials by one or another of them.

4. While earlier myth theorists such as Jung, Eliade, or Campbell think that myth is needed in our time or invoke the need for a fully spontaneous mode of awareness man once had, Ricoeur and Frye do not think this possible. Ricoeur says that the "direct relationship" between "myth and "action" is unproductive for us today (1991, 483).

If we were primitives, perhaps we could spontaneously enter into the story line of myth and enact it without a thought. Yet, "we are no longer primitives, living at the immediate level of myth," so this possibility is not ours (1991, 485).

While Frye observes that "there is justification in Aristotle for the identification of '*praxis*' (action) with '*mythos*'" or of "events and narrative," he does not choose to connect them (*RW*, 129). It is rather Aristotle's *mythos* and *dianoia*, plot and theme which, as Ricoeur says, form the "basis of Northrop Frye's 'Archetypal' criticism" (1991, 110). For Frye, there is both an internal "thought-form" and an external "event-form" (*RW*, 129). The *Anatomy* juxtaposes "idea" and "event" which in a literary action are united in the kind of symbol he designates as the "image" (*AC*, 184).

Both Ricoeur, in the first volume of *Time and Narrative*, and Frye, in the *Anatomy*, start from Aristotle. Ricoeur's reader has a "power of configuration" (1984, I, 53). Lived experience is a closed horizon which can open through "the mediating of the imagination [which] is forever at work in lived reality" (1991, 470). The *Anatomy* begins with the Aristotelian phrase (close to language occurring in the *Rhetoric*) "power of action" (33). The very sentence in which this enigmatic Aristotelian expression is introduced swerves away from limiting myth to action by using *ethos* or character in a dual manner. His comparative scale or typology of characters' power of action is constituted by the "reader's reflective act," as Ricoeur says in another context, his relating of himself and his world or setting to fictional figures and their settings (1991, 109). The reader is crucial to the typology of the *Anatomy*'s first page—in fact, typologizing is the book's characteristic activity. The reader is present in Frye's later constructions as the secret agent of the theory of symbolism and as the hero who turns the "Theory of Myths" into a set of reading practices. Though almost submerged in the second essay, he rises as the ideal reader, in the "Theory of Myths," as the practitioner of "archetypal criticism," reading any work in the light of the mythopoetic heritage and from within one or another of the literary traditions.

5. The reader's entry into or transaction with texts, is, for Ricoeur and Frye, a search for deliverance. The reader is, for Ricoeur, initially like a "narcissistic ego" with an "avaricious" attitude in that he sets

out to devour the text; eventually, though, it is just such a disposition "from which literature can liberate us" (1991, 437). The sequence of reading practices outlined in the *Anatomy* sets out from an avaricious, aggressive reader, the person who in Jung is depicted as a Freudian ego. Such a picture of the ego is much the same as the myth theorist mentioned earlier who gazes in sullen detachment and is suspicious of everything he sees. Frye sets out from this point, and, half way through his phases of reading, says that a literary or "liberal education" allows something within us to be "liberated," echoing similar language in Cassirer (*AC*, 93).

Frye does draw upon what he calls Jung's "private myth," his "myth of individuation" (*WGS*, 203); and he interrelates it to Jungian typology. One might say that a Jungian allegory of psychological development and Jungian typology become stages of reading leading into Frye's *mythoi*. The joining of allegory and typology itself has a long history and what Frye does might equally well be related to its first Christian practitioner, Origen. In any case, Ricoeur's suggestion that "we should not rush to denounce the latent 'Jungianism'" in the *Anatomy* is apposite (1991, 250). For one thing, there is not in Frye just a romantic-centered account of an individual journey of an ego on its way to personal selfhood. Instead, just as in Ricoeur, the reader's quest for deliverance from himself also involves the other, the traditional or Aristotelian understanding of character as setting in what is an opaque world (Ricoeur) or a world of ordinary experience (Frye). Jung works at the level of lived experience, while Ricoeur and Frye are concerned with textual worlds. For Ricoeur texts magnify and help clarify our world. For Frye texts belong within traditions each of which is a distinguishable mythic world or a way of reading the world. For another thing, Jung's particular contrast between what Frye calls an "egocentric consciousness" and an expanded "imaginative consciousness" is "one of the major cultural trends of our time" or century (*MM*, 74).

6. A mythic narrative has often been assumed by modern myth theorists to describe "in dramatic form" either "origins or transformations," according to Cohen. Freud and Frazer present their own "dramatizations" through the technique described as the "temporalizing of essence." They reengage in "the characteristic

mental habit of the nineteenth century" when they are "translating 'essence' into origin," so that the statement 'This is the essence of the situation' becomes in them the statement 'This is how it began'" (Hyman, 366). For them, "origin myths" of their own devising, like the one in *Moses and Monotheism*, provide a "genesis in the past" on which to attach an account of an extended development growing out of it (Hyman, 139).

"It apparently takes social scientists much longer than poets or critics to realize that every mind is a primitive mind," according to Frye (*GC*, 37). What Freud and Frazer set within some pre-historical past Ricoeur and Frye place within us. Both use latent-to-manifest patterns such as Freud does: but it is from opaque (Ricoeur) or ordinary (Frye) experience through imaginative structuration ending in capacity of action in our world (Ricoeur) or greater power of perception (Frye). Ricoeur's model of threefold *mimesis* in *Time and Narrative* sets the entire theory of symbolism of the *Anatomy*, "Frye's stages of the symbol," as he says, within his own second stage of *mimesis* or within the midst of his own framework. Frye's anti-mimetic theory is appropriate to an account of literature that is attempting to display secular literary works as continuously re-presenting Biblical and Classical myth.

Gerald Bruns suggests that literary texts, in Ricoeur's second stage of *mimesis*, have the "bare narrative function" of "projecting a possible world."[3] The literary work is "only an incomplete sketch, a fragment," which requires an interpreter or reader to become a "complete world" (240). In *Fearful Symmetry*, myths are "rough drafts" requiring writers to complete them by their incorporation of them into literary works" (424). Texts in Ricoeur help magnify our world so that it becomes legible, while in Frye they help intensify our "consciousness," our imaginative powers of "concentrating," or are "techniques of meditation" that are "designed to focus our minds" so that we get beyond the vagaries of ordinary experience that belong to life as seen through the filters of "time and space" that Kant said were built into perception (*MM*, 77; 254). Power of action comes in Ricoeur's final stage of *mimesis* when a text has been fully understood, completely restored by its interpreter, and opens upon some line of action in his world. "Power of action" is what the gods have at the beginning of the *Anatomy*, but the rest of the book is more concerned with ideal readers developing their divinatory powers of reading. Frye's stages of reading might be called his myth or they may be said to constitute an "allegory" for a literary education in the sense of that word which Bruns provides: the recreation "of the dark or recalcitrant text is all that allegory has ever meant."

If Ricoeur has what Bruns speaks of as a "magical looking-glass theory of textual meaning," so that the interpreter of a text is an Alice stepping through a looking glass, entering a wonderland world, and then stepping back into her own world and seeing it imaginatively, then Frye leaves his ideal reader in wonderland at the "still center of the order of words" (*AC*, 117). Ricoeur seems to require a reader to appropriate entirely a single text without saying how it is the only appropriate text for that reader. Frye's anagogic experience of literature is perhaps more transfigurational than transformational. If Ricoeur takes us back and forth through a looking glass or single text, Frye's reader, with a single text before him, enters into all texts, and arrives at a moment of at-one-ness, which is the goal, fulfillment, and atonement for an entire life-time of reading.

7. Earlier myth theorists thought of myth as a "sacred communication" from gods to humans in primitive times; the theorists in our time perceive this communication in the reverse direction with such descriptions based upon projection by man. Cohen's description of myth as communication from god to human is characteristic of what Frye thinks of as our impoverished "descriptive" phase of writing. Such a view presents a one-way channel of "information from an objective divine source to a subjective human receptor" (*WP*, 29). Because Ricoeur and Frye alike focus upon myth as it occurs in written language in sacred or literary texts, they can return to an understanding of the initiative that "words with power" have. The conventional topic, here again, has been shifted, in this case, from the context of objective communication to the communion of texts and interpreters or readers. Both men are concerned with a succession of distinctive interpretative communities or with writing and reading cultures. Both work their way back through an understanding of what for Ricoeur is the tradition of hermeneutics which starts out with Biblical hermeneutics and what for Frye is our Western mythopoetic tradition. Both men return to the initiatives or powers our foundational texts have partly in order to

contest the characteristic ideologies or one-man myths generated by writers such as Rousseau or Marx or Freud.

8. "Cultures create themselves by telling stories of their own past" by Ricoeur's account (1991, 475). "What human societies do first," Frye thinks as well, "is to make up stories" (*MM*, 88). For Ricoeur, "in our Western culture, the myth making of man" is accompanied and at no time without continuous interpretation of myth (1991, 486). The very "survival of myth calls for perpetual historical interpretation"; myth has "constantly" been "interpreted and reinterpreted in different historical epochs" in Western culture (1991, 486). Myth is often associated with stories of the founding of our culture, but for Ricoeur it is indispensable that we "relate our own time to this other time," the time of myth before our history or perhaps our present historical horizon began (1987, 273).

For Frye the "myth of concern" and the "myth of freedom" are continually in tension with each other, yet "interpenetrate" (*CP*, 109). This dual vision is relatable to earlier writers on myth who focus upon myth as social charter, though Frye's version of it ends with "the conception of the social contract" or the story a culture tells itself about its founding (*CP*, 109). Then there is the myth of "the Utopia or ideal state," which might be realized at some future time or exists as an ideal for our time (*CP*, 158). Suspended between the social contract and the future vision of an ideal state is the "educational contract" that mediates between them (*CP*, 162).

9. Writers on myth vary in what they say or assume about the relationship myth has to its world and our own. Earlier theorists often engage in some form of demythologization that reduces everything in myth's world to our own. Others seek to recover for our own world what once belonged to a primitive world of myth. Cassirer was the first, among modern myth theorists, to abolish the assumption that "the same neutral and underlying world" that contemporary science investigates" is not only our world but also that of myth (1991, 201). When "somebody asks out of what worlds are made, we have," after Cassirer, "to answer: from other worlds"; for Cassirer, the initial world that man inhabits is made of the world of myth or of myth and language together, and our other cultural worlds are also versions of the world (1991, 201-02). For Cassirer, unlike Frazer, we cannot move

from myth's world to a basic, underlying physical world. While he does not situate a physical world prior to all others, Cassirer tends to place a neutral world at the end of his sequence of the symbolic forms of the world that start with myth as if all of them were governed by a "teleological development" and as if they were expressions of "the mind's thrust towards objectivity," with objective or "scientific knowledge" as man's crowning cultural achievement (1991, 201). The Frye of the *Anatomy* has a similar teleological pattern since for him literary criticism becomes the latest symbolic form. With the help of Cassirer, he starts from the idea that Western literature can be seen as the remaking of Classical and Biblical myth. It is "from worlds already on hand" that literary works are made: "the making is a remaking" (1991, 202). This Cassirean assumption is brought together with the opening of the *Poetics* where poetics and poet have to do with making: "how the Myths ought to be put together if the [poetic] making is to go right."[4]

Up through the 1950's, Cassirer and Frye were among the few major thinkers in the old humanities to have chosen myth as a major category. Cassirer is Frye's predecessor not as a myth theorist, but as one who preceded him in dismissing earlier thinkers' reification of theory over practice. Cassirer, too, undercuts the earlier habit of introducing subject and object frameworks, as with Jung's *Psychological Types* where the relation of subject and object, applied throughout his types, is what makes his discussion so "opaque" (*MM*, 178). Then again, Cassirer is helpful to Frye in helping him to "avoid the scholar's mate" that Frye finds in a causal thinker such as Freud or Frazer which is to assume "we have explained the nature of something by accounting for its origin in something else" (*NFCL*, 70). The "causal thinker" when "confronted with a mass of phenomena," views them as "effects, after which he searches for their prior causes" (*GC*, 81). Such points as these rehash what has been said in earlier chapters, but I repeat them here because of my conviction that the Frye of the *Anatomy* owes a debt to Cassirer on myth.

CHAPTER FIFTEEN

BIBLICAL HERMENEUTICS
AND FRYE

"Many issues in [literary] critical theory today had their origin in the hermeneutic study of the Bible," according to Frye (*GC*, xix). Our exploration of Frye's relationship to Biblical hermeneutics will encounter some of the topics in twentieth-century myth theory discussed in the last chapter. Our particular interest is neither with literary nor myth theory, but with the practices in Frye's Bible and literature books, especially with his effort to work from "the more traditional approaches of medieval typology" (*GC*, xvii). "Typology," Frank Kermode suggests, "is at the heart of *The Great Code*," and is even "the principle" of its structure.[1] While Kermode and others have related Frye to writers towards the end of the hermeneutical tradition of the Middle Ages, I find it more productive to relate him to a figure prior to the time when medieval hermeneutics became a tradition.[2] I have chosen Origen because much of that tradition grew out of him and since he joins typology to the allegorical practices he inherited. My comparison is based upon chapter two of Origen's *On First Principles*.[3] The context for my discussion is Ricoeur's "*Preface to Bultmann*" in *Essays on Biblical Interpretation*.[4]

Ricoeur's essay outlines three successive modes of Biblical hermeneutics from St. Paul to the present. When we juxtapose his modes with some of the principles the final chapter of *The Great Code* works at, it is easy to perceive that both are working with similar concerns.[5] Ricoeur's first mode is the question of the "relation between the two Testaments" (50). Frye says that the relationship between them is that "the Bible is a gigantic myth" (*GC*, 224). "The more traditional approaches of medieval typology" are "congenial" to Frye "because they accepted the unity of the Bible as a postulate" (*GC*, xvii).

Ricoeur's second mode has to do with an effort "to decipher the movement" of the reader's "own existence in the light of the Passion and Resurrection of Christ" (52). Like Ricoeur, Frye too starts from St. Paul and contrasts " the world of death" with "the world of life" (*GC*, 231). The second mode has "Scripture" as a "total interpretation of the world" which is the world of "secular culture" (53). Frye speaks of the confrontation of the "Bible of myth and metaphor" with "its opposite or secular knowledge" (*GC*, 228).

The third and more recent mode of Biblical hermeneutics involves what for Ricoeur is the relation between divine and human speaking or what Frye calls "the antithesis between divine and human" (*GC*, 232). For Ricoeur, "as soon as the whole Bible is treated like the *Iliad*, ... the letter is desacralized and the Bible is made to appear as the word of humans" (55). One might say that Frye's entire writing career belongs to this "mode" in the sense that "the meeting point of the sacred book and the work of literature" is the setting he stands upon from his book on Blake to *Words with Power* (*GC*, 216). When early Christians began their novel practice of reading the Hebrew Scripture through the event of Christ, they brought together the "Christ-event" and Judaic Scripture in the relationship of interpretation and text. They understand that book through Him; they understand what the event of Christ means through it. For Ricoeur, "the problem of allegory" was constituted by this text and the interpretative relationship between "one Scripture and one event" (50). The relation "is expressed quite well in allegorical terms," since the interpretative situation is "entirely contained in the relation between the letter, the history ... of the old Covenant and the spiritual meaning which the Gospel reveals after the event"(50).

Among the allegorizing approaches then available was that "of Philo," while another, Origen's, adopts "quasi-Platonic language" to express "the opposition between flesh and spirit" (50-51). Philo retains the practice of allegorizing the Hebrew Scripture in the manner in which Greek philosophers allegorize Greek myth. Philo allegorizes because he can no longer read the Scripture literally.

Origen finds that the Old Testament is filled with gross events. Many events in it are indistinguishable from secular romance:

> The exploits done by certain righteous men along with their crimes
> as men; [episodes involving sex or] unchastity [and] wickedness;
> spectacular battles [described in a] marvelous way, [and] the dif-
> ferent fates, now of those who conquer and now of those who are
> conquered. (187)

All such gross events, marvelous deeds, and spectacles are undeniably in Scripture just as they are in epic poetry or romance. Origen
says these events are in Scripture for the sake of the majority of readers
who are simple or slothful. These literal events are for one-
dimensional readers, but "the letter itself" or any literal and historical
event is the Bible's concession so that "a great many" readers "can be
edified," and so that all readers will have open to them the possibility
of learning to "progress" or read at a deeper level (187). [6]

The question of what the relationship is "between the letter, the
history" in the Old Testament "and the spiritual meaning," Ricoeur's
first mode, is Origen's point of departure (50). The reader is to
"inquire into the hidden meaning of God's Spirit" that underlies all of
Scripture in looking at "an ordinary narrative" and its gross events.
Throughout Scripture the literal and Christological senses, the fleshy
and spiritual, are in tension.

It is not just this contrast, but "the typological value of the events,"
that is significant in this first mode (51). These events are not just
"things, but also persons and institutions of the old economy in relation
to those of the new" (51). There is for Origen not just a sequence of
gross events all the way through Scripture, but also, underneath each of
them, "forms and types" (187). The "entire narrative" as a whole
consists of a continuous sequence of "forms and types of hidden and
sacred matters" (181). Origen (and later Frye) looks at the "relation
between the two Testaments" as a unity in which the units are spiritual
forms and types. Together the two Testaments are a single mega-
narrative or an "entire narrative" (181). For Frye, too, the acceptance
of the "unity" of Scripture is an essential "postulate" (*GC*, xvii).

The contrast of fleshly (literal or historical) and the spiritual is only
the point of departure in Origen.[7] His last principle is his cardinal principle, one which affects most of his previous ones. As with many of
the others, he grounds this rule in Paul. An interpreter's relation to the
Scriptural text involves him in a death and resurrection. A reader be-

gins with a search for the literal meaning, but the letter is never ful-
filled. The spiritual meaning is to be found in any passage the reader
starts from in the entire narrative. At whatever point the reader enters
the text, if he dies to the literal, he rises to the spiritual. Hermeneuti-
cally, Origen enjoins the allegorical with the typological: both are universalized.

Origen's final rule for reading Scripture is neither a closing argument nor a concluding point; it is a metaphoric picture of literal and
spiritual "ways" of reading. The *hubris* of the literalist leads into humility; only after the reader has emptied himself of his pretense to understanding does the possibility of rising to the spiritual sense occur.
The aggressive quest for literal explanation ends in an impasse of
"impossibilities and contradictions" (187).

The imagery in what follows consists of Pauline "stumbling
blocks," the Gospel's contrast of the two "ways" with a "narrow footpath" becoming a "higher and loftier way or road," and the reader
eventually looking out upon an "immense" horizon or revelatory
panorama. There are

> certain stumbling blocks or interruptions of the narrative meaning
> [because the Spirit has inserted] in its midst certain impossibilities
> and contradictions, so that the very interruption of the narrative
> might oppose the reader.

These intrusions by the Spirit are intractibilities by which the reader
is brought to a halt. One "way" of reading the Scripture is barred. By
intruding these obstacles, Origen continues,

> Wisdom denies a way ... and, when we [readers] are shut out and
> hurled back, [then Wisdom] calls us back to the beginning of an-
> other way, so that [wisdom] may open for us [into] the immense
> breadth of divine knowledge. (187-88)

The spiritual "way" begins as a "narrow footpath," perhaps because a solitary reader must move along the single file of his own perceptions; this becomes "loftier" than the literal "way," because it is an
ascent, while the literalist can only descend. The way down of the literalist leads to a dead end in which meaning has closed down; the way

up of the spiritual reader opens upon a revelatory landscape (187-88). Origen's language is such that when we read this final rule for reading Scripture as if it were just another point, we miss the point; if we follow his imagery, we perceive the Christian metaphor: any reader " is on the wrong path to begin with," and so must "find" the "way back to the real starting point" (*WP*, 93). "The figure in the Sermon on the Mount" contrasting the way of destruction with the straight and narrow way to salvation is for Frye "the basis of a number of sustained allegories in literature (*WP*, 92).

The second Biblical hermeneutical mode is created by "Paul when he invites the hearer of the word to decipher the movement of his own existence in the light of the Passion and Resurrection of Christ" (52). In this mode, "hermeneutics is the very deciphering of life in the mirror of the text" (53). The Christian vision of life is one in which, as Frye says, "everyone is on the wrong path" or moving in the wrong direction "to begin with," and must turn around. Origen applies this view to the reading of Scripture (*WP*, 93). This pattern is reflected in Paul's conversion experience. Perhaps Origen's extension of Paul has more to do with Paul's telling the various episodes of his life as a self-dramatization by which to align his experience to the landscape of the cross as seen by the light of the resurrection. The plot line of the story Paul continually tells himself and others becomes Origen's cardinal principle of reading. Paul's self-dramatization in witnessing becomes in Origen the basis for reading experience, which continually involves us in death and resurrection. Origen starts with a book and only by relating our lives in the world to it do its pages become the mirror in which our lives become legible (52-54). Scripture is the landscape upon which the reader, on his journey through this world, understands himself on his way to life in God. "Only from the divine words of the book do we "learn" from its "words what this world is" (186).

The topic from the last chapter bearing upon this is the perception that prior to any physical world is a symbolic one. "Myth," Ricoeur says, gives "worldly form to what is beyond" any "known and tangible reality" (61). "Myth expresses in terms … of the other world or the second world," and its "objective language" helps us understand limit situations or intractibilities such as life in time, by relating our cultural world to a time before it, a time of myth (60-61). Earlier in the book, we noticed a related and crucial perception by Ricoeur relative to the "Theory of Myths" in the *Anatomy*. Frye's cycle of seasonal myths is divested of "every naturalistic characteristic" because it, from the beginning of the essay, has been placed "under the sign of the Apocalypse" (1991, 252).

Origen's cardinal principle assumes that the literal and historical sense and the spiritual sense are in tension with each other, yet complimentary reading activities. He assumes that there are two levels of narrative throughout the Scripture. A sequence of gross events constitutes the entire "ordinary" narrative. The same mega-narrative has a subterranean level with "forms and types" embedded in it. Metaphorically, the first is an opaque outer "garment," and the level underneath is a transparent "veil," and the two are "interwoven" in the book (187). Hence, underneath a manifest sequence of events is a latent sequence of forms and types.

The medieval hermeneutical tradition constructed a sequence of levels out of Origen's relatively fluid rules of reading. While Origen has a two-leveled Scriptural narrative, his contrast of literal with spiritual more nearly consists of two directions or dimensions of reading. A reader begins by looking at the literal or historical, yet invariably is forced by the text to go "looking in another direction" (186).

For Frye, "every work of literature has to die," and then "to be reborn in the individual studying it." He often contrasts opposing but complimentary directions or processes: one first reads a narrative and then stops, and looks up as part of another process. Many of these accounts are related to Aristotle's *mythos* and *dianoia* distinction. While there is no source-derivation connection between Origen and Frye, his recurring principle that "some death and rebirth process" is at the core of reading is productively related to Biblical hermeneutics, and the first exponent of our dying into and rising from texts is Origen (*SM*, 119).

"The New Testament is a text to be interpreted"; "the literal meaning is itself a text to be understood": such formulations belong to Ricoeur's third mode of Biblical hermeneutics (55). Both arise from the earlier modes. The New Testament "is not simply an interpreting with regard to the Old Testament," as in the first mode, or "an interpreting of life and reality as a whole," as in the second, but "it is itself a text to be interpreted" (55). His supposition that "the literal meaning is itself a text to be understood," is also successive (55). Initially, "the New Testament" is the means by which to "decipher the Old"; in the second mode, the New Testament "remains an absolute norm as long as its literal meaning serves as an indisputable basis" or point of departure for "all the other levels" that the medieval tradition of hermeneutics established or "constructed"; yet, in our time, "the literal meaning" has become "itself a text to be understood, a letter to be interpreted" (55).

Origen constructed a set of interpretive principles mainly from Saint Paul. One oversimplifies an immensely complex process by saying that his extraction of Pauline principles led to and became the schematization of Origen in the elegant four-level medieval tradition. The idea that Scripture contains its own set of rules of interpretation is an idea with an extended history, and Origen's assumption involves applying mainly Pauline texts which are, from Ricoeur's viewpoint, "already an interpretation" (54).

For him, this third hermeneutical mode is modern, while the others are "two ancient forms," or "roots," and those "contributed to concealing what was radical": the "problem that was present from the beginning of the Gospel but hidden" (57). As soon as the Gospel came to be written, it became "a new letter, a new Scripture," and thus "itself a text to be interpreted" (55). "The kerygma" was initially "the announcement of a person," but our relationship to the message is that "we ourselves are no longer those witnesses who have seen." We are instead dependent upon witnesses who responded to a message that is embedded "in stories" and so "can believe only by listening and by interpreting" the text (54).

> As a text, it expresses a difference and a distance, however minimal, from the event that it proclaims. This distance, always increasing with time, is what separates the first witness from the entire line of those who hear the gospel. Our modernity means only that the distance is now considerable between the place I myself occupy at the center of a [scientific and historical] culture and the original site of the first witness. (56)

147

"The product" of our modernity, this mode is the expression of "the backlash of the critical disciplines ... on the sacred texts" (55). Frye's version of this situation points to "vast expansion of comparative data" collected from cultures adjoining or outside the Biblical culture" (*GC*, 91). The tendency of "Frazer and others" has been to look at the Bible centrifugally instead of as he does: to start from the Biblical landscape and work from within the Biblical hermeneutical tradition by returning to some of its core issues (*GC*, 91). He calls for a reversal of perspective or a return from "taking mythology in general as a key to the Bible" to taking "the Bible as a key to mythology" (*GC*, 92). "Myth in general" for Ricoeur and "mythology in general" for Frye belong to earlier twentieth-century conventions of social scientific theorizing (1991, 485; *GC*, 92). Such approaches often begin directly with myth through some conceptual notion rather than assuming its symbolic dimensions; and proceed quickly to lock myth into whatever procrustean explanatory framework is momentarily fashionable in the social scientist's particular discipline: with the origin or the causes (in earlier writers), the structure or function (in later ones), and the meaning or content of myth as the more commonplace categories. An analogous habit among historical critical scholars of the Bible is to lock themselves into "their historical reconstructions" as if they "*are* the reality" (*WP*, 99).

Our notion of the "literal" is at the crux of present-day Biblical hermeneutics for Ricoeur. Frye has engaged in extensive efforts at the revision of it. Both deliberately start from the fourfold hermeneutical scheme of medieval exegesis. Both characterize the demise of the literal sense in the recent past. Both attempt to restore or recreate the literal sense.

While the traditional Biblical approach engaged, Ricoeur thinks, "in the construction of a spiritual meaning on the literal meaning," our twentieth-century efforts typically bore "under the literal meaning" with the result of a "de-struction" or "deconstruction" of the literal or "letter itself" (57-58). The story of "The Purloined Letter" is for Frye the parable of all these efforts because the sense of the literal, "a letter that is a verbal message," has become anything whatever "except what it really is" (*GC*, xxi).

Ricoeur, reworking Cassirer's notion of the "symbol," says it is "any structure of signification in which a direct, primary, literal meaning designates, in addition [to it], another meaning which is indirect, secondary and figurative and which can be apprehended only through the first sense" (1974, 12). In tandem with the dual vision of the symbol is the return to a contemporary version of the medieval hermeneutical tradition: "Interpretation ... is the work of thought which consists in deciphering the hidden meaning in the apparent meaning, in unfolding the levels of meaning implied in the literal meaning" (1974, 13).

Origen's initial rule for reading Scripture is based upon Paul's contrast of "the letter which kills and the spirit which gives life" (II Cor. 3:6). His final rule for reading is that a reader is invariably or inevitably involved, if he is to move from the fleshly to the spiritual, in a descent into the literal and an elevation towards the spiritual or in the process of death and resurrection. This rule can be called his cardinal rule since it affects all of the others.

Origen is an initiator of some of the rules or principles that became the medieval hermeneutical tradition. Yet the tradition founded upon Origen perhaps departed from him when it made the literal sense foundational, since in Origen the literal is more a direction or dimension of reading rather than a solid, distinct step leading up a staircase with other rising levels of meaning. In Origen, the reader founders with the first step he takes. The reader starts with some literal sense, with some historical or "gross event," but he sees what it means only when he has died to his natural desire to explain the event. In Origen, the reader turns away or turns around.

In the *Anatomy*, the turning around or "imaginative revolution" begins in the formal phase of meaning and is completed in the universal or anagogic phase (119). His formal phase is related to Aristotle. He can also be, indirectly, related to Origen, for this phrase, as Ricoeur suggests, is "allegorical" in that it consists of "the very movement from the literal sense" to "another kind of sense" (1991, 249). We noticed in the chapter on symbolism that Frye's phases belong to two groups: one leading up to an Aristotelian sense; the other starts with the allegorical sense belonging to medieval hermeneutics, which leads into his archetypal level, and issues into his universal level. Yet, all along, these are flexible "contexts or relationships" which are perhaps as comparable to Origen's as they are to the levels of medieval interpretation (*AC*, 73).

Frye says that his return to a "true literal sense of the Bible [which] is metaphorical is not even his idea, for it is not "new or even modern," but belongs to the Biblical hermeneutics of the past (*DV*, 69). For him, "primary and literal meaning" in the Bible is the "poetic" or the "metaphorical meaning" (*GC*, 61). For Origen, the literal and historical sense comes first simply because the reader starts with the words that are in the text, but these are incidental, secondary, and subordinate to the Christological or spiritual sense. Paul's observation that Scripture is to be "spiritually discerned" (I Cor. 2:14) is construed by Frye as a directive for readers to wrestle with every word of the passage, follow the imagery, and read the metaphor (*GC*, 56). Origen's chapter opens with a typology of readers and ends with his metaphoric picture of reading as *metanoia* or turning away from the literal sense, dying to it, so that one is open to the spiritual.

In Origen's dual vision of the unified Scripture, everything in it is "allegorical" in Gerald Bruns' sense. There is a text before the reader that is "dark and recalcitrant," or opaque, which is "all that allegory has ever meant." There is another narrative that has forms and types all the way through. Origen universalized the typological by suggesting that individual passages eventually open out on some spiritual truth for its reader, whether about his relationship to the body of Christ on earth, or his particular relationship to God during this life, or our life in God to come. Origen elicits these typological meanings somewhat as the Frye of the *Anatomy* exercises his ingenuity in finding "archetypes" which are roughly elements or organizing significance that the reader notices in secular literature on the basis of his reading experience of Classical and Biblical myth. His archetypal criticism, however, is a distinct phase of literary critical activity preceding his universal or anagogic criticism. His archetypal criticism, one might say, is typological, in contrast to the phase of allegorical criticism that precedes it. In this phase, "all commentary is allegorical interpretation" (*AC*, 89); all this "commentary ... continues the tradition of allegorized myth" (*AC*, 342).

The Great Code universalizes the typological by presenting a sequence of reader-oriented Biblical phases that extend from Creation through Apocalypse with "each phase being a type of the one following it and an antitype of the one preceding it" (*GC*, 106). This Scriptural internalization of the typological, Frye suggests, is now preferable to the extended practices "of the past" when "doctrinal structures" were assumed to be or "make themselves the antitypes of Biblical narrative and imagery" (*GC*, 227). The universal, for Frye, is an open and global "community of vision" (*GC*, 227). Entrance into this community seems to require the suspension of the prejudgments of the reader relative to his setting, whether in some particular faith or interpretative community, and self, his prejudgments of belief or value (*MM*, 96-97). Dying to our own positions and assumptions opens the possibility of rising to an imaginative apprehension of the Bible's "total verbal structure," so to "receive" its "revelation" (*MM*, 240) and to experience a "resurrection of the original speaking presence" (*WP*, 114). Gadamer says that "the technical term for the form in which sacred texts speak" is "myth," and for Frye as for Origen the myth of the death and resurrection of Christ is the cardinal rule of reading. In Origen as in Frye, there is first the "annihilating" of "everything we thought we knew," and then the "restoring" of "everything we have never lost" (*WP*, 313).

Our final chapter is as introductory as the others. Most of them have, to borrow Ricoeur's word, consisted of an extended "detour." Frye on myth is placed in conversation with the five "myth theorists." No doubt my comparisons tend to make him seem entirely of their company. The chapter comparing him with Ricoeur attempts to indicate his departures from them. The present chapter has related Frye to a figure in whom allegory and typology come together. Perhaps, as we review the earlier chapters, we can discern that Frye's synthetic recreations of the myth theorists in the *Anatomy* are typological in character. In any case, our brief glimpse at Frye on typology shares Kermode's view that "his affinities" are "with certain visionaries who carried the typological habit to extremes" (1989, 76). Kermode traces Frye back to Joachim of Fiore; for him, Frye belongs to a "speculative tradition, as Blake had before him" (1989, 77). I have related him to the tradition of medieval hermeneutics by looking towards its beginning rather than its end. Whether Frye carried the "typological habit to extremes" or not, perhaps he has continually engaged in this habit. In his earlier books, Frye seems to participate in the deployment of the comparativism the various myth theorists use. With hindsight, one might relate this "method" to "the panchronic approach," both "synchronic and diachronic," which Ricoeur says "characterized the hermeneutical method" (1991, 484). Still, Frye's Bible and literature books engage us in practices from the past rather than theoretical speculations; in fact, as Frye later perceived, the *Anatomy* does: he, like Gadamer, thinks that, if we are to quest for truth, we eventually let go of our methods. "Like a knight errant who finds himself in the middle of a tournament," Frye has "left his lance" or method "at home" (*GC*, ix).

Our book is a detour as a whole in the sense that it never answers a question that came up long ago. This question has silently been sitting like a sphinx overlooking my entire commentary. What does Frye mean when he says he engages in "rewriting my central myth in every book?" (*CP*, 9). Or, to put it another way, "What one does not understand" is what commentaries such as mine omit (Balfour, 3). I have often tried to answer this question or riddle, usually by turning to others who provide insights about his myth. Kermode says that Frye is relatable to the "ancient myth that the world is like a book," and that each of Frye's books is in itself a "whole myth" (72, 73). As we read them, they take on what Hamilton calls a "dialectical" and Todorov a "dialogical" cast. As I read him, in the light of my theological education and practice, I am sometimes tempted to explain Frye's myth by some theological category: Denham suggests "incarnation" as a possibility throughout. Perhaps there are other choices: reconciliation, our twentieth-century version of the myth of the Atonement, or recreation, or death and resurrection. Then again, there is probably "something dismally corny about isolating a myth," after the fashion of Frazer, and explaining away Frye's books. If we lived in a world where our elemental questions had answers, would we even call upon myth and literature?

NOTES

Chapter One: Life and Works

[1] Richard Kostelanetz, "The Literature Professors' Literature Professor," 431.

[2] Frye, "The Classics and the Man of Letters," *Arion* 3 (Winter 1964), 49.

[3] See Jonathan Hart, "The Critic as Writer," in his *Northrop Frye: The Theoretical Imagination*, ch. 9.

[4] In an interview in *A World in a Grain of Sand*, Frye said the Blake experience occurred in 1935, not in 1934 (237). His designations of the time of the occurrence vary slightly (see *WGS*, 275; *SM*, 17; and Ayre 1989, 92, 411).

[5] See C.G. Jung, "Psychological Types," in *The Portable Jung*, ed. Joseph Campbell (New York: Viking Press, 1971), 262.

[6] Margaret Atwood, "Fifties Vic," *CFA Critic* 42 (November 1979), 21. The subsequent references occur in the same paragraph

[7] See G. E. Bentley, Jr., "Blake on Frye and Frye on Blake," in *The Legacy of Northrop Frye*, eds. Alvin A Lee and Robert D. Denham, 177-90.

Chapter Two: Frye and His Myth Theorists

[1] Stephen and Robin Larsen, *A Fire in the Mind*, 177. Starting in 1932, Campbell "read the entire opus seven times over the next decade," in part for the "mythological foundation" of Spengler's ideas. He "credited Spengler's insightful historical mythologizing with opening to him the inner logic" of cultural patterns in history. Campbell places Frazer's *Golden Bough*, along with Spengler's *Decline*, among the books that were "bibles" to him (48).

2 Ayre suggests that Frye first encountered *The Golden Bough* in his hometown public library. It didn't circulate, but Frye was able to read it when he worked at the library not long after it opened "in early 1927" (1989, 48, 124).

3 See Ayre 1989, 105. The passage occurs in a letter from Frye to his fiancée, Helen Kemp, written October 19, 1934 (Ayre 1989, 412). Robert D. Denham said that the entire correspondence, "more than 340,000 words," between Frye and Kemp is to be published (*NFN* 6 [Fall 1994], 4).

Chapter Three: Spengler

1 Spengler distributes what he says about the prime symbol across both volumes. The passages can be tracked by locating the references under "Symbolism" in the index to *Decline*. The most illuminating of them is perhaps that in I, 174, which I work from later in this chapter.

2 Frye's review essay on Cassirer (*NFCL*, 67-75) works with the philosopher's "general conception of symbolic form" by distinguishing between an epistemological sense of it and the sense in which it is a form of culture. Despite Cassirer's contempt for Spengler, Frye probably would have observed the similarities and differences between Cassirer's more epistemological sense of symbolic form and Spengler's prime symbol. Both theorists relate their constructs to Kant's *a priori* – his seminal notion that man makes the world he perceives. (See Spengler on Kant's construct in I, 59-60 and 74.) He historicizes Kant. If Kant thinks any and all individuals see through the forms of space and time they impose, Spengler assumes all the individuals of a specific culture see reality through their unique form of culture, which will have its particular understandings of space and time. They see through their unique prime symbol; what they see when they look through the inner prism of their own culture is like the graded colors, which are for Spengler the expression-forms of the culture. As Hughes succinctly states, Spengler delineates these "expression-forms" in the order of their closeness to the prime symbol: "first art and music ... then religion and philosophy, then natural science, and finally politics and economics" (Hughes, 80). The prime symbol is "prime" because the culture is born through or with it; after this entirely fortuitous birthing, the prime symbol, now called a "Destiny-idea," displays itself through a course of teleological development. In this sense the prime symbol is "prime" because it initiates the course a culture takes as the culture

plays itself out or unfolds along Spengler's one thousand-year grids. An utterly fortuitous occurrence sets in motion an entirely controlled development. I find it helpful to look past Spengler's philosophical jargon and read his imagery, especially his botanical imagery. Briefly, he thinks of the development of culture as a power of growth that is set off by the birthing of the prime symbol as the *seed* which grows out of a particular cultural landscape. A symbolic form in Cassirer is a way of world-making in which the form of what we see comes out of our entire mental consciousness, including feeling and imagination as well as rational thought, and the content comes out of, but is not the same as, the objects in the world around us. More important, a symbolic form is the "structure" of such human cultural activities as "language, myth, religion, art, science, [and] history" (Cassirer 1994, 93). These activities begin with myth and language; thereafter, according to Paul Ricoeur, the "symbolic forms taken together constitute" for Cassirer "a teleological development ruled by the mind's thrust towards objectivity, i.e., scientific knowledge" (*A Ricoeur Reader*).

3 Robert Denham discusses Frye's elastic construct of myth, as used in *Anatomy*, in *Northrop Frye and Critical Method*, 206-7.

4 The procedure is briefly described in Frye "Levels of Meaning in Literature," *Kenyon Review* 12 (Spring 1950), 256.

5 Frye's frequently recurring posture is to suggest that he anchors his use of the word "myth" in Aristotle's *mythos* in the *Poetics*. In the *Anatomy*, Frye refers to the translation by Ingram Bywater: *On the Art of Poetry* (Oxford: Clarendon Press, 1920), which has a preface by myth theorist Gilbert Murray. Frye quotes Aristotle's first paragraph (*AC*, xiv-xv), which Murray construes as "how the Myths ought to be put together if the Making is to go right" (6). Since we are the heirs of Kant in assuming the mind makes the reality it sees, Murray's observation about "making" is helpful. He suggests that making, in Aristotle, means less making up than taking up and giving shape to myth: "the poet who was 'maker' of a Fall of Troy clearly did not make the real Fall of Troy. He made an imitation Fall of Troy" (8). He also observes that, despite the Greeks' habit of assuming that comedy was something the plot of which the writer made up and tragedy something the content of which was taken up from the "sacred myths or heroic legends," Aristotle's use of "the word *mythos* practically in the sense of plot" is atypical (17-18). Another of Murray's observations that might have affected Frye's perception of the *Poetics* is his statement that Aristotle's distinction that tragedy imitates good and comedy bad men strikes moderns as absurd (9). However, "the truth is that neither

'good' nor 'bad' is an exact equivalent of the Greek; Frye notes that "the importance Aristotle assigns to goodness and badness seems to indicate a somewhat narrowly moralistic view of literature" (*AC*, 33). It would be nearer the truth, Murray suggests, "to say that, relatively speaking, you look up to the characters of tragedy, and down upon those of comedy. High or low ... or many other pairs of words" could be used (9). Frye chooses to say that "fictions" can be classed, "not morally, but by the hero's power of action, which may be greater than ours, less, or roughly the same" (*AC*, 33). Two of his levels upon which writers present characters to us are the "high" and the "low mimetic mode" (*AC*, 34). High and low are for Murray relative to our way of looking at the characters of tragedy and comedy; "'high' and 'low,'" in Frye, "have no connotations to comparative value, but are purely diagrammatic" (*AC*, 34). Chapter six will discuss Frye's indebtedness to Murray's ritual pattern, which Murray succinctly summarizes as: "the god was torn in pieces, lamented, searched for, discovered or recognized" and then mourned by his followers during which "a sudden Reversal turned into joy" (15). Several passages in Aristotle's *Metaphysics* deal in passing with myth. Frye regrets that it "dismisses" without sufficient consideration "the nature of mythological thinking" (*GC*, 64). He also observes "the contemptuous reference to the mythological way of thinking" (*WP*, 33). In neither case does Frye cite the passage, which presumably is *Metaphysics*, Book III, chapter four, in which "the subtleties of the mythologists"—identified as "the school of Hesiod and all the theologians"—are dismissed.

Significant for its bearing upon Frye's theory of the displacement of myth is the passage at the end of *Metaphysics*, Book XII, chapter eight: "Our forefathers in the most remote ages have handed down to their posterity a tradition, in the form of a myth." The "myth" is that "the first substances" or the heavenly "bodies are gods," and that "the divine encloses" or envelopes "the whole of nature." Aristotle then contrasts this myth to "the rest of the tradition," which was "added later in mythical form" for reasons of civic and religious "expediency." The earlier form of the myth is for him both an "inspired utterance" and an extractable portion from the later "additions" to it. For him, then, the poetic, or mythological, kernel of truth is the idea that "the divine encloses the whole of nature." For Frye, "myths" appear "to provide a kind of containing form of tradition" (*FI*, 31). For Aristotle, later "additions" to myth remain in mythical form, yet are attached merely for "expediency" and "the persuasion of the multitude." For Frye, myth is subject, in later eras, to readers' demands for persuasiveness, or "plausibility."

6 The final essay closes with a section called "The Rhetoric of Non-Literary Prose," but the penultimate section, like those before it, treats literature ("Specific Encyclopedic Forms," 315-25).

7 A. C. Hamilton says that "The Bible provides explicitly or implicitly either the beginning or the end of each of the four essays" (Hamilton 1992, 259).

8 I have not included the cluster of definitions of myth from the second essay's section entitled "mythical phase: symbol as archetype" (AC, 95-115). Frye says, for instance, "The union of ritual and dream in a form of verbal expression is myth," which, he acknowledges, "is a sense of the term myth slightly different from that used in the previous essay" (AC, 106). Though he places myth in between Frazer's "ritual" and "dream" in Freud and Jung, he says nothing about Cassirer. Frye's effort to expand Aristotle in an expressionist direction is aided by the most expressionistic of the theorists of myth; his recurrent joinings of Frazer and Jung are accomplished through Frye's use of a Cassirean symbolic form, which unites adjoining areas in a single containing form.

9 My remark about an "imaginative game" owes much to Frank Kermode's perception that "*Frye's* systems are mnemotechnical in character, a way of making fruitful connections between disparate activities of an extraordinary mind" (Kermode 1967, 16). See also Kermode 1990, 95.

10 During the *Anatomy*, Frye glides across whatever separation there is between primitive and historical cultures. He begins by suggesting "the possibility of seeing literature as a complication of a relatively restricted and simple group of formulas that can be studied in primitive culture" (AC, 17). Later he says that he is "suggesting the possibility of extending the kind of comparative and morphological study now made of folk tales and ballads into the rest of literature" (104). Yet he then assumes that the stories belonging to his mythical mode belong within cultural times, as when he says that stories in that mode are like "religious Byzantine painting," which is a cultural and not primitive epoch in art history (134). And then his real assumption comes to the fore: that "the Bible ... and Classical mythology" are the starting-points for the study of literature (135). He presumably follows what he calls "Spengler's distinction between primitive and historical culture" from the beginning, since myth for both of them is confined to the historical culture, though he is, in the *Anatomy*, trying to make alliances with other groups of scholars (*SM*, 185). After the *Anatomy*, he

is more explicit. "Oral" societies are for him as well as Spengler "pre-mythical cultures"; he has little interest in the "pre-literary" use of myth in society (*WP*, 30; *MM*, 238).

11 A difference between the two thinkers is that Spengler's project be-gan with his reflections on art, where Cassirer's would have ended, had he lived to complete it, with a volume on art. Roger Scruton suggests Spengler is in the tradition of comparative art history of Heinrich Wolfflin (Scruton, 20-21). Andre Malraux, in remarks to which Frye calls our attention (see *NFN* 3[Spring 1989], 6), says that the *Decline* "started as a meditation on the destinies of art forms, a meditation which gradually amplified in scope and depth" (Maulraux, 619). In Cassirer's original plan of his philosophy of symbolic forms, "a vol-ume on art was proposed," but "postponed"(Krois 233 n. 92; see also 31-32). Krois and Donald Phillip Verene are preparing the manuscript for the fourth volume of *The Philosophy of Symbolic Forms* (Krois, 224, note 8; 31).

12 One might compare the fact that Spengler's first volume sold 100,000 copies in four years with Frye's comment, made twenty-one years after it was published, that the *Anatomy* has "sold well over 100,000 copies" (*WGS*, 169).

13 See Ayre 1989, 65-66, 68.

14 Scruton says that "Spengler's three favorite cultures are defined so as to cross promiscuously the boundaries between religious faiths. Christianity, for example, has its Magian, its late classical, and its Faustian manifestations, and in all its manifestations it is the culture, rather than the religion, that takes precedence" (Scruton, 28). While Scruton thinks Spengler's assigning "precedence" a weakness, Malraux thinks it the strength of Spengler's work. It is, he says, "by subordinating all religions to the organic life of the cultures assumed to have engendered them [that Spengler's] theory can in its dealings with religious civilizations assign to religion a secondary place" (Malraux, 619). Frye, in effect, takes both points of view. In accounting for re-ligion, he prefers Arnold Toynbee's *A Study of History* to the *Decline*: "Toynbee sees that an internal proletariat (the exploited members of the society) and an external one (the barbarian nomads outside) com-bine to form a 'universal Church,' which becomes at once the coffin of the old society and the womb of a new one, so that a real spiritual pro-gress from one society to another can occur" (*NFCL*, 79). "This," he adds, "gives Christianity a far more satisfactory historical explanation than Spengler gives it." (See also *SM*, 195-96, where Frye turns from the metahistorians to Giambattista Vico, a thinker who tends to dis-

place both Spengler and Cassirer in Frye's thought starting roughly with *The Critical Path*.) At the same time, Frye agrees with Malraux that Spengler's subordination of religion allows other "forms" of culture to be seen on the same plain with it. In his notebooks Frye says that "the great intuition I got from Spengler, and later from Vico, was the sense of every historical phenomenon being symbolic of every other phenomenon contemporary with it" (*NFN* 5 [summer 1993], 29, item 554). Then again, he says that "Spengler shows how" history evinces his synchronic "notion that things don't get reconciled, but everything is everywhere at once. Wherever you are is the center of everything" (*NFN* 3 [Winter 1990-91], 6). From Spengler's point of view, everything in the history of a culture is the expression of the prime symbol that has constituted that culture; everything throughout his eight or so cultural areas, of which religion and art are two, is equally an "expression-form." Or, as Frye says, "everything a culture produces" is seen by Spengler "as characteristic of that culture: in other words as a symbol of it" (*RW*, 321).

Chapter Four: The Myths of Frazer and Spengler

1 Robert D. Denham discusses Frye's view of the imagination in his introduction to *NFCL*, 18-23.

2 Frye's ultimate phase of literary critical activity is anagogic criticism (*AC*, 115-28). He says that "in the greatest moments of [reading] Dante and Shakespeare, in, say *The Tempest* or the climax of the *Purgatorio*, we have a feeling of converging significance, the feeling that here we are close to seeing what our whole literary experience has been about, the feeling that we have moved into the still center of the order of words" (*AC*, 117). It is the reader who moves through the various phases of literary critical activity, arriving at the experience which is foundational for Frye's literary critical enterprise though available only to the individual reader.

3 A. C. Hamilton says that "the circle of *mythoi* is not static as the metaphor of the circle implies, but moving" (Hamilton 1990, 135). He then remarks that "unfortunately, such movement is bound to appear teleological." Unfortunate or not, all the myth theorists with whom my book is concerned are teleological thinkers. Freud, according to Stanley Edgar Hyman, "assumed without question an ontogenetic teleology, a progress of the lucky individual to the ideal of the heterosexual genitality, productive sublimation, and ego capacity" (Hymen, 428). Frazer's version of teleology is in keeping with that of most

nineteenth-century theorists' view of progress. Similarly, Cassirer's symbolic forms, according to Paul Ricoeur, "taken together constitute a teleological development ruled by man's thrust towards objectivity, i.e., scientific knowledge" (Ricoeur 1991, 201). In Spengler, a historical culture is driven by the teleological force he calls its "destiny." Individuation in Jung, according to Frye, is a "growing force within the psyche, ... and, being a biological force, it behaves teleologically, just as an acorn behaves as though it intended to become an oak tree" (*NFCL*, 119).

4 The phrases occur in the section headings of his four story types (*AC*, 163, 186, 206, 223).

5 The citation is from page 316 of Frazer's own abridgment of *The Golden Bough* (London: Macmillan, 1922). All subsequent citations are from this edition.

6 Frazer 1922, 62-65, 824-25. Frazer, like Frye, sometimes uses the word "displacement," which is usually associated with Freud's *Interpretation of Dreams*. See Frazer 1922, 188, 377, 825.

7 This topic is treated in chapter five.

8 Cassirer can be included, for he is an intellectual or cultural historian. Several of his diatribes against Spengler are to be found in *Symbol, Myth, and Culture: Essays and Lectures of Ernst Cassirer, 1935-1941*.

9 On Frazer see especially Robert Ackerman, *J. G. Frazer: His Life and Work*; Ackerman, *The Myth and Ritual School: J. G. Frazer and the Cambridge Ritualists*; Robert Fraser, *The Making of "The Golden Bough": The Origins and Growth of an Argument*; Fraser, ed., *Sir James Frazer and the Literary Imagination: Essays in Affinity and Influence*; Stanley Edgar Hyman, *The Tangled Bank: Darwin, Marx, Frazer and Freud as Imaginative Writers*; and John B. Vickery, *The Literary Impact of "The Golden Bough."*

10 Ackerman says that "these gods and the repetitive rhythmic pattern that constitutes their myth lie at the heart of the third edition" and that they, along with Dionysus, have a "central placement" that "is symbolic of their importance" (1991, 63).

11 Frye finds Frazer helpful in bringing together "a vast number of 'dying god' myths" (*WP*, 43). Frazer "treats myths as interlocking story patterns like a literary critic," instead of relating them to the "functions" they have "within their various cultures," as most anthropologists would do (*GC*, 35). It is when Frazer recounts the stories of

Adonis, Attis, Osiris, and Dionysus one after the other that he is treating myths "as interlocking story patterns." Apparently, then, it is his presentation and interrelation of myths, not his interpretation of myth, that Frye finds useful.

12 This statement, which applies to the Mediterranean gods as a class of dying and rising gods, is then applied to each in turn. "The ceremony of the death and resurrection of Adonis" is "a dramatic representation of the decay and revival of plant life" (Frazer 1922, 391). "Attis was to Phrygia what Adonis was to Syria," in that he was "a god of vegetation, and his death and resurrection were annually mourned and rejoiced over at a festival in spring" (403). Osiris, in Egypt, belongs to the same class: the god who is a "personification of the great annual vicissitudes of nature" (420). In Greece, Dionysus "reflect[s] the decay and revival of vegetation," and "the myth of Demeter and Persephone" represents it (456).

13 Klaus P. Fischer says that "perhaps the most important idea which Spengler borrowed from Goethe was the metamorphosis of plants" (Fischer, 94). The phrase is the title of a book Goethe wrote in 1790; Frye directs the reader to a study of it, *The Poem as Plant* by Peter Salm (*SS*, 193). Fischer says that Goethe assumed that there was a "universal Primal Type" that was the "common ancestor of all plants" and that Spengler employed this idea in his view of "cultures as the expression forms of certain underlying prime symbols" (Fischer, 95). He also discusses the idea in Goethe and Spengler and relates it to comparative morphology (see 162ff).

14 "The common pattern" in the myths or life-stories of the gods Frazer treats "might be called 'the tragic rhythm,'" according to Ackerman, (1991, 62).

15 Hughes observes that Spengler's "biological metaphor provided the conceptual frame giving unity and coherence" to his view of a culture as an organism moving "through a regular and predictable course of birth, growth, maturity, and decay" (Hughes, 10). Spengler's "whole 'morphological method' ... is simply an elaborate metaphor drawn from biology" (153). Spengler constructs history through "inspired metaphors," while others are non-metaphorical or descriptive writers (159). Finally, Hughes writes of Spengler's "pictorial, figurative language, his talent for finding the images and personalities that set off in high relief an entire epoch of the past" (162).

16 Frye's citations are from: Apollodorus, *The Library*, tr. Sir James George Frazer, Loeb Classical Library (London: William Heinemann,

1921), I, xxvii; and Friedrich Max Muller, *The Science of Language,* rev. ed. (New York: Scribner's, 1891), I, 21.

17 Frye echoes Frazer's use (1922, 58) of this traditional religious distinction (*NFCL*, 90).

18 Foreword to Jessie L. Weston's *From Ritual to Romance* (1993), xxiv.

19 I have borrowed the categories which Frye uses in *SS*, 65ff. Both, however, are applicable to Frazer's initial stage of magic.

20 Frazer says that "incarnate human deities," who for him precede the figures of gods that myths present, "may be said to halt midway between the age of magic and the age of religion" (Frazer 1922, 188). The myths, or god-stories, are to be found fully *in* the stage of religion. But only in the combined stage are they tied to rituals.

21 The reason the king is put to death, says Frazer, is that "the fertility of men, of cattle, and of the crops is believed to depend sympathetically on the generative power of the king, so that the complete failure of that power in him would involve a corresponding failure in men, animals, and plants, and would thereby entail at no distant date the entire extinction of life, whether human, animal, or vegetable" (Frazer 1922, 313). All this, he adds, "correspond[s] very nearly to the theory and practice of the priests of Nemi, the Kings of the Wood."

22 Frazer varies both on myth and on the relation of myth and ritual in the three editions of *The Golden Bough* and in his work as a whole. See Ackerman 1987, ch. 5, 13; Fraser 1990a, ch. 11; Hyman, 239-42, 275-76.

23 Chapters 57 and 58 of *The Golden Bough* (1922 ed.) are on scapegoats; "carrying out death" is discussed on pp. 357-67 and mentioned on pages 144-45, 351, 668, and 711; chapter 25 is on temporary kings.

24 See, for example, William Wimsatt, "Criticism as Myth" in *Northrop Frye in Modern Criticism*, ed. Murray Krieger, 102-4.

25 Frye's "conception of literature as existing in its own universe" (*AC*, 122) can also be related to Cassirer and others.

26 See *NFN* 3 (Winter 1990-91), 6 and *NFN* 5 (Summer 1993), 29, item 554.

27 Though Frye takes us to these higher and lower worlds only briefly in the theory of myths, the theory of archetypal meaning which precedes it (*AC*, 141-58) treats all three worlds at some length. The theory

of myths takes us up to his higher world or down into the lower one; the theory of archetypal meaning presents first apocalyptic, then demonic imagery before the analogical imagery characteristic of most of secular literature.

28 Michael Maigent's *The Holy Blood and the Holy Grail* (London: Jonathan Cape, 1982) is the work to which Frye refers (*NFN* 5 [Summer 1993], 4, item 49). The polarized figures with whom Frye opens and closes the third essay of the *Anatomy* recur in many of his books. In his first book, "Blake's conception of Jesus" extends to "the parody of Christ by Antichrist" since "truth clarifies error into the negation of itself" (*FS*, 214; see also the other twenty or so references to "Antichrist" in the index of his book). His book on Milton similarly finds a negative crystallization within Christ's mind as he refuses the temptations of Satan (*RE*, 123). Both his Bible and literature books treat the polarity, but perhaps his most interesting comment occurs in his notebooks. He voices his "uneasy suspicion that I'm making the same oversimplified mistake I made in *FS* and *GC*: establishing the polarizing of the apocalyptic and demonic and not paying enough attention (a) to the contraries (b) to the analogy of generation identified by Christianity with the Old Testament" (*NFN* 5 [Summer 1993], 4, item 58; see also items 49, 50, 123, and 512).

Chapter Five: Christianity and Classical Culture

1 The title of this chapter comes from Charles Norris Cochrane's Christianity *and Classical Culture* (London: Oxford University Press, 1940), which Frye places among the "the finest scholarly studies ever written by a Canadian" (*NFCL*, 142).

2 In the first essay of the *Anatomy*, Frye only gradually introduces the expression "mythical mode" (*AC*, 56). Cassirer uses the expression of "mythic mode" (Cassirer 1946, 62) and refers as well to the "mode" of "mythical thinking" (32). Philip Wheelwright says that "myth," in Cassirer's definition, is taken as synonymous with the mythopoeic mode of consciousness." What needs to be added to Cassirer, he says, is that myth "characteristically involves expressions of that [mythopoeic] outlook in the form of particular, concrete narratives" (Wheelwright, 133). What Frye adds to Cassirer are four *mythoi* or narratives.
Spengler speaks of the "mythopoetic" (Spengler, I, 399). The indices to the *Decline*, which are not Spengler's, are unreliable guides to his use of the term "myth" and its variants; they also belie the frequency

with which such terms occur. "Myth" is a crucial term for him. In I, 187, myth is synonymous with "prime symbol" when he says "our [Western] myth develops itself in steady opposition to the Classical." In volume II, he refers in turn to our "mythic world," "Mary-myths," the "Devil myth," and "Gothic myth" (289-90).

3 Nietzsche taught Classics at Basle, where he wrote such works as *The Birth of Tragedy from the Spirit of Music* (1872) and the posthumously published *Philosophy in the Tragic Age of the Greeks*. "Myth" and "archetype" are for him important categories. Frye also points to the changes in Frazer's readership, which tend to make him of more interest "to literary critics than anthropologists" (*NFCL*, 88). It might be added that the best work done on Frazer has been almost entirely by literary scholars such as Ackerman, Fraser, Hyman, Manganaro, and Vickery.

4 Studies of nineteenth-century English attitudes toward Greek culture include Richard Jenkyns, *The Victorians and Ancient Greece*, and Frank M. Turner, *The Greek Heritage in Victorian Britain*.

5 No simple, straightforward relationship between Frye and any of the theorists considered is being assumed. Whatever he inherits from any of them he proceeds to modify. As far as I know, Frazer and Spengler had little influence upon each other. Spengler mentions Frazer once in passing in the *Decline* (I, 404). From the early 1970s onward, Frye turned from several of his earlier mentors, Spengler and Cassirer, to Giambattista Vico. Whether Spengler read Vico is unknown. H. Stuart Hughes, who calls Vico the founder of "the comparative study of civilizations" in the preface to his 1991 abridged edition of the *Decline* (New York: Oxford University Press), finds it "incredible" that Spengler knew nothing of Vico (Hughes, 53). Yet Frye finds "no evidence that Spengler had read him" (*SM*, 196). John F. Fennelly, (Fennelly, 65), also thinks Spengler was "unacquainted" with Vico (65).

6 As Frye says of his use of Frazer and Spengler, "Their conceptions seemed to get into and inform everything I worked on" (*SM*, 111).

7 Frye means, of course, that Spengler ignores the birth of a new society out of an old one. For Frye, Arnold Toynbee's "main improvement on Spengler" is his perception "that an internal proletariat (the exploited members of the society) and an external one (the barbarian nomads outside) combine to form a 'universal Church,' which becomes at once the coffin of the old [Greco-Roman] society and the womb of a new one" (*NFCL*, 79). Toynbee treats "Universal Churches" in Part

VII of the second volume in D. C. Somervell's abridgment of *A Study of History*. The phrases Frye uses occur towards the beginning of the first volume (12-13).

8 The old Roman society, the last stage of classical culture, dies and a new Western society eventually emerges. Between them, and incorporating elements of both, is Christianity. Frye's starting point is the Christian Bible, presumably because only the form canonized by the Church, which was completed during the fourth century, influenced most Western writers.

9 Frazer "treats myths as interlocking story patterns," as Frye does, "rather than in terms of their functions within their various cultures," as most anthropologists do (*GC*, 35). Spengler is the source of Frye's idea of "interpenetration," which means that "wherever you are is the center of everything" (*NFN* 3 [Winter 1990-91], 6). Spengler, he adds, shows how interpenetration "operated in history." Perhaps he means that Spengler assumes everything looks differently, for a person in any particular culture, than it would to a person in another culture, for everything is seen through the prism of the culture's prime symbol. Furthermore, everything is perceived in similar ways by everyone else in the culture.

10 Harold Mattingly reminds us that "the history of the [Roman] Empire is very commonly studied in two distinct compartments, secular history on the one side, Church history on the other" and that this "curious system of division" is merely the "result" of the way moderns teach history   (Mattingly, 229). An analogous "cleavage" occurs "between pagan and Christian literature" (246). The two are distinct until the fourth century, "when Christianity had become an integral, recognised part of the imperial scheme"; it is only then that we can "readily compare pagan and Christian" literature (246).

11 My procedure is to begin with the discussion of the Bible that Frye gives toward the end of the *Anatomy*: "Specific Encyclopedic Forms" (315-26) is the penultimate section of Frye's final essay, but the last on literature. I treat related passages until arriving at the opening version of the modal table, his account of tragic and comic forms. This crablike procedure is necessary because Frye, like others my book treats, delineates his assumptions or argument only gradually. Freud and Frazer are, like Frye, masters of this stylistic technique. Here, as elsewhere, I am indebted to A. C. Hamilton's observation that "The Bible provides explicitly or implicitly either the beginning or the end of each of the four essays (Hamilton 1922, 259).

12 Frye says that in his books on the Bible and literature he "wanted to suggest how the structure of the Bible, as revealed by its narrative and imagery, was related to the conventions and genres of Western literature" (*WP*, xi).

13 Frye notes that, in "G. R. Levy's *The Sword from the Rock* (1954), three types of epic structure are recognized: mythical epics, quest-epics, and conflict-epics. As far as the epic material is concerned, these correspond roughly to [Frye's] mythical, romantic, and high mimetical encyclopedic forms" (*AC*, 363).

14 A crucial passage for construing Spengler's "primary symbol" is *Decline*, I, 174 where he suggests that it is like a seed falling into a culture's initial mythopoetic landscape. It mysteriously and spontaneously drops into the external or "mother-landscape" and then rises with the whole destiny of the culture inscribed within it. What the prime symbol discloses, to those living within the springtime stage, is a "mythic world" different in kind from the natural landscape those people had previously been living upon (*Decline*, II, 288). Though Spengler sometimes uses the image of the seed (e.g., *Decline*, I, 105), he typically views it from the end point and calls it by such terms as "destiny-idea." Frye's "points of epiphany" (*AC*, 203-6), from a developmental perspective, are forms waiting to grow. When he suggests that "there may be analogous [interrelatable] forms of epiphany," he is associating these seeds with the things into which they grow: the four story types. He assumes that there is a "place of seed into which everything subject to the cyclical order of nature enters at death and proceeds from at birth" (*AC*, 205). The seeds of his story types exfoliate from the center of his circle of story types and become four equidistant points on the circumference of it. This process closely resembles the "center with radiating points" that, according to Frye, is Spengler's "central symbol" of Western culture (*SM*, 183). The movement that Frye attributes to Spengler's primary symbol of our culture is the same as the movement of his points of epiphany. An innate drive leading outwards in dynamic movement, a "drive into infinite distance that makes it unique," is as inherent in Frye's circle as in Spengler's primary symbol for the West (*SM*, 183). Perhaps the most important passages from the *Decline* that would have led Frye to designate Spengler's primary symbol as a "center with radiating points" that expand "into infinite distance" are the following. Certain medieval religious and literary works, Spengler says, "have rhythms" embedded in them, each of which "radiates immensities of space and distance" (I, 186). Then again, the autumn stage of our culture produced a

"Faustian group" of arts at the center of which is "instrumental music": "from this centre, fine threads radiate out into all spiritual form-languages and weave" other areas of cultural expression "into one immense totality of spiritual expression" (I, 282). Finally, he says that Western man exists "*in* an extension that encircles us" and that, for us, "there is only one true 'dimension' of space, which is direction from one's self outwards into the distance, the 'there' and the future" (I, 172).

15 Still, Frazer brings the rituals and myths of primitive cultures to bear upon the Classics and the Bible, where Frye treats the myths of classical culture and Christianity as they inform later Western literature. Frye's focus is upon the "gradual transformation of mythology into literature" in the West (*DV*, 62). He traces "the great evolution of what we now call literature [because the notion of literature as a whole is a conception that begins only with poets and thinkers of the Romantic period] out of mythology" (*DV*, 43).

16 Perhaps Frazer chooses the priest-king ritual to show that primitive features, which others had usually placed in early Roman religion, continued to exist throughout the Empire. It would probably be a feather in any revisionist's cap to prove that such a ritual was practiced so close to Rome. As Ackerman describes Frazer's view, neither Judaism nor Christianity had "been immune from the widespread bloody worship of the procreative principle that peoples like the native Canaanites knew" (Ackerman 1987, 169).

Chapter Six: The Rhythm of Romance

1 See Frazer's recounting of the lives of the Mediterranean gods of vegetation in *Golden Bough*, one-volume abridgment (London: Macmillan, 1922), chapters 29-39.

2 Frye "unites" the organic rhythms of Spengler and Frazer. He deliberately conflates their rhythms.

3 One might say that Frye's initial act, in the presentation of the story types in the *Anatomy*, is to draw a line, the plot line of romance, across "the natural cycle" so that it now has a "top half," the "world of romance," and a "lower half" in which belongs the "literature of experience" (*AC*, 162).

4 Frye says that "all other cyclical patterns" in his list "are as a rule" [i.e., by Frye's rule] assimilated" to the first of them (*AC*, 159). In

other words, he supplies us with a rule or guideline for reading and interpreting his list. I call it a "metacyclical pattern" because it informs the others. The other metacyclical pattern is the sixth in his list of seven. It is the only one linked to a modern theorist, Spengler, though most of them probably stem from other myth theorists or poets. Spengler's cyclical pattern depicts "civilized life" as "assimilated" [the same verb he uses for Frazer's pattern] to the organic cycle of growth, maturity, decline, death, and rebirth in another individual form" (*AC*, 160). Following his list, Frye immediately makes an observation that turns his Spenglerian cyclical patterns into a metacyclical, or informing, pattern. The "cyclical symbols" that occur throughout the list "are usually divided into four main phases." The symbols have as their "type" the "four seasons of the year," which accounts for their having a fourfold poetic organization, as in a poetic account of a life through the "four periods" of "youth, maturity, age, death" (*AC*, 160).

5 The *Anatomy* repeatedly alludes to dying or rising gods, usually to both: see, for example, 36, 42, 43, 121, 137, 138-39, 140, 148, 158-59, 160, 179, 183, 185, 187-88, 189-92, 193, 194-95, 199, 205, 207, 214, 215, 222-23, 238-39, 292, 314, 315-26.

6 The paragraph following Frye's list of cyclical patterns does not explicitly mention Spengler; who nevertheless seeps into the passage when Frye comments that the reader has to "add," in order to apprehend an organizing device used by Eliot in *The Waste Land*, the "medieval, Renaissance, eighteenth-century, and contemporary" periods (*AC*, 160). In his last essay on Spengler, Frye presents a chart that includes these periods and remarks that "the Spenglerian analogy is there [in *The Waste Land*] in full force" (*SM*, 188; see also, *TSE*, 8-9).

7 In Frye, the social precedes the individual: an individual is born into a society (see, e.g., *AC*, 96-97).

8 That is to say, Frye combines the organic rhythms of Spengler and Frazer; one could equally well say he deliberately conflates them. Spengler's rhythm runs through cultural history. Frazer's runs through the rhythm of the seasons of the year, or the annual decline and revival of vegetable life. Frye's rhythm runs through the body of secular literature, but is particularly embodied in romance. In "the history of literature," romance continually arises after more sophisticated literary "conventions" die out (*SS*, 28). "Popular literature, with romance at its center, comes again into the foreground": this dying and rising pattern occurred "with Greek literature after New Comedy, when Greek

romance emerged," and it recurred "when the Gothic romances emerged," as part of the movement called Romanticism (*SS*, 29).

9 While Frye expands Frazer's "three-day rhythm of death, disappearance, and revival" into four parts in his section on romance, the *Anatomy* begins with a contraction of Frazer: "stories of dying gods" are "tragic stories" (*AC*, 35-36); stories of rising gods are comic—these are not resurrection stories, though, but of a "hero being accepted by a society of gods," or of "assumption" (*AC*, 43).

10 Conflict is the recurring feature in romance. It enters into the three parts: death, disappearance, and revival.

11 Frye borrows "the terms employed by Sir Gilbert Murray in his Excursus in Jane Harrison, *Themis*, 2d. ed. (1927), 341 ff." (*AC*, 361). In Murray, the terms refer to the ritual elements of Greek tragedy; in Frye, they refer to the elements of romance in Western literature. Three elements of romance are presented on page 187 of the *Anatomy*; a few pages later, he gives another account, in which there are now four of them. Here he takes the "*sparagmos* or tearing-in-pieces," which is a "form" subsumed under Murray's second ritual element, death or disaster, and elevates it to equal status with his other elements (*AC*, 192). In between a "death-struggle" (which becomes associated with tragedy) and "discovery" (associated with comedy), he now has "the disappearance of the hero, a theme which often takes the form of *sparagmos* or tearing to pieces" (which becomes associated with satire). Murray, together with F. M. Cornford, might well have been included as a theorist of myth who influenced Frye. Murray traces the rise of tragedy from early Greek religion. Frye, while borrowing Murray's terms, places them in a synchronic account of the archetypal themes expressed fully only in romance. What Murray does for tragedy, Cornford does for comedy. On both Murray and Cornford, see Ackerman 1991, ch. 7. Though influenced by both, Frye changes the developmental approaches that Murray and Cornford inherit from Frazer into a more synchronic approach.

12 While the distinction between plot and theme is one of the staples of Frye's literary criticism, it is helpful in our present context to view it in the light of other myth theorists. Frye assumes that "the cyclical sequence in a [generic] romantic hero's life" can be spread out in time, like a plot line. Here he is in keeping with others who have drawn a composite hero, a "hero with a thousand faces," as in Joseph Campbell and, before him, Lord Raglan. By presenting the "cyclical sequence," Frye identifies particular thematic patterns in romance. Frye also looks

at romance as a typical, recurring plot rather than thematically, and isolates—and this is another composite drawing—the "normal quest theme" (*AC*, 200). From the perspective of its plot, Frye makes contact with another group of myth theorists. He can relate the typical plot of romance to the terms that Freud applies to dream: "displacement" and "condensation"; alternatively, romance can be perceived in the vocabulary of Jung, in which case "the quest-romance is the search of the [human] libido or desiring self for a fulfillment that will deliver it from the anxieties of [human] reality but will still contain that [human] reality" (*AC*, 193). In between theme and plot is character, and Frye's discussion of comic character types is largely an effort to work with the character types that Cornford (1914) finds throughout Aristophanes, and extend them from Classical to Western comedy.

13 Frye says that "the natural form of the point of epiphany is called in Spenser the Gardens of Adonis"; they are like "Eden in Dante" in being "a place of seed, into which everything subject to the cyclical order of nature enters at death and proceeds from at birth" (*AC*, 205). In the Classical tradition, the image representing this point of epiphany is "Venus watching over Adonis"; in the Christian tradition, its "analogue" is depictions of "Madonna and Son" (*AC*, 205).

14 Literary forms are compared with seeds throughout the *Anatomy*. In the first essay, Frye advances the "principle" that, in every one of his five modes, "we may attach a special significance to the particular episodic form that seems to be the germ [an embryo in its earliest stage of development, which is like the bud on a flower or a seed] out of which the encyclopedic forms develop" (56). The germ of the mythic mode is the "oracle," which somehow "develops a number of subsidiary forms, notably the commandment, the parable, the aphorism, and the prophecy" (56). The second essay has, near its end, the passage cited in the text—a passage that I attribute to Spengler's influence. Yet the notion that there is a "seed-plot of literature," from which a few seeds develop into literary forms is similar to what he says in his essay on Frazer: ritual, for Frye, is a "potential work of art," which "can grow into drama or romance or fiction or symbolic poetry" (*AC*, 122; *NFCL*, 90). The discussion of romance, in the third essay, has a multitude of references to seeds. The image of the birth of the hero can be seen, from a psychological perspective, as an image of "the embryo in the womb"; anthropologically, the image is "of seeds of new life buried in a dead world" (*AC*, 198). The discussion of the point of epiphany (203-6) is filled with seed imagery. For example, the end of Dante's *Purgatorio* conveys "the sense of being between an apocalyptic world above and a cyclical world below"; it suggests that it is "from the

Garden of Eden" that "all seeds of vegetable life fall back into the world" (204). The fourth essay returns to the point that Frye had made in the first: that "the growing points of prose," which he called "the commandment, parable, aphorism, and oracle" (56), "reappear as the kernels of scriptural forms" (324). His essay on "Charms and Riddles" begins with an elaborate "botanical analogy," in which "there are generic seeds or kernels, possibilities of expression sprouting and exfoliating into new literary phenomena" (*SM*, 123).

15 Klaus Fischer says that "Spengler was indebted to Goethe for three important ideas" besides his organic approach to history (Fischer, 93-94). The three are: "the idea of the life cycle, the metamorphosis of plants, and the image of Faustian man" (94). Of the three, "perhaps the most important" is the conception of "'the metamorphosis of plants,'" the title of Goethe's *Die Metamorphose der Pflanzen* (94). Frye himself mentions "Goethe's essays on the metamorphoses on plants" (*SS*, 184). See also Fischer's comments on the relationship between Goethe's primal type and Spengler's prime symbol (95), and upon their respective morphological approaches (162 ff.).

Chapter Seven: Myth and Culture

1 Schilpp, 25. There is no biography of Cassirer in English, and no reliable study of his life in any language. By far the best study of his thought is John Michael Krois, *Cassirer: Symbolic Forms and History*; subsequent citations are to it.

2 A fourth volume of *Philosophy of Symbolic Forms* is being prepared by Krois and Donald Phillip Verene (Krois, 224, n. 8). While that volume is on the metaphysics of symbolic forms, Krois says that "his plan to write a volume on art" never materialized (31). Though not a part of the series, Cassirer hoped to write, near the time of his death, a book on Shakespeare which would have treated the topic of "the correlation of the comic and tragic" (32).

3 Quoted in Krois, 13. In the same place, Krois draws from Lewis White Beck the observation that "men entered and left" the neo-Kantian movement as if it were a church or political party; members of one school blocked the appointments and promotions of the others."

4 Language eventually extricates itself from myth. When it does, the sheerly—people in the humanities might prefer to say "merely"—conceptual language of science becomes possible. Art, however, con-

tinually releases primitive language and the expressive power of myth into our lives.

5 William K. Wimsatt, Jr., and Cleanth Brooks, *Literary Criticism: A Short History.* Brooks wrote the chapter "Myth and Archetype," in which these points are made (xi). He relates Frye to Cassirer, but on the basis of Frye's 1951 article, "The Archetypes of Literature" (reprinted in *FI*, 7-20). That essay serves to indicate the direction Frye's thought was then taking or as "to some extent a summarized statement of the critical program worked out" in the *Anatomy.* Yet it is an illegitimate procedure to use the essay as if it were an epitome of *AC*, as is still occasionally done.

6 For Cassirer, there is a direct connection between myth and art be-cause artists, musicians, and writers employ the expressive power of myth. When he writes of writers, he focuses on lyric poets. For Susanne Langer, who was greatly influenced by him, the individual arts are treated as autonomous symbolic forms. In her *Feeling and Form*, every one of them, from dance to the latest symbolic art-form, the cinema, occupies a "virtual" field of its own. Frye reviewed her book in *The Hudson Review* in the summer of 1953 and Cassirer's work there a year later (*NFCL*, 111-16 and 67-75). Frye's view that "literature" is "the only one of these arts" to have a "direct connec-tion with myth" is perhaps a point of disagreement with Langer. In any case, his immediate difference from Cassirer consists in substitut-ing for his generic term, "art," a specific term, "literature."

7 On the same page Frye says that he encountered the notion of "interpenetration" not only in Spengler but also "later" on in Alfred North Whitehead's *Science and the Modern World.* That book pres-ents a notion of "organicism" in which events are grasped synchronic-ally, since an event organizes not only time, but space, within itself. In the chapter entitled "Abstraction," he says that "no one man" or soci-ety or age "can think of everything at once" (Whitehead, 142). While his exposition is historical or developmental, he attacks the idea of the material that science progressively generated by opposing to it his idea of "organic synthesis" (142). The chapter ends with his principle that "any eternal object is just itself in whatever mode of realization it is involved" (155; see also 144). According to Frye, Cassirer occasion-ally uses the word "interpenetrate" or interpenetration" (1946a, 90, 97).

8 As Krois explains, "The whole idea of 'nature' is foreign to mythic thought because in myth the world is seen in terms of a living society in which man is a member. The inanimate objects, vegetation, and

animals are conceived in animism and totemism to be man's relatives"
(Krois, 137).

9 A springtime culture, the first three hundred years of Classical culture (1100-800 B.C.) or of the age of chivalry (900-1200), is "the first
formative act" of the "awakening spirituality" of a culture (Spengler,
I, 399). These are "form-worlds of great myth," epic ages, in which
the "great world image of a new religion" comes to be (I, 399). Classical mythology takes form in the Classical culture and "*Faustian mythology*" in Western culture (I, 398, 399).

10 Spengler contrasts his view that the categories of space and time are
different in every major world culture to Kant's that they are universal:
(I, 174). Jung studied Kant intensively, according to his *Memories,
Dreams, Reflections*; Freud mentions Kant implicitly in *New Introductory Lectures on Psychoanalysis* (Lecture XXXI) when he writes of
"an exception to the [Kantian] theorem that space and time are necessary forms of our mental acts," because "there is nothing in the id that
corresponds to the idea of time" (74).

11 Hazard Adams says that "one was not simply to return to Kant to
accept all he said, but to start *from* Kant again" (Adams, 206).

12 "Imagination is the primary talent of the human mind," according
to Langer, "On Cassirer's Theory of Language and Myth," in Schilpp,
386.

13 The topic is addressed at the close of the following chapter.

14 Compare the passages in Cassirer's *Language and Myth* In which
art is brought together with his initial cultural forms (7, 98), with
Frye's comments about them (*NFCL*, 69).

15 Here, again, Frye's review of Langer is helpful (*NFCL*, 111-16).

Chapter Eight: Cassirer and the Anatomy

1 An indispensable book for the study of Cassirer and Frye is Hazard
Adams, *Philosophy of the Literary Symbolic*, chs. 8, 10.

2 Cassirer locates myth through his spatial metaphor "lower original
stratum" (Cassirer 1944, 109). Perhaps the characteristic action of
early twentieth-century myth theorists is to lower their readers into
myth. In any case, Cassirer considers the mythical world not only the
earliest or original symbolic form but also the lowest. His "mythical

world" stands in contrast to the view of the world offered by science. As Ricoeur says, Cassirer "put the scientific version" of reality "at the top of the ascending scale of [symbolic] forms" (1991, 209).

3 In *Myth, Rhetoric, and the Voice of Authority*, Marc Manganaro contends that "Frye's representation of a broad spectrum of literary critics with limited views approximates Frazer's description of field-workers whose critical acumen is realized only when their observations are brought together" by him (Manganaro, 114). Manganaro also maintains that Frye inherited "the essentially Addisonian tendency of Frazerian comparativism" (116). Manganaro wants to overturn the too frequent view of Frye as a sheerly systematic or synchronic thinker by placing him within a developmental species of comparativism. In actuality, Frye incorporates both kinds. Yet I agree with Manganaro that "Frye's rank as the greatest myth critic" in literary criticism accompanies his resistance to that "label"; he does endeavor to be a "master comparativist" (114). Manganaro rightly suggests that "archetypal criticism is prominent" in the *Anatomy* "because it concerns the interconnection of varying methods, the potential for synthesis, and as such it is an important correlate of that fundamental synthetic mechanism, the comparative method" (116).

4 See Ricoeur's discussion of the phases of symbolism (1991, especially 252-53). He says that "literary symbolism does not imply a category of symbols" for Frye "in the broad sense that Cassirer gave this term" (1991, 247). Certainly Frye does not locate literary symbolism within a symbolic form. As Krois notes, "Cassirer uses the term *symbolic form* in a variety of ways: to refer to particular occurrences of meaning" or to indicate "pervasive kinds of symbolic relations," which is presumably what Ricoeur means by the "broad sense," and "to cultural forms or ways of having a 'world' such as myth, language, art, or science" (Krois, 44).

5 Kermode designates Frye's view of literary meaning as continually hypothetical or imaginative as a "symbolist" perception; Frye's term, "hypothetical" is similar to Susanne Langer's term "virtual" meaning (1959, 320). One might say that for Langer aesthetic meaning is always virtual meaning. In Frye's review of her book *Feeling and Form*, he says that she classifies each of the "arts according to the virtual fields that they occupy" (*NFCL*, 112). These virtual fields are in accordance with Cassirer's sense of a cultural form. Langer's innovation is her specification of his principle: each of the arts has a virtual or symbolic form of its own. On this point, Frye agrees with her: similar but autonomous fields are characteristic of each of the arts. Literature

has a self-contained, autonomous universe; "similar inverses exist for all the arts" (*AC*, 122). What Frye considers "disappointing" is Langer's haphazard application of "the ideas of Cassirer" (*NFCL*, 111). Her "main idea" is based upon Cassirer's "central assimilating form," but she uses his idea merely as a "touchstone," which implies that Frye thinks it could be put to better use, as he himself does in organizing the second essay of the *Anatomy* (*NFCL*, 113).

6 "Constitutes" is a word which Cassirer takes from Kant. We constitute, found, establish, set up the world; with the Romantics, it becomes more frequent to say that we make up or create the world.

7 Frye's theory of reading is the subject of chapter eleven. In the present context, the closing sentence in the preface of *The Secular Scripture* is pertinent: "Even if there is ultimately only one mythological universe, every reader sees it differently." Frye is echoing Heraclitus' aphorism: "although the Logos is common to all, most men live as if each of them had a private intelligence of his own" (Wheelwright, 1966, 69, fragment 2). Heraclitus is a significant figure for a number of those who influenced Frye: Spengler, who wrote his doctoral dissertation on him, Eliot, and Cassirer, who says, "Heraclitus likes to use the image of the circle to express his doctrine," and which, he says, set a precedent for Plato and Aristotle (1955, 133 ff.). The expression of thought with the help of a circular diagram occurs in Cassirer, Jung, and Frye. The circle has the same function in all three of them. It represents the goal they seek rather than something they have indubitably established. Hence the depiction of circles in their commentators, including myself, is inevitably misleading. For Cassirer, the goal is to display all the symbolic forms as an "organic whole," a "circle" of the activities that comprise humanity's work, so that "language, myth, religion, art, science, and history are the constituents, the various sectors of the circle" (1944, 93). For Jung, according to Frye, individuation, when achieved, presents "the self" as "the center of a circle with four cardinal points" (*NFCL*, 119). Like Cassirer in *Essay on Man*, Frye briefly mentions a circular arrangement in his discussion of the circle of story types, but only to offer the reader a glimpse, a possibility (*AC*, 162). Frye's circle of story types is structurally similar to Jung's theory of individuation. Just as the containing form of the first essay of the *Anatomy* comes from Spengler, and the form of the second essay comes from Cassirer, so the containing form of the theory of reading, in Frye's theory of story types in the third essay, comes from Jung.

8 "On Cassirer's Theory of Language and Myth, "in Schilpp, 393. The second essay of the *Anatomy* draws upon three articles he wrote.

The main difference between the second essay and the articles is that the articles restrict everything to a *single* symbolic form. Frye's first article, "Levels of Meaning in Literature" has three such levels *contained* within a fourth. In the next, "Three Meanings of Symbolism," the antithesis of naturalism and *symbolism* is dissolved by the Romantics' use of the symbol as an archetype and is dissolved, in Frye's literary criticism, by a "fourth conception of the symbol as monad or unit of total poetic experience" (*AC*, 19). Finally, in "The Language of Poetry," myth is presented as a symbolic form. It is a central term which contains and unifies flanking terms: ritual and dream (*AC*, 48). Three kinds of scholarly activity, or fields, are united by the literary critic such as Frye, who works with Frazerian anthropology and Jungian psychology (*AC*, 49). The three articles are: "Levels of Meaning in Literature," *Kenyon Review* 12 (Spring 1950), 246-62; "Three Meanings of Symbolism," *Yale French Studies* 9 (1952), 11-19; and "The Language of Poetry," *Explorations: Studies in Culture and Communication* 4 (February 1955), 80-90. The *Anatomy* has five phases of symbolism, with the hinge coming with the distinction between "two aspects of form," with which he begins both the last article and the mythical phase of the *Anatomy*. These aspects of form differ insofar as the "formal phase" is restricted to the notion of imitation of nature and so belongs to his first symbolic form. The formal phase in his second symbolic form begins the journey in which imitation is gradually eclipsed in what Frye later called this "anti-mimetic theory of literature" (*NFN* 5 [Summer 1993], 34). Adams says that "to all his phases" except the literal phase "Frye assigns some mode of imitation" (Adams, 266). He adds that "as we pass up the chart from descriptive to anagogic we discover the term departing from its usual meaning to indicate metamorphosis or liberation of material into a new form" (Adams, 266). Metamorphosis, as seen in the last chapter, is one of Cassirer's "laws" of myth; and Frye's language about "liberation" comes directly from Cassirer (*AC*, 93; Cassirer, 1946a, 98). In Frye, however, the gradual movement away from imitation comes with the Aristotelian term "*ethos*," which permeates the formal phase, pervades the mythic phase, and floods the anagogic phase and sweeping out imitation in the process.

9 *NFN* 5 (Summer 1993), 34. Though he calls it a "theory of literature," he refers to the theory of symbolism.

10 For Cassirer, Dante's version of medieval exegesis "preserved" the four-level theory of the interpretation of the Bible "unchanged," and Dante's "poetics is no less rooted in it than his theology" (1955, 256). Frye, too, suggests that Dante is responsible for having "taken over

from theology" a "scheme of literal, allegorical, moral, and anagogic meanings," and "applied" them "to literature" (*AC*, 72). There are, however, two widespread conventions in medieval interpretation. Both stem from Origen, according to Henri De Lubac (*Exegese Medievale*). What both have in common is that they take the whole landscape of Scripture as the provision by which our lives become spiritually legible or morally readable. Their shared assumption, as Brevard Childs says in his discussion of Origen, is that "Scripture is a word from God to us on the way toward life in God" (Childs 1993, 35). Origen's *On First Principles*, Book IV, ch. 2, consists of a sequence that might now be described as rules of reading. Origen's ideal reader of Scripture is much like Frye's: the reader understands scriptural meaning to the extent that there is death to the literal meaning, followed by a resurrection and ascension to spiritual meaning. Another of Origen's rules is that "the entire narrative" of the Bible as a whole consists of a continuous sequence of "forms and types of hidden and sacred matters" (*An Exhortation to Martyrdom, Prayer, First Principles*, tr. Rowan A. Greer [New York: Paulist Press, 1979], 181). For Origen, as for Frye, the reading of Scripture is the pursuit of a lifetime; for both, the vision of ultimate meaning belongs to an individual reader's revelatory experiences. For Origen, the buried treasure of types, enigmas, and forms runs like an extended vein of gold throughout the hidden meganarrative of the Bible as a whole; for Frye, literature as a whole constitutes a landscape from which the reader is constantly extracting archetypes. For Origen, only from "the divine words" of Scripture do we "learn" from its "words what this world is" (Origen, 186); for Frye, the purpose of reading the Bible and literature is to enable us to read the world as it really is by deconstructing the temporal world.

11 On these three phases, Krois says that "Cassirer identifies three states in the development of symbolic forms, stages he terms "mimetic," "analogical," and "purely symbolic"; Krois calls this development "an ideal, not a historical, progression" (Krois, 80).

Chapter Nine: Displacement and Condensation

1 Since Frye says that he takes the concept of "displacement" from Freud, the normal way to approach Frye on the displacement of myth is to compare him with Freud on the displacement of dream. I have chosen not to follow this well-worn procedure for three reasons. First, Frye's last remark on the topic is that "for some mysterious reason, I left out any discussion of condensation [a term that works in tandem

with displacement in Freud] in the *Anatomy*" ("E-CS," 245). He omitted it, he adds, despite the fact that "when I read Freud on dreams and learned that the major operations of the dream were condensation and displacement, it struck me that the same operations took place within literature." The *Anatomy* assumes that there is a process at work in literature that is analogous to that which Freud's *Interpretation of Dreams* calls "condensation" but that is not named in Frye's book. If so, then it seems to follow that the discussions by others are limited in their validity since they do not take into account the condensation process, which works together with displacement in Freud and Frye. Second, the framework of Frye's discussion is not myth alone. As he says, "condensation" in literary language means "a concentration on metaphor," whereas displacement for him means adapting myth to ordinary, everyday experience ("E-CS," 246). Hence the full context for discussion should be that of literary myth and literary language, or "the study of the mythical and metaphorical elements of literature" ("E-CS," 246). Finally, even if one wished to limit discussion to myth and not metaphor, the concept "displacement" has to be related to it and not, as Freud does, to dream. A myth for Freud is more like a daydream than a full-sleep dream; and Frye follows Cassirer and Spengler on the topic of myth. Freud takes the view, Frye says, that "the dream and the myth were the same thing," which he dismisses as "nonsense" (*NFN* 4:2,10).

2 Frye explicitly identifies Freud as the source of his use of displacement ten years after the *Anatomy* in his essay "Literature and Myth." Referring to his book, he says parenthetically that he has "borrowed from Freud" the term "displacement, though naturally the context is different in him"; for Frye it refers "to the process by which mythical stories, about gods who can do anything, or become romances about heroes who can do almost anything, or heroines of tantalizing elusiveness or unshakable fidelity, and from there become stories of the foundling Tom Jones, the whorish but unquenchable Moll Flanders, or the virtue-rewarded Pamela" ("L&M", 38-39). In *The Secular Scripture* he says the "romantic tendency" embodies condensation: the focus of the writer is one of "concentrating on the formulaic units of myth and metaphor" (37). Conversely, "the realistic tendency moves in the direction of the representational and the displaced" (37). The dual patterns together constitute a "kind of reversible shuttle" operative in "the fiction-writing of the last four or five centuries" (37). Frye speaks explicitly of condensation for the first time in *Words with Power*. He again opposes this process to displacement, but now defines condensation as occurring when "the similarities and associations

of ordinary experience become metaphorical identities" (149). While the *Anatomy* upheld Joyce's *Ulysses* as a prime example of condensed, or ironic, myth, now he calls Joyce's *Finnegans Wake* "the most extreme form of condensation" in literature (149). What is condensed is not myth in that work, for there is "apparently no continuous sequential narrative"; instead, the *Wake* is condensed, since "we have a huge body of words and verbal sounds echoing one another" (149). It is possible that more will be learned about condensation and displacement as Frye's notebooks are published. For an account of this project, see *NFN* 5:2, 1-2.

3 I cite Reed's later book as an example of a work that displays the merits of a roughly approach (Reed, 490). For instance, both Reed and Ann Colley treat the theme of "madness" in Tennyson. Colley grounds what she says in the life of the Tennysons and the medical literature of the time; Reed focuses upon other writers' treatments of the theme and shows that Tennyson is working with it, though doing the same sort of thing better than most of the others.

4 Frazer and Freud tend to assume nineteenth-century developmental patterns of thought. Peter Allan Dale suggests that "the nineteenth century was dominated as no period before or since ... by the 'historical sense'" (Dale, 2). Stanley Edgar Hyman says that "the characteristic mental habit of the nineteenth century was translating 'essence' into 'origin,' so that the statement 'This is the essence of the situation' becomes 'This is how it began'" (Hyman, 366). Frank Kermode's chapter, "Freud and Interpretation," in *An Appetite for Poetry*, gives an excellent account of Freud as an evolutionary thinker and the contrasting patterns of thought of his time. Marc Manganaro discusses Frazer's "evolutionary comparativism" in *Myth, Rhetoric, and the Voice of Authority*; a later chapter on Frye attempts to relate him to this kind of comparativism. In this attempt Manganaro seeks to overturn the too common view of him as an entirely systematic or synchronic thinker. I think the truth is more nearly that Frye works through both kinds, as do Spengler, Jung and Cassirer.

Chapter Ten: The Forces of Convention

1 The "containing form" of his first essay is the "organic rhythm of cultural aging" that Frye finds in the *Decline* (*AC*, 343). In Spengler, a culture has what Frye calls a "rhythm" that is developmental (birth, growth, maturity, and death) and a "key" (its primary symbol). The introduction to his third essay says that literature can be seen in relation

to "the literary equivalents of rhythm and key" (*AC*, 133). The rhythms turn out to be his four story types. The keys turn out to be the archetypes of imagery, or what I call the forces of convention. They are the means by which we read his classification table of imagery. Or, following his musical metaphor, the metaphoric structures which his table displays are like the notes in a musical score, and the forces of convention are like a pair of keys to reading the score. The containing form of the second essay has a dual structure. The phases of symbolism are organized into a set of symbolic forms. Each set consists of a threefold structure: a content area affected by a shaping form, and between them a unifying form. The easiest way to apprehend the structure of the third essay is to begin by perceiving its several parts in the same way as we did the second.

2 Both of Frye's shaping forms have the same construction. The relationship between apocalyptic and demonic imagery and between the Christian myth of a higher world and a demonic world consists only of the stark contrast that he draws between them. These are polarized constructions.

3 It might seem that the container for the latter part of the essay is the "natural cycle" upon which Frye begins imposing his story types (*AC*, 162). He does confine most of his discussion to his "comparative study of the story type[s]" (*AC*, 137). However, it is for the sake of his comparative study of comedy, romance, tragedy, and satire that he tends to confine his discussion to his circle. His interest is mainly in treating the recurrent aspects of secular literature from his archetypal perspective. Nevertheless, he has a dual perspective. He takes us to the poles of his circle on a regular basis, as will be seen; when he does, he shifts into his "anagogic," or universal, perspective. He takes us toward that perspective. Frye gives us only momentary and synchronic glimpses of the polar areas above and below his circle. Ricoeur says that "from an archetypal and an analogical perspective, ... all imagery is inadequate in relation to the apocalyptic imagery of fulfillment and yet at the same time in search of it" (1991, 252). This and the further remarks he makes are among the most perceptive ever addressed to the third essay.

4 Frye relates the imagery to only three of his literary historical modes: romantic, high mimetic, and low mimetic. His selection of structural elements in the later part of the essay is usually from the same literary eras as those three modes: medieval through nineteenth-century literature. He treats Renaissance works most frequently, nineteenth-century works less often, and least often Restoration and eighteenth-century

works. His range, however, is broader here than in the discussion of analogical imagery, for he is viewing each of the story types as an autonomous literary tradition. He includes Classical works in his sections on comedy and tragedy because those traditions are so heavily affected by Classical works; Classical works also figure in his discussion of satire. His discussion of romance includes the Bible more often than any of the other sections do.

5 It is Frye, not Jung, who thinks so. For Frye, the Bible's "typology" provides both "the definitive alchemical myth for alchemists" and "the definitive grammar of allegory for allegorical poets" (*NFCL*, 128).

6 Another way of thinking about Frye's project would be to distinguish between his survey of the structures of poetic imagery and the "structural principles" that account for those structures (*AC*, 133). Such a distinction would be like that in the first essay between the "survey" he makes in the first essay and the list of "inferences" he draws from his survey (62). There the inferences are generally comparative observations. In the third essay, however, comparativism has been promoted over anything resembling an historical approach. The closest we get to history is the metahistorical version of it on which the first essay is based upon and which the third essay takes for granted: the adaptation of Spengler by which Frye joins Classical and Christian metaphoric language and myth together and has them affecting the whole of what for Spengler is Western culture and for Frye Western secular literature.

7 I am thinking of Liddell-Hart's *Strategy*.

8 The third essay of the *Anatomy* assumes that literary conventions and genres together constitute a continuous tradition that descends from or is shaped by Classical and Biblical mythology. In later literary critical works, he works with different assumptions. He writes that Romanticism initiates a "change in the structure of literature itself" (*SER*, 4). He introduces an entirely new and Romantic form of his four story types (*SER*, 35). He assumes a pair of continuous traditions, "a double tradition, one biblical and the other romantic" (*SS*, 6).

9 The Great Chain of Being is the subject of Arthur O. Lovejoy's book by that title; see also C. S. Lewis's *The Discarded Image: An Introduction to Medieval and Renaissance Literature* and E. M. W. Tillyard's *The Elizabethan World Picture*. Tillyard attempts a brief outline history of the construct. "The idea began with Plato's *Timaeus*," he suggests, "was developed by Aristotle," then "adopted by

the Alexandrian Jews" and "spread by the Neo-Platonists," and settled
into its stable form (Tillyard, 26). It presents "an ordered universe arranged in a fixed system of hierarchies" (5-6). The Frye of the *Anatomy* takes intuitive leaps from Revelation to the Great Chain, and from
it into the whole of secular literature (*AC*, 141-42, 161-62). The remarks he makes there, however, are developed in later works. *The
Great Code* presents the "structure" of the Bible's imagery in the form
of a "double table" (165). A "Table of Apocalyptic Imagery" is followed by one of "Demonic Imagery" (166, 167). Yet the categories
he presents in his tables come not from the Bible but from the construct
that developed out of it, the Great Chain. The construct has a metaphorical basis in Jacob's vision of the ladder in Genesis 28:10-22, but
is itself a post-Biblical development; it is also an extra-Biblical development, for even in the *Anatomy*, Frye points to another metaphorical
origin in the golden rope that Zeus describes in the opening lines of the
eight book of the *Iliad* (*AC*, 142). The Great Chain, in its traditional
form, extends from God, who is pure form, down through various levels to a baseline of inorganic matter (*GC*, 155; *MM*, 165). Frye begins,
in the *Anatomy*, with six levels: apocalyptic, human, animal, vegetable,
mineral, and demonic. However, he later includes a "fire" and a
"water" world (*AC*, 145, 146).

10 Take, for instance, Keats. Like other low mimetic poets, Keats presents, or according to Frye's table ought to present, realistic situations
dealing with everyday experiences by using "the ordinary images of
experience" (*AC*, 154). Such poets "anchor" their poems in
"empirical psychological experience," so that their images are concrete and sensuous (*AC*, 154). In "The Eve of St. Agnes" Keats de-
votes nine lines to a detailed description of a window frame, or case-
ment. Yet the Spenserian stanza he employs points to the convention
he deploys. The function of the "charm'd magic casements" that recur
in Keats is to open out upon romance "fairy lands," as they do toward
the end of his odes to the "Nightingale" and "Psyche."

11 Frye follows up the expression by speaking of the "conventions of
literature [which] are enclosed within a total mythological structure,"
even though that structure "may not be explicitly known to anyone"
(*SER*, 5). John Reed, who quotes this remark, works at the problem of
convention within a single period (Reed, 490).

12 In his notebooks, Frye writes of his "uneasy suspicion" of repeating "the same oversimplified mistake" he had made in *Fearful Symmetry* and in *The Great Code* of "establishing the polarizing of the
apocalyptic and demonic" (*NFN* 5 [Summer 1993] 4, item 58). I think

his polarizing of apocalyptic and demonic imagery as well as the polar worlds just above and beneath his circle of story types are also "oversimplified." Yet comparativists, at least the ones treated here, often achieve their effects by some simple dichotomy. For example, there is Spengler's contrast between Classical and Western cultures. It seems to me, however, that such contrasts are not necessarily a "mistake." They are, rather, part of the aesthetic approach these poetic thinkers take or of the approach poets often take, or of the ethical approach the Biblical prophets take. Frye, at any rate, suggests that many of the people that shape the thought of an era have a "massive simplicity" (*RW*, 323). Poets often have a "vision" which is "penetrating because it is partial and distorted" (*C&R*, 9).

13 "Twenty Questions" begins with a person's thinking of something. Like an archetype in Frye, it can be anything that happens to interest him. Others begin their questioning by asking, "Is it animal, vegetable, or mineral?" Like Twenty Questions, "archetypal criticism" is a game rarely played today; like it, Frye's game depends upon the play of the imagination. Were his archetypal criticism to be played in the future, I imagine that it would reappear under the banner of some emerging literary critical enterprise. I think it could easily be adopted by the literary critical followers of the hermeneutical philosophy of Gadamer and Ricoeur. When Frye says that the essential things about a literary work are "that it is contemporary with its own time and that it is contemporary with ours," he is taking the view that almost any hermeneutical critic would endorse (*AC*, 51). Frye's readings of literary works are almost always sensitive both to our age and to the era to which they belong.

14 See *AC*, 136, 140. Later, Frye mentions Aristotle's "list of *six* elements of poetry" (*AC*, 244). These occur, in the Bywater translation, which has a preface by myth theorist Gilbert Murray, in section six. Frye takes the first three elements that Aristotle lists and uses them in his first three essays; the other three are his point of departure for the fourth essay.

15 The conception has an origin in Frazer, according to Ernest Jones. Discussing the third essay in *Totem and Taboo*, entitled "Animism, Magic, and the Omnipotence of Thoughts," he quotes Frazer's description of the process of thinking in magic as "men mistaking the order of their ideas for the order of nature, and hence imagining that the control which they have, or seem to have, over their thoughts, permits them to exercise a corresponding control over things" (Jones, II, 358). Freud wanted to turn this "static description" into a more dynamic

one, so that "the basis of magic" resides "in man's exaggerated belief in the power of his thoughts, or more exactly his wishes, and he correlated this primitive attitude with the omnipotence of thoughts" (358). While Jones says that Frazer's notion is merely reflective of "the association psychology of the nineteenth century," he nevertheless observes that Freud accepted "the usual division of the stages of human development into the animistic, the religious and the scientific," which is characteristically a nineteenth-century grid and the same as the Frazerian scheme of magic, religion, and science (358, 357). Freud differs with Frazer only in postulating a premagical stage (357). For Freud's account of the omnipotence of thoughts in *Totem and Taboo*, see *Complete Works*, vol. XIII, 83-91, 186, 188; he mentions it as well in XVII, 139, 240-247, 250, and in XX, 66. Cassirer refers to Freud when writing of the "omnipotence of thought and the omnipotence of desire" and of the "omnipotence of the will" (1955, 157-58). See also (1944, 124).

16 Cassirer contrasts "mythical thinking" with modern logical, scientific thinking. Mythical thinking colors objects in the world with whatever the mind wills. Science endeavors to see the objects of the world as they really are. Mythical thinking is expressive; scientific thinking, objective. Frazer compares magical with scientific thinking. The aim of both is practical. Both assume that the order of external nature can be understood. They differ in that magical thinking is interested thinking and scientific thinking disinterested thinking: a magician approaches nature to manipulate it, perhaps because of the crudeness of his ideas about nature. As Frye says, "magic is wrong about natural law and science right," so that Frazer invites us to "enter on an age of science, or true magic" (*NFCL*, 92). The difference between Frazer and Freud is that Frazer attributes to earliest man the wish to know nature so as to manipulate it, where Freud attributes to him "the omnipotence of thoughts." In Frazer, the wish to master nature comes out of the wish to abolish any separation between oneself and nature. In Freud, the wish comes out of the hope that one's thoughts are all-powerful. Freud's discussion of primitive man, in *Totem and Taboo*, elicits likenesses between the thinking of primitives and children on the one hand and modern, neurotic adults on the other. In Jung's first essay in *Symbols of Transformation*, "Two Kinds of Thinking," archaic thought is imaginative, natural, and spontaneous; modern thought is linear and logical thinking. *Psychological Types* has a four-cell typology that starts with a "thinking" person and ends with an "intuitive," since the thinker or rational ego tends to be the person most unaware of his unconscious, where the intuitive is the person who

is most responsive to the unconscious. For Jung, according to Frye, "the logical and discursive structures of rational consciousness" are one-dimensional, in contrast to the "structures of symbolism" which come from a "collective unconscious" (*NFCL*, 95). Where Jung contrasts forms of awareness within people, Spengler writes of the different worlds or settings. Jung and Spengler are alike for Frye in presenting the same contrast: "The objective world, the world that we know and perceive, the phenomenal world, is essentially a spatial world: it is the domain of Nature explored by science and mathematics, and so far as it is explored, it is a mechanical world, for when living things are seen objectively they are seen as mechanisms. Over against this world is the world of time, organism, life and history. The essential reality of this world eludes the reasoner and experimenter: it is to be attained rather by feeling, intuition, imaginative insight, and, above all, by symbolism" (*SM*, 180). The difference between Jung and Spengler is that Jung assumes the structures of symbolism come from the collective unconscious; by contrast, they come, for Spengler, from the primary symbol a culture has.

17 The notion of "magic" can be traced from Frazer to Cassirer to Frye. In *Essay on Man*, Cassirer says that Frazer's view of magic being replaced by religion is "untenable," because the belief in magic is very much a part of "our own European civilization" (Cassirer 1944, 135). It is in fact retained by the leading "thinkers of the Renaissance," who each held "their own philosophical scientific theories of the magic art" (135). In *The Individual and the Cosmos in Renaissance Philosophy*, the same argument is given at some length. He asserts that "the natural philosophy of the Renaissance had sought nothing less than an *epistemological* foundation and justification of magic" (Cassirer 1963, 169). For instance, he quotes Pico della Mirandola, whose idea was that "we may apply the name of magic to the whole of science and the whole of philosophy with as much right as we call Rome 'the' city, Vergil 'the' poet, Aristotle 'the' philosopher" (169). In short, magic for Cassirer is what Frye calls an "organizing idea."

18 One might compare the organizing idea of "form" with Cassirer's remark in *The Question of Jean-Jacques Rousseau*: "In its literature as well as in its philosophy and science, the eighteenth century had come to rest in a fixed and definite world of forms" (Cassirer 1954, 36). For Cassirer, Rousseau "repudiated and destroyed the molds in which ethics and politics, religion as well as literature and philosophy were cast" (36).

19 Here again, a comparison with Cassirer helps. Cassirer says in his book on Rousseau that eighteenth-century men rejoiced in "the basic power of reason" (Cassirer 1954, 36). The comment by itself is a commonplace, for everyone thinks of the century as the age of reason. However, his further reflections in *The Philosophy of the Enlightenment* bring us closer to Frye's view of reason. The intellectual history of the period is for Cassirer "held together in a common center of force" (Cassirer 1951, 5). Reason is conceived, then, as a "formative power" (5). "When the eighteenth century wants to characterize this power in a single word, it calls it 'reason'," so that, for Cassirer, "'Reason' becomes the unifying and central point of this century, expressing all that it longs and strives for, and all that it achieves" (5). To say the same thing in Frye's terms would be to say that reason is both expressive of desire, yet works in the world, the world of nature. Hence, Frye's "analogy of reason and nature."

20 Some context for these organizing ideas is provided in *SER*. In the Romantics, "the reason founded on a separation of consciousness from nature" is subordinated (*SER*, 12). While "the artist" had traditionally been said to imitate nature, this expression is taken by Romantics such as Coleridge to mean that he imitates the "living process of nature by seeking a union of himself, as a living and creating being, with nature as a process or genesis" (*SER*, 12).

Chapter Eleven: The Myth of the Ideal Reader

1The argument of this chapter is based upon the recurrent terminology Frye employs in the theory of myths. His exposition of a story type such as comedy provides a set of interrelated terms. For instance, in the second paragraph, he begins with the term "plot structure" (*AC*, 163). Then, in a sub-section of his discussion of comedy, he says "we pass on to the typical characters of comedy" (171). Next, he indicates a transition by saying, "let us now look at a variety of comic structures," which he designates during this section as "phases" and are thematic phases (177). He insists upon our accepting a sequence of five phases, on the analogy of the "circle of fifths in music" and yet declares that he actually recognizes "six phases" in each story type (177). This flat contradiction is dissolved only distinguishing between different stages in what is tantamount to a theory of reading. As I suggest later, there are five phases in the first stage of Frye's developmental theory of reading, and the sixth is significant only in his third stage. The second stage in his theory is indicated by his recurring generic designations, such as "ironic comedy" (176). He says that "the distinction between an ironic comedy and a comic satire, or between a romantic comedy and a comic romance, is tenuous, but not quite a distinction without a difference" (177). And indeed it does make a difference in our account of his theory of reading, for his second stage consists of these recurring generic distinctions. His third set of terms consists of the expressions "total *mythos*" (171) and "mythic world." He speaks of a "mythical world" above that of comedy, and he continually uses the word "world" toward the end of his sequence of thematic phases (185). Once we learn to distinguish among these three stages, we begin to see that Frye's seemingly unrestrained terminological outpouring has more precision than is usually attributed to the theory of myths, which is in fact the climax of his book.

2 We explored this particular sense of myth in chapter three. As we saw, Frye employs "myth" as an expressive configuration in Frazer's *Golden Bough* and Spengler's *Decline*. Myth means not only something that those thinkers deploy as a line of their own thought; it means a line of thought or configuration that articulates what many other people in their time had been assuming, which is why I call it "expressive." My chapter title merely applies to Frye himself the sense of the word "myth" he applies to other myth theorists. I think we should see him as a pioneer in what, subsequent to the *Anatomy*, became the burgeoning area of reader response criticism, though, doubtless, his theory of reading may seem primitive relative to the host of reader response theories available at present.

3 *NFN* 5 (Summer 1993), 27, item 461

4 Since reader-response theories of all kinds have been proliferating profusely in recent decades, it is natural that the *Anatomy* has occasionally been used as a point of departure. In such a freewheeling situation, any of the *Anatomy*'s four theories—modes, symbols, myths, or genres—can be related to a particular reader--response theory. Most reader response theories ignore Frye altogether. Some invoke the *Anatomy* only to dismiss it, as do Jonathan Culler and E. D. Hirsch, Jr., whom I mention in a later note in regard to genre. In his reception theory, Hans Robert Jauss uses Frye's theory modes. "Frye's typology of the hero" becomes a typology or "system of receptional modes" in "Levels of Identification of Hero and Audience," *New Literary History* 5 (Winter 1974), 296. A. C. Hamilton's book shows that reading is a concern through all four essays in the *Anatomy* (see his section on "Reading, Criticism, and Creation," 196-99, and its companion piece, "Reading and Criticism," 25-29). It appears, however, as the *locus* of

many of his remarks about reading. For him, Frye's literal level is the "level of reading" (92). Frye 's theory of symbolism as a whole "begins and ends in the act of reading" (103). The final anagogic phase "describes the ideal experience of reading" (111). Hamilton adds that it is a "post-critical", yet he has said that "in establishing his critical method," Frye deliberately set out to duplicate" his own personal reader response to Spengler (56). It would seem to follow that the ideal experience of reading literature, which serves as the goal of reading for Frye, is grounded on the experience or experiences he had as an undergraduate. However this may be, Hamilton says that "it is Frye the reader, not the critic, or rather ... the reader-critic, who places the individual literary work at the centre of the literary universe constructed by criticism" (112). The question is, whose criticism is it? Here the difficulty is that Hamilton means Frye's criticism, yet he wants to preserve the entire *Anatomy* as the ground upon which contemporary literary criticism can be played. Hamilton introduces the reader into the last sentence of his account of the second essay. He prepares for it by saying that "the anagogic phase" is "the end of the critical path," in "Frye's theory of symbolism," when he is also aware that it is "post-critical" (118; 111). Then he says that "the journey" through the five phases of symbolism "is sustained by the faith," which is Frye' faith, though it has not been the shared faith of other literary critics since the *Anatomy*, "that the structural pattern found [by Frye] in literary works" are expressive of identity. The phases become expressive in the sense that they have become an objective totality somehow simultaneously the expressive counterpart of what Hamilton calls "the reader's" distinctive identity (119). The post-critical phase of the journey of the reader-critic ultimately becomes "existential" (119). If so, one could relate his final phase to the final phase of Jung's individuation theory. Frye observes that he does not want "*literature* to be turned into a psychological allegory of individuation," but says that "once I move back from literary to existential metaphor" he comes "very close" to doing so (*NFN* 5 [Summer 1993], 9, item 138). "In Jungian terms," the "way of reading literature," which we can apply to Frye's second essay, stands opposed, at the outset, to the view of the reader as a "conscious ego"; by the end of Frye's account of reading, the reading process has become one in which "the superconscious individual directs" (*NFN* 5 [Summer 1993], 17, item 273). The difference between these initial images and the final ones of the reader would be like the difference between a traffic cop, who directs without becoming involved in the flow of traffic, and a symphony director who is involved and who "directs" the music. For Hamilton, contemporary literary criticism has become a wilderness wandering, in which confused tribes have forsaken the Moses who wrote the *Anatomy*. Hamilton's is a brilliant defense of Frye. Nevertheless, I agree with Thomas Willard that Hamilton "de-emphasizes the development of Frye's theories" and his concentration on the *Anatomy* has the unintended effect of undercutting the "resilience" of his later thought "in response to newer developments" in literary criticism (Willard, review of Hamilton, in *NFN* 3 [Winter 1990-91], 27-31).

5 "The Ideal Reader: A Critical Fiction," *PMLA* 93 (May 1978), 469. Frye is discussed on pages 468-70. He is set within a comparative study of the ideal readers of John Dryden, Samuel Johnson, and Samuel Taylor Coleridge. DeMaria's citations of Frye's works are few but well chosen: *FS*, 418, 427-28; *AC*, 117-18, 132, 344, 345-46; *FI*, 263-64; *CP*, 125, *St. S*, 164. Notice that several of them cite the end of a book (*FS*, 417-18 and *FI*, 263-64). And observe that the latter is a recapitulation of the last paragraph of the *Anatomy*: both passages quote Joyce's remark about "the ideal reader suffering from an ideal insomnia" (*FI*, 264; *AC*, 354). Frye says that "eventually it dawns on us that it is the *reader* who achieves the quest" and so is the real hero of *Finnegans Wake*. In the last paragraph of *SS*, Frye says that Edmund "Spenser thus passes on to his reader the crowning act of self-identity as the contemplating of what he has made, including what one has recreated by possessing the canon of man's word as well as God's" (*SS*, 188). Similarly, the last paragraph of GC is explicitly about the Bible and implicitly about the heroic reader, who, like Samson, can recreate the Bible in an imaginative context rather than using it as the grist "in a mill to grind our aggressions and prejudices" (*GC*, 233).

6 One of the brilliant comparative passages in Hamilton's book suggests that each of the four essays of the *Anatomy* comprise a distinct stage in the response of literary criticism to literature. They are tantamount to literary critical stages of reading. He packs his "stages," with one for each of the successive essays, into a single sentence (197). The first stage, related to Frye's first essay, consists of "reading a literary work within the history of literature both as a sequence of displaced myths and [as] analogies of revelation." The next involves "understanding" a literary work's "meanings in their sequence as they make it the centre of the literary universe." His third stage, which concerns Frye's third essay, allows the literary critic to perceive the work's "place within the circle of *mythoi*." His final stage comes when the critic recognizes the literary work's "place within a specific genre in relation to all other works in their genres." These stages seem faithful to Frye's ideal reader. They envision the literary critical enter-

prise as a corporate activity. They are stages by which literary criticism as an organized, progressive activity, "produces an active but disciplined, informed but imaginative, and therefore creative response to literature" (197). The pathos I experience, when reading Hamilton, is that only by remembering the 1950s, which seem now so tranquil and orderly, and by an accompanying obliviousness to present-day literary critical activity, can I even imagine the *Anatomy* now as a guidebook for literary criticism.

7 Previous essays of the *Anatomy* have prepared us for his related set of terms—plot structure, character type, and thematic phase. On pages 52 and 53, Frye "lists," on the basis of Aristotle's Poetics, ch. six, "*mythos* or plot, *ethos*, which includes both character and setting, and *dianoia* or 'thought,'" (52-53). He then remarks that there are "four ethical elements"—namely, the hero, the hero's society, the poet, and the poet's readers (53). While in Frye's first essay Aristotle' three terms serve as related "elements," the second essay reintroduces them within a conceptual framework. They become, as such, a sequence of distinguishable "phases" of symbolism (73). The third essay proceeds to take us a step further. *Dianoia* now becomes "the structure of imagery," which he considers as his comparative unit in the first half of the essay. The other part of his comparative study is his treatment of "*mythoi* which are these structures of imagery in movement" (140). Just as *ethos* is the secret agent of the theory of symbolism, so his expansion of *ethos* in a symbolist direction, in the third essay, is quite as significant as his expansions of *mythos* and *dianoia*, plot and theme. The starting point for the theory of myths is his view of plot structure, character type, and thematic phase as symbols of the reading process. His synchronic finale comes when these symbols have fully developed into archetypes: archetypal narratives, archetypal themes, and, between them, points of epiphany.

8 If the third essay has remained the least understood of the essays of the *Anatomy*, the sections on character types have tended to attract the least discussion. Even Hamilton thinks Frye's Aristotelian source "does not serve him well, and he redefines Frye's comic characters relative to the cycle of thematic phases" (Hamilton, 1990, 139). In his sections on each story type, he leaves out discussion of the character types. Denham, however, gives a good description of Frye's comic and romantic character types (*NFCM*, 73-76). As both Hamilton and Denham observe, a source for three of Frye's recurring character types is the brief document called "Tractatus Coislinianus," which is reprinted in Lane Cooper's *An Aristotelian Theory of Comedy* (New York: Harcourt, Brace, 1922), 226. The three character types from the

"Tractatus" are the "self-deprecator," "impostor," and "buffoon" of comedy, which Frye thinks of as recurring types in romance and tragedy. These three types, Frye says, are "closely related to a passage" in the *Niomachean Ethics*—evidently, book four, chapters seven and eight—in which Aristotle contrasts the self-deprecator to the impostor in chapter seven. In chapter eight, he contrasts the buffoon to a character whom Frye terms the "churl" or "rustic" (*AC*, 172). After we have traced these Aristotelian sources, we have done but half the work in identifying the basis upon which Frye's discussion of character types proceeds. We must then turn to the various myth theorists. For comedy, his main source is F. M. Cornford, who himself works from the Frazer's *Golden Bough* and who presents various character types in *The Origin of Attic Comedy*. For romance, the most important source for Frye is Jung. For instance, he writes of "the figure of the old wise man, as Jung calls him"; and Jung also calls him the "magician" (*AC*, 195). "The feminine counterpart," in both Jung and Frye, of the magician or wise old man is for Jung the "great mother" and for Frye the sibylline wise mother-figure" (*AC*, 195). Both male and female figures, in Jung and Frye, have their demonic counterparts, whom Frye calls "the evil magician and the witch"—the latter "is appropriately called by Jung the "terrible mother" (*AC*, 196). Perhaps the figure whom Jung calls the "golem" (Jung 1966, 96, 304), a figure whom he connects with both the shadow and the magician archetypes, is relatable to the figure Frye names the "golux" (*AC*, 197). This figure becomes one of Frye's four romance character types. He "represents" the "shrunken and wizened form of practical waking reality," which is close to Jung's "wizard" (*AC*, 197; Jung 1966, 96).

9 Frye says that a "forbidding piece of symmetry turns up in our argument," then follows this up with a remark that obfuscates the problem (*AC*, 177). First he says that his thematic phases "have some literary analogy to the circle of fifths in music," an arrangement of pitches or chords by successive fifths (*AC*, 177). By this analogy, there are five of his phases. Yet he adds: "I recognize six phases of each *mythos*" (*AC*, 177). The best that I can do with this puzzle is to suggest that the five phases belong to the first stage of his developmental account of reading, while the sixth phase become pertinent within the context of his third stage. He recognizes initially five thematic phases, which together are the typical plot structure of a story type; a sixth thematic phase, later on, is a stage of dissolution in comedy, of complete contemplation in romance. With tragedy and satire, the sixth stage comes when the tragedy "shocks" the reader with its "world of shock and horror" and when the satire "presents human life of largely

unrelieved bondage" (*AC*, 222, 238). While a thematic phase involves a theme, and a theme has a point, Frye's final stage of reading is not the end point, the final vision a story type offers us about a world of story, but a turning point, a reversal of perspective from it to another world, which opens up and which the reader is led up to only by following the total structure of story all the way through.

10 See *AC*, 77-78, 83, 104-05, 120. In this sequence, Frye inflects his plot and theme distinction through his phases of symbolism. When he says that the "common factor" between ritual and dream will be reserved for "later treatment" (107), he associates the word *ethos* with "identification." After the *Anatomy*, "identity" tends to replace what the *Anatomy* calls *ethos*.

11 Johnson speaks of "the common reader" at the end of his discussion of Thomas Gray in *Lives of the Poets*; Virginia Woolf takes up his phrase in *The Common Reader*.

12 The developmental stages move from the acceptance of the common reader's perspective toward that of the increasingly literary critical, sophisticated reader, but these stages are followed with what, borrowing Ricoeur's expression, is a second naïveté.

13 That is to say, a reader's response to genres is not well developed in the theory of myths. Of course, the writer's entry into and use of genres and convention is the topic, respectively, of the entire fourth essay and of a section in the second essay (*AC*, 95-105).

14 Of all the material from earlier essays incorporated into the *Anatomy*, Frye's essays on satire are the earliest: "The Anatomy in Prose Fiction," *Manitoba Arts Review* 3 (Spring 1942), 35-47 and "The Nature of Satire," *University of Toronto Quarterly* 19 (October 1944), 75-89). Frye's ideal reader is equally familiar with the entire traditions of all four story types. While even literary critics often tend to be partial to one or the other of them, just as persons in Jung tend to have a "primary function" or to be a certain "type" of person, the ideal is to draw upon all four traditions in Frye and to draw upon all four areas of one's psychic resources in Jung.

15 A great divide between the *Anatomy* and later writings is Frye's growing willingness to accept the discontinuities of Western literature, especially the major shift that occurred with Romanticism. Example: "The Romantic movement transforms all the generic plots of literature: there is a new and Romantic form of tragedy, of irony, of comedy . . . [and] of romance" (*SER*, 35).

16 Robert Denham observes that "the degrees of variation" of a thematic phase "are determined by a number of criteria, which is why the term phrase is difficult to define precisely. Sometimes Frye distinguishes the phrases from each other in terms of the total plot pattern" (*NFCM*, 78). What Denham calls the "total plot pattern" is an apt expression for what I am designating as the third stage of the developmental theory of reading, which has, as its symbol of the reading process, the "total *mythos*." Frye sometimes speaks of "types of comic structures" or "types" of satire and romance. These types belong to his first stage of reading. Genres such as comic romance belong to the second. The total *mythos* belongs to the third. There is an equivalent distinction to Frye's "types" of literary structure and his "total *mythos*" in Jung's psychological distinction between "type" and "function." Applied to Frye's theory of reading, a plot structure can be seen as a "type" of literary structure, where a total *mythos* is a function that the reader has internalized and learned to see through. In Frye, four story types are gradually assimilated and internalized, so that they become equally the lens through which the reader sees what he is experiencing when he reads. In Jung, the four functions are equally the resources upon which a person, an individuated person, draws, so that the reader identifies himself, potentially and quite as synchronically as Frye's ideal reader, with everything outside him.

17 The three related terms in this stage of reading can be seen as a reconfiguration of the terms of Frye's first stage: plot structure, character type, and ethos. There is the movement in comic action toward the formation of a fictive comic society. Then there is a movement through three generations of characters. Next, there is a thematic movement across the seasons. The archetypal action of comedy is elemental. Once upon a time, society enjoyed harmony. The action of comedy returns us to this harmony by ending with a kinder, gentler society. "Normal" comedy displays a transfer of power, either social or sexual or even both. This transfer involves three generations of characters. The eldest of these is often only implicitly suggested and precedes the action. At the beginning of the comic action, another generation has already displaced the one before it. The entire action of comedy is a restoration of the stable social order that existed once upon a time. It is a return to "a golden age in the past before the main action of the play begins" (*AC*, 177). Each of the three concepts that Frye takes from Aristotle (plot, character, and theme) relates to the normal action of comedy. First *mythos*: the entire movement of comedy is from a "stable and harmonious social order" to its disruption by a usurping generation and to the renewal of society by means of a

younger generation. The second term, "generation," is applicable to *ethos*: both to the "characters" and to the audience or the reader. Third is *dianoia*: Frye describes the thematic development recurrent in typical comedy by use of a complex seasonal simile. "The action of the play" is "like a contest of summer and winter in which winter occupies the middle action" (*AC*, 171). In this simile winter is akin to the generation in power at the beginning of the action—that is, the second, usurping generation. Summer is akin to the youngest generation, which comes into power by the end of the action. Yet often implicit—this is something that the audience or reader confers on the action—is what might be called a grandfather. This person is like winter. Perhaps the main reason for Frye's complex analogizing is that the recurrent thematic concern of comedy as a whole is with rebirth. Comedy is the *mythos* of spring because it represents *all* this seasonal movement. Comedy is the *mythos* of spring since the renewal (*mythos*), regeneration (*ethos*), and rebirth (*dianoia*) of society are its perennial thematic concern. Comedy is like the other story types in that it involves a *total* movement through the seasons. Yet comedy receives its specific identity from a particular season, just as the other story types do. Identify is an aspect of *ethos*, which gives shape to what otherwise would be endless cyclical recurrence (*AC*, 105, 159).

18 One might possibly compare Frye's "settled order which has been there from the beginning" (*AC*, 185) with the "settlement" of Jung's archetypal personages (persona, shadow, anima, and counselor) into a new psychic perspective or "attitude" that has also, in the potential that every person has to become an individuated person, been there from the beginning (Jung 1966, 99). I discuss what Jung calls a "settlement" and what Frye, describing Jung, refers to as a process by which archetypes "settle into" psychological types in chapter 12, note nine.

19 Ricoeur likes to write of a single text's presenting a world he might inhabit. Frye likes to make this point intertextually: there are for him four possible worlds, four places that the reader through imagination has the capacity to inhabit. He says that, while "we know very little about our own imaginative worlds," yet between "actual worlds, and fantasy worlds," there is "a world of possibilities" (*OE*, 116). Initially, we are "totally inarticulate about what we can imagine," but literary works provide means of expression (*OE*, 116). Then he describes his four mythic worlds. Romance, for instance, is an "idealized world," where satire is the "world" that is "opposed" to it (*OE*, 117).

20 DeMaria finds three stages in the "quest" of the "ideal reader" (469). The first stage begins with the reader entering a text and is characterized by pre-critical and experiential response to it. The last is "again a kind of experience." In between these stages is one belonging to literary criticism (De Maria, 469). DeMaria helpfully indicates that there is a synchronic element in a preliminary stage of reading and a final stage. His second stage is a sequence of three developmental stages. He says that the reader initially "experiences literature as a participant rather than a spectator" (469). I would put it the other way around. He says that the reader "moves 'into' the narrative and follows it in a fundamentally unreflecting way. In a flash, however, he perceives the total form of the narrative" (469). The way I have presented it, the reader moves into texts by their narratives, character types, and thematic phases, and, in this first developmental stage, is relatively unconscious of what he is doing in relation to the succeeding stages. In the third developmental stage, to borrow from the Frye essay that DeMaria cites, "the productive or creative effort is inseparable from the [reader-critic's] awareness," because the "either/or" dilemma between a "detached spectator" and a "preoccupied actor" has been overcome (*St. S.*, 174). The creative and the critical become the reader's unified "vision" in this stage: "there is no division, though there may be a distinction, between the creative power of shaping the form [total *mythos*] and the critical power of seeing the world [mythic world] it belongs to" (*St. S.*, 174).

21 Hamilton relates the term "monad," in Frye's final phase of symbolism in the second essay, to a "religious term now secularized", namely, epiphany, to Joyce and to some earlier and romantic conceptions" (Hamilton 1990, 114). For Hamilton, the point of epiphany in the theory of myths in the third essay is ambiguously related to (it "may be identified ... with") "the anagogic phase of symbolism in the second essay" (143-144). Here again, he provides a comparative approach to Frye: he compares the meaning of the point of epiphany as it seems to apply to each of the four essays (143). He then contrasts its meaning in the *Anatomy* and *The Secular Scripture* (144).

22 The point of epiphany provides a recognition scene for the reader. Hamilton says that, in using Aristotle's term "*anagnorisis* or recognition," Frye "refers to a structural device explicit in sixth-phase comedy" (Hamilton 1990, 136). His comment that sixth phase satire comprises a "surprising reversal" is helpful (152). However, he views the reversal as issuing into a simple renewal of the rotation of Frye's story wheel (152). I think that when the reader undergoes the surprising re-

versal of which Frye, and before him Aristotle, speaks, the situation is the same for the reader of satire as it had been for the reader of comedy. But the scene has changed, and so what the reader recognizes has altered. The reader is no longer confined, as he had been with the point of epiphany of comedy, to the Christian mythic landscape or worldview. Instead, with satire, he has a fresh vista: mythic, no doubt, but this recovery of myth is sheerly individual and entirely imaginative. We can also compare the points of epiphany of romance and satire. The one associated with romance has the reader "arriving at the summit of experience in nature" and looking down upon the turning or "cyclical order" there (*AC*, 205). The reader of satire, having revisited the places of the three preceding points of epiphany, "is in a position to look down on its rotation," which refers not to the still point in Frye's turning story wheel but to the whole massive turning wheel itself (*FI*, 264). What the reader sees is the story wheel's "total form," which involves "something more than rotation" (*FI*, 264). Frye is talking about the reader of *Finnegans Wake* here, but his remark that "it dawns on us" that "the reader" is the one "who achieves the quest" applies to the theory of reading (*FI*, 264; see also *AC*, 354). Besides Hamilton, I am also indebted to Terence Cave and Robert Caserio. Caserio suggests that "Frye transforms Aristotle's point of recognition into epiphany" (68). "The epiphanic point," he adds, "reveals the mythic world" (68).

23 For DeMaria, the quest of the heroic reader is the "critical fiction"—or myth, I would say—throughout Frye's works. He compares the "critical fiction" (the subtitle of his essay) with other figures of the ideal reader: Dryden's judicious reader; the reader as everyman in Johnson; and Coleridge's reader, who enters into creative collaboration with the writer. The difference for DeMaria between Coleridge and Frye is that, while in Coleridge writer and reader are "reconciled," in Frye they "have crossed paths and reversed their traditional roles" (DeMaria, 468). For my part, I think writer and reader cross paths within the *Anatomy*. Frye presents a theory of the writer's production of myth down through time with the help of Freud's notions of "displacement" and "condensation," a theory which has its locus, in the first essay. And he presents a theory of the reader's assimilation of literary archetypes, recognizable elements in the reader's literary experience, in his third essay, this time with some help from Jung. While Caserio complains that Frye's point of epiphany or "revelation" is merely "a point of seeing" or an access or increase of perceptual power, and not an enhanced or renewed power of action, I think it helpful to have a dual vision of Frye's theories of writing and reading.

Power of action applies to the levels of characters in the theory of modes; power of perception applies to the levels in the theory of myth's reading process. The god of the mythic mode has complete power of action, and the reader at the end of his theory of reading has a synchronic and momentary glimpse into a story type. The difficulty is to get from this revelation about the way of a storied world, which becomes internalized in the reader, to the anagogic level. The theory of myths is mainly concerned with secular literature, where the theory of symbolism, of which the anagogic stage is a culminating, post-critical vision, is not confined to the fictional or mythic "worlds," but instead extends to a greater literary "universe." Frye's final developmental stage of reading is concerned with the internalization of individual story types, but the last page of the theory of myths takes us beyond that limitation, since he recapitulates the previous points of epiphany, in relation to their places in his circle of story types, on that page (*AC*, 239).

24 The definition of point of epiphany in the glossary of the *Anatomy* is double-edged. Frye says that it is "an archetype presenting simultaneously an apocalyptic world and a cyclical order of nature, or sometimes the latter alone," as in the case of romance (367).

25 Toliver also has an interesting pair of diagrams of genres (144) and the self (145).

Chapter Twelve: Jung and Frye

1 Frye's interpretation is given in the opening pages of a review essay on Jung. Originally appearing in *The Hudson Review* 6 (winter 1954), it has been reprinted in Robert D. Denham's collection of review essays: *Northrop Frye on Culture and Literature* (Chicago: University of Chicago Press, 1978), 117-29. The occasion for Frye's review was the publication of several volumes in the Bollingen Series XX: the second editions of *Two Essays*, which is volume seven in the Series, and *Psychology and Alchemy*, volume twelve. Both were published in New York by Pantheon in 1953. Frye, however, adds another book to his discussion. His review essay begins by treating *Two Essays* (*NFCL*, 117-18), then presents several "differences between Jung's thought and Freud's" (119-20), and moves into a broad discussion of Jung and the world religions (120-21) before turning to another of Jung's books. This second book is *The Psychology of the Unconscious*, which Frye discusses on pages 122-23, and then compares with Frazer's *Golden Bough*, and subsequently moves into a discussion of the relation of

Jung and Frazer to his "archetypal [literary] criticism" (123-25). The final section of his review treats *Psychology and Alchemy* (125-29), though Frye is at least as interested in presenting his own views on Jung's topic and in suggesting how Jung can be helpful to literary critics as in that particular book. Frye's review essay, though occasioned by the English translations of two of the three books mentioned above, and by what was then the forthcoming publication of *Symbols of Transformation* (which Frye says was "soon to be republished as volume five" in the series and "was previously known in English as *The Psychology of the Unconscious*" [*NFCL*, 122]), is an overview of Jungian thought. Frye's reading of Jung's works, prior to this 1954 review essay, probably extends back more than fifteen years. His rather casual references to Freud and Jung in a 1938 essay on modern painting, written when he was 26, already suggest familiarity with their works (*RW*, 36).

2 While the present chapter endeavors to track the developmental processes of Jung and Frye, the next one focuses upon another dimension of their individuation and reading theories: both men crown developmental processes with synchronic conclusions.

3 See chapter two, "The Conception and the Genetic Theory of Libido," in *Psychology of the Unconscious* (New York: Dodd, Mead and Company, 1963). Frye says that the psyche in Jung "is built on a Freudian foundation of a conscious ego, trying to be rational and moral and adjusted to the demands of society and nature, and a subconscious 'shadow' (not far from Freud's 'id'), formed of one's suppressed or ignored desires" (*NFCL*, 117).

4 At no point in the theory of myths does Frye explain how he expands Aristotle's concepts or why he has chosen to do so. However, his preparation for the use of those terms has begun as early as pages 52-53 and 73 in the *Anatomy*.

5 Commentators who have discussed the relationship between Jung and Frye have tended to focus their attention upon whether or not Frye's term "archetype" is Jungian. Both Robert D. Denham and A. C. Hamilton treat the term as it is used in Frye's second essay, while I have chosen the theory of myths in his third essay as the basis of my discussion. Denham says that "Frye's review of Jung's *Psychology of the Unconscious* ... develops a view of [literary] criticism which makes its way later, some of it verbatim, into his account of the archetypal phase of symbolism" in the second essay (*NFCL*, 45-46). He interrelates pages 122-25 of the review to the *Anatomy's* section on the "Symbol as Archetype" (95-115). My concern, at present, is not with

Psychology of the Unconscious, but with *Two Essays*, and not with the section on the archetypal phase of symbolism, but with the theory of myths. Hence, I draw upon the opening portion of the review essay which treats *Two Essays* (*NFCL*, 117-21).

6 See *Two Essays on Analytical Psychology*, 188-211. Frye speaks of the "personal and anima" as being "kept in balance"; Jung speaks of a "centre of balance" (*NFCL*, 118; *Two Essays*, 196).

7 See *Two Essays*, 227-28 and 90-92.

8 See *Two Essays*, 227-38 and, for the "magician," 93-100. Another of his names for the "magician" is the "wise old man," who is mentioned only twice in the book: on page 97, where a note refers us to *Archetypes of the Collective Unconscious*, paragraph 74 (in the Bollingen series, it is the first essay in volume nine, part one), and page 110. What Jung calls the "loving and terrible mother" is discussed in *Psychology of the Unconscious*, especially in part two, from chapter five through the end of the book.

9 One might compare Jung's "darkly discerned potencies" and "world-pictures" with Frye's "*mythoi* and mythic worlds" (*Two Essays*, 237).

10 Someone remarked that Frye uses the word "total" so frequently that it comes to resemble the hiccup of an after-dinner speaker. A precedent for his usage of the word is set by Jung, who speaks of the "total personality." See, for instance, *Two Essays*, 221 and 223 or *Psychology and Alchemy*, 106 (and notice Jung's circular diagram of the "total personality" on the following page) and 329.

11 Perhaps it might be helpful to think of the entire third essay, not just the theory of myths in the second part of it, as an account of how readers inherit and assimilate literary tradition. The first part of the essay, roughly speaking, addresses archetypal imagery inherited by readers. The forces of convention we looked at in an earlier chapter shape these imagery patterns. The second part, the theory of myths, presents four traditional genres: "four narrative pregeneric elements of literature," which he calls "*mythoi* or generic plots" (*AC*, 162). In any case, if we think of the story types as literary traditions, we have to start from Frye's observation in the *Anatomy's* introduction, which singles out T. S. Eliot's "principle": "the existing monuments of literature form an ideal order among themselves, and are not simply collections of the writings of individuals" (18). While Eliot is concerned with how the "individual talent" or writer is affected by and affects literary tradi-

tion, Frye's theory of myths is concerned with how the individual reader assimilates and internalizes literary traditions. The earliest of Frye's efforts to think of a story type as a literary tradition were "The Anatomy in Prose Fiction," *Manitoba Arts Review* 3 [spring 1942], 35-47; "The Nature of Satire," *University of Toronto Quarterly* 14 [October 1944], 1-16). These essays are descriptions of its tradition, the tradition which he identifies as "Menippean satire." The several essays were, to a large extent, merely incorporated into the *Anatomy's* section on satire (223-39). The result, as A. C. Hamilton says, is that he presents "not a *mythos* [of satire] but the tradition" of it as well as "the nature of satire as a genre" (1990, 149). While these early efforts are helpful in suggesting that Frye is working at the problem of tradition, his view in the *Anatomy*, at least relative to the other story types, is that they are dual-edged. They have an inward and outward aspect: there is a subjective element, which the reader recreates within himself or a *mythoi*, and a relatively objective element, the mythic world. A story type has both elements at once. The unideal reader who attended only to the *mythoi* would be the reader who saw all of literature as a single tradition, like F. R. Leavis' *The Great Tradition*; on the other hand, the reader who saw all of life relative to a single mythic world would be the reader who projects a vision of life on the basis of whichever one it is (e.g., with the tragic *mythos*, one might read reality as though it were a Hardy novel).

12 The anima is especially important, in Jung's theory of individuation, because it becomes the gateway to the unconscious after the ego has established continuity with the shadow. The anima provides the means for tapping into the personal unconscious. The possibility of drawing upon the archetypes of the collective unconscious then exists. The anima is thus the initial channel through which the power of the primordial images can be released into the psyche.

13 Any such visual aid inevitably distorts or omits some of what it seeks to represent. In the case of my chart, over-simplification occurs because a two-dimensional illustration seeks to present what, for both thinkers, is more like a three-dimensional process.

14 What Frye designates as the "balancing point," the "center," and the "center of personality," in Jung's stages are quite in keeping with the terminology in the second of his *Two Essays*. There Jung says that mental patients' "psychic equilibrium" becomes upset and speaks of a "loss of balance" (161). Then, in the chapter on the anima, he speaks of a "centre of balance" (196). Next, in the chapter, "The Mana-Personality," he speaks of the "establishment of a balance of power

between the two worlds" (229). Even more important is his discussion of what he calls "the mid-point of the personality" (221). Finally, what Frye refers to as the destination of individuation, "the real center," is, in Jung, a "virtual centre" (*NFCL*, 118, *Two Essays*, 237). Also, what Frye refers to as "the self" as "the center" is in Jung "this centre" which he calls "the self" (*NFCL*, 119; *Two Essays*, 238). All this suggests that he is following Jung quite closely.

15 C. A. Meier, in *Soul and Body: Essays on the Theories of Carl Jung* (Santa Monica, CA: Lapis Press, 1986), has a discussion of this sequence, though only mentioning the last, on pages 90-106. The "figures and motifs," Jung discovered during the course of treating patients, "appeared in regular succession" (90). "As a rule, it is necessary" for the person "first to assimilate" an archetypal figure "before the contents" of another of them "can appear" and "this appearance then becomes the next step in analytical" treatment (90). The sequence of shadow, then persona, anima, and counsellor constitutes a "continuous process" or a "development," because there are "successive stages" in which these archetypal figures "turn up one after the other" (105). As Frye says, "they turn up on the way to 'individuation'" (*SM*, 119).

16 Meier says that "in the course of a longer, more thorough, and more complete analysis, it was possible to outline a hierarchy of figures" (90). The figures or archetypes of the shadow, persona, and anima, and the great mother and wise old man, according to the spatial metaphors Jung employs, come from successively deeper levels of the mind; even Frye retains that spatial metaphor when he speaks of the great mother and magician or wise old man as "two deeper powers" that come "from the unconscious" and "which move up to reinforce" the figures in the second stage of development, the "persona and anima" (*NFCL*, 118). The spelling of the work "counsellor" is that used by the translator of *Two Essays* and by Frye. The usual spelling of the word is "councilor."

17 For example, his list, on page 110, includes: "the shadow, the animal, the wise old man, the anima, the animus, the mother, the child, besides an indefinite number of archetypes representative of situations."

18 As the final three words of the following sentence suggest, almost anything can count as the "units" in one's view of the "total structure" of literature: these units, he emphasizes, are "*archetypes*," the "recurring formal elements of literature"–"its conventions, genres, symbols, rhetorical patterns, plot and character types, and so on" (*NFN* 1 [Spring 1989], 26). Robert D. Denham observes, reasonably enough,

that his definitions of archetype tend to "expand outward" and he cites others with similar complaints (*NFCM*, 208).

19 Discussions by others of the relationship of Frye to Jung have largely been confined to a single question: whether or not Frye's notion of the archetype is the same as or different from Jung's. Frye says that he was "continually asked about my relation to Jung, and especially about the relation of my use of the word 'archetype' to his" (*SM*, 117). Then he adds that he has "tended to resist the association" for the reason that "whenever anyone mentions" the seeming congruity of their usages of the same term, their "next sentence is almost certain to be nonsense." Another interesting observation is that "my objections to Jung are not to him but to my being called Jungian" (*NFN* 5 [Summer 1993], 9, item 138). This time, though, he seems more perplexed when he adds that, on the one hand, "I don't want *literature* to be turned into a psychological allegory of individuation," and, on the other, when "I move back from literary to existential metaphor I'll come very close to it." (He puts this in the future tense when he says "I'll come," but perhaps the remark can be read relative to a number of such attempts in previous writings: e.g., *SM*, 119, *EI*, 79-81.) Another interesting observation is his comment about the origin of his use of the term, which he says he took "not from Jung, as is so often said, but from a footnote in [James] Beattie's [*The*] Minstrel (*EAC*, 94). (He quotes the lines and the footnote in *St. S*, 82.) In *GC*, he says that he has, in his writings, "used the term 'archetype' to describe" such "building blocks" or "structural units" in literature that are repeated; while he assumed that he was using the term "archetype" "in its traditional sense," he found he had not realized "how completely Jung's more idiosyncratic use of the same word had monopolized the field" (48). However, he appends a note to his comment: "It should however be added that in one very unlikely place (*Civilization in Transition* [Eng. Tr. 1964], par. 847), Jung does characterize an archetype as I should do: 'The myths and fairy tales of world literature contain definite motifs and which crop up everywhere'" (*GC*, 238).

20 His phrase, "reasoning and sensational ego," it seems to me, is helpful. The ego is not just, as Frye had said in an earlier essay, "a rational ego," using such structures as concepts (*NFCL*, 95). And it is not just caught up in the midst of "haphazard and involuntary perceptions," which I take to be the equivalent of the word "sensational" (*SM*, 116). Instead, it is both at once.

21 The verb "directs" implies a contrast. The conscious ego directs in the midst of a confusing situation, like a traffic cop; the

"superconscious individual directs" in the transformed situation of his rapport with his setting, like a conductor does with a symphony.

22 When Frye says that "the point" at which the four archetypes "now settle into" four psychological functions or types "comes somewhere in between the two books," what does he mean? On the verso of the title page of *Two Essays* we find that "the two principal works in this volume are translated from *Uber die Psychologie des Unbewussten* (1943) [*On the Psychology of the Unconscious*] and *Die Beziehungen zwischen dem Ich und dem Unbewussten* (1928; 2nd edn., 1935)," which, as the second of the *Two Essays*, is "The Relations between the Ego and the Unconscious." So far, then, it seems clear enough that what Frye means is that what became *Two Essays* were "two books" in German. That is the literal bibliographical answer to the question I raised. Yet there is an interpretative question as well. Here we are helped by looking at several of the editorial notes which explain why they have included a pair of appendices. These are the "original drafts" of the *Two Essays* and these drafts are significant, because they "contain the first tentative formulations of Jung's concept of archetypes and the collective unconscious, as well as his germinating theory of [psychological] types" (v). Another editorial note to the second appendix suggests that Jung's discussion "was greatly developed in *Psychological Types*" (279). Our next interpretative step is to notice Jung's notes and comments about *Psychological Types*. He refers to that book twice in the text (6, 138), but quite regularly in the notes: 5, 44, 54, 57, 58, 100, 134, 147, 154, 155, 189, and 196. This sequence of notes, though it subordinates *Psychological Types* to the main topic the *Two Essays* addresses—the archetypes—invites us to think about the relation two books (*Psychological Types* and *Two Essays*) have to each other. Frye's interpretation does interrelate them: for him, the four archetypes presented in each of the *Two Essays* "settle into the four functions of psychic life: though, feeling, intuition, and sensation," which are presented in chapter ten of *Psychological Types*.

23 Meier takes us one step further than we went in the last note. Relative to the question of the relation of Jung's discussions of archetypes and his *Psychological Types*, Meier takes the position, which he emphasizes, that "*Individuation begins and ends with typology*" (242). Typological concerns, according to him, are the starting-point in the development of Jung's thought. He takes the perhaps radical position that Jung's 1902 doctoral dissertation, with its discussion of the mandala, eventually leads in to *Psychological Types* (257). If so, he started with a circular diagram as a means of considering the relations of psychic functions or types of person to each other. However, "later in his

life, when he wrote about the mandala in the individuation process, he
always omitted hinting at the connection with the typological pattern,
which [for Meier] constitutes the dynamics of the process itself" (257).
He makes an effort to trace the development of Jung's thinking about
typology even before he began writing *Psychological Types*, which
was begun in 1913 and published in 1921 (245). I find Meier's thesis–
that Jung's interest in typology preceded his concern with individuation in the development of his thought, that typology is, as it were, the
crown, or the end towards which individuation leads, even though
Jung's regularly segregates these two concern--valuable for the understanding of Frye on Jung. He, too, thinks the dual concern--
individuation and typology--together. Moreover, the theory of myths
(*AC*, 163-239) is preceded by a circle of story types (*AC*, 162). That
circle is an organizing device or containing form for the theory of
myths. Finally, the theory of myths ends, as we shall see, with a reversal that can only be understood by visualizing his circle of four story
types.

Chapter Thirteen: Circle of Story Types

1 *NFCL*, 118-21. My primary passages are this one, in which he inter-
prets Jung's *Two Essays in Analytical Psychology*, and *SM*, 116-22,
which contains an account of Jung's influence upon him.

2 *AC*, 162. Notice that his description of what he later came to call his
circle of story types is not in the theory of myths (*AC*, 163-239), but is
the last page of his introduction to it.

3 In the *Anatomy's* fourth essay, his discussions of " Specific Forms of
Drama" (282-83) and "Specific Thematic Forms" (293-303) are organized by circular diagrams. Each has four "quadrants" with four
"cardinal points" marking the transition from one quadrant to another
(287, 292, 293, 295, 297, 300). Moreover, his next section, " Specific
Continuous Forms (Prose Fiction)," probably also has a connection
with Jung, for, in it, he is working with ideas from *Psychological
Types*. He adopts Jung's terms, "extraversion" and "introversion,"
and adds to them another pair of opposites, the "personal" and the
"intellectual." These four terms become somewhat like Jung's four
types of person, and, just as Jung has a fifth type or function, the
"transcendent function," so Frye ends with a "fifth and quintessential
form" that binds all the other four together (*AC*, 314). My book does
not cover any of these sections, because I regard them as little more
than earlier drafts of the third essay's theory of myths, insofar as Frye

is working from Jung. I also think Hamilton's discussion of the fourth essay provides unsurpassable commentary on it. As he notes, the *Anatomy's* section on the four prose forms of fiction is an "expansion" of his 1942 essay, "The Anatomy in Prose Fiction," *Manitoba Arts Review* 3 (spring 1942), 35-47 into what became "The Four Forms of Prose Fiction," *Hudson Review* 2 (winter 1950, 582-95). He also says that Frye "incorporates the 1951 article "A Conspectus of Dramatic Genres" (*Kenyon Review* 13 [autumn 1951], 543-62), without taking advantage of the perspective provided by the circle of *mythoi*" (Hamilton 1990, 172). It seems to me that each of the fourth essay's sections can be seen as efforts over time to assimilate Jungian individuation and typology to his literary criticism. From a developmental standpoint, his circle of mythoi is the latest of these attempts.

4 Frye contrasts "thinking" and "feeling," and then says that "for Jung there is an ideal of "individuation" beyond them both" in *MM*, page 178. "The 'thinking' type, if he is primarily that [i.e., has thinking as his primary type or function], is often," according to Frye, "a hard-driving aggressive person, impatient with the untidiness of people who never seem to understand that the shortest distance between two points is a straight line." The thinking type is "the direct opposite of the 'feeling' type," who is the kind of person that more often "would make a good chairman [because of his capacity for] collecting the sense of a meeting, or a good teacher, ... but his record of accomplishment in the world might be less impressive." Frye redefines Jung's "feeling type" as "a receptive thinker" in contrast to Jung's "thinking type," who is for Frye an "aggressive" thinker. In his notebook, Frye says that he himself can be characterized as "one of Jung's feeling types," but, in saying so, his point is really that feeling or that which he calls receptive thinking is his way of relating to public situations. In Jung's jargon, feeling is his secondary function, which he uses so as to relate to others, since his primary function is introverted intuition. See *NFN* 5 (Summer 1993), 35, item 718.

5 The order of Jung's presentation of these kinds of person, in *Psychological Types*, chapter ten, is: thinking, feeling, sensing, and intuition. Frye regularly reverses the final pair, so that intuition comes before sensing. See *NFCL*, 118 and *MM*, 178. Jung does use this ordering of his terms in *Psychological Types*, in his definition of "Type" in chapter eleven. It appears to me, though, that Frye is again adapting what he adopts from Jung.

6 The same ambiguity is attendant upon both their uses of the word "experience." By "experience," Jung means not only his clinical ex-

perience of observing many kinds of people, but our experience of them as well. When Frye speaks of our "experience," he means our reading experience of four kinds of story types (just as Jung thinks there are essentially four kinds of person or four psychological types), and he assumes that other readers' experience will be much the same as his own. Ricoeur makes the suggestion that Frye's "typologies of employment" properly belong either to "the self-consciousness of the [literary] critic" or "of the poet" (1991, 459). The way I would put it is that the circle of story types belongs to the self-consciousness of the individual reader; the circle, in a sense, is no more nor less than a private reader's assumption that everything he has read somehow fits together. It provides a backdrop for the exercise of his memory of what he has read and especially for the possibility of interrelating his more significant experiences of reading. Perhaps this is what Frank Kermode means when he says that Frye's circle is "a mnemonic device" and that the theory of myths is a "memory theory" (1990, 95).

7 Jung is not among those Frye says are participants in this twentieth-century cultural trend: Julian Jaynes and Marshall McLuhan. Nevertheless, if we set his description of Jung next to the accounts he gives of them, we can see how close the three men are, in Frye's view of them. Here is his account of Jung for whom: "structures of symbolism are seen as emanating from a collective unconscious through a consciousness which has accepted the Jungian shift from a rational ego, opposed to the unconscious, to an individuality in rapport with it" (*NFCL*, 95). Next, Jaynes, who contrasts "our egocentric consciousness," which is "our present form of consciousness, with its ego center," with a "more intensified form of consciousness" (*MM*, 74). Finally, there is Frye's description of his colleague at Toronto, McLuhan: "who also contrasted a linear, causality-bound, tunnel-vision type of perception with a simultaneous type capable of taking in many aspects of a situation at once" (*MM*, 74). In Jung, one can find this contrast in the first chapter, "Two Kinds of Thinking," in *Symbols of Transformation*, or in the last chapter (chapter ten) of *Psychological Types*. In *Symbols of Transformation*, a "directed" or linear kind of thinking, prized or rewarded in places like academia thanks to the prestige of the sciences, is contrasted with an earlier, more mythical mode of apprehension: a spontaneous, empathetic, and imaginative kind of "thinking." In *Psychological Types*, he starts with an extroverted or aggressive thinking type and he ends with an introverted intuitive type.

8 Another way of saying this is that Frye himself makes the same kind of contrast, in his theory of reading and elsewhere, that I have outlined in my last note. He regularly contrasts chaotic ordinary experience

with the streamlined organization of experience that comes through the reader's assimilation of the story types, which are "four fundamental types of imaginative experience" (*OE*, 117). We are "at first, totally inarticulate about what we can imagine, until something in literature," for instance a poem that resonates for us, "comes along and expresses it" (*OE*, 116). In *The Educated Imagination*, he makes the same contrast. In the "dissolving flux" of ordinary experience, the reader is initially "in the position of a dog in a library, surrounded by a world of meaning" the reader does not "even know is there" (79). This situation is comparable to the ego in Freud, which is surrounded by forces hostile to it as well as to the Freudian ego with which Jungian individuation begins, though in Jung the ego is oblivious, like Frye's dog, to the forces around it. The contrasting situation in Frye comes when the reader, having "devoured whole libraries," as Boswell says of Johnson, or having assimilated four whole narrative traditions of literature, finds himself no longer enclosed.

9 Jung uses the word "settlement" in *Two Essays*, page 99. He explains the "effecting" of "this settlement" with the help of his "transcendent function," which is his name for or "is called" the transcendent function. When he arrives at the same place, in the second of the *Two Essays*, he does not use the word "settlement," but attributes the final change in movement towards individuation by referring to the transcendent function (219, 223). Unfortunately, for his reader, Jung describes the transcendent function differently almost every time he mentions it during the course of the book: see pages 80, 99, 109, 116, 219, 223. In a note on page 134, he refers the reader to his definition of "Symbol" in chapter eleven of *Psychological Types*; his penultimate paragraph there introduces still another version of what he means by the transcendent function. I am not trying to disparage his term, but suggesting that it is important to notice the varied contexts in which he presents it. Still another of his accounts of the transcendent function is presented in his discussion of "The Type-Problem in Poetry" in *Psychological Types*. It transcends the other four functions in that it comprises "a new attitude towards the world," which occurs upon the death of the ego and the rising of the self from the ego: with the emerging self, a new way of experiencing "the world" then "arises" (*PT*, 313). This account might be compared with Frye's assumption that the literary work, like the ego, dies within the reader, and then "revives within" him (*SM*, 119). "Some death and rebirth process has to be gone through" by the reader, according to Frye (*SM*, 119).

10 C. A. Meier offers an interesting account of the interrelationship of the relationship of *Psychological Types* to individuation (242-46).

11 C. A. Meier says (the emphases are his): "Individuation begins and ends with typology" (242). Jung's practice is to implicitly or indirectly bring in his type theory when talking about individuation and vice-versa. For instance, even though a subtitle of *Psychological Types* is *The Psychology of Individuation*, 'the term individuation' is hardly used and is only discussed rather timidly in the last chapter, where it is given a tentative definition," according to Meier (246). Similarly, in *Two Essays*, typology appears from time to time (see pages 5, 6, 44, 54, 57, 58, 100, 134, 138, 147, 154, 155, 189, 196, 279—all of these references are to notes except those on pages 6 and 138).

12 In the first of the *Two Essays*, Jung seems to be saying that the four archetypes become unified; in the second, he says the "four functions' are unified: compare the passages on pages 109 and 223.

13 I am indebted to Robert Caserio for his statement, in *Plot, Story, and the Novel*, that "Frye transforms Aristotle's point of recognition into epiphany" (68). Aristotle discusses recognition and reversal in *Poetics*, ch. eleven. Recognition, for Aristotle, Is "between persons" in the play and is defined as a "change from ignorance to knowledge." "Reversal of intention" is defined as "a change by which the action veers around to its opposite, as when the messenger expects to free Oedipus from his anxieties about Jocasta and does the opposite." The point of recognition, for both Aristotle and Frye, is a surprise. In Aristotle, it comes as a "surprise" to some character within the work; in Frye, it is a surprise to the reader or critic. It is an insight or glimpse of the way a literary world is and, specifically, a surprise or synchronic perception about the nature of a particular narrative world or mythic world. Frye arrives at four interrelated points of epiphany. Those of comedy, romance, and tragedy are cast by him in a developmental pattern; with satire, however, reversal occurs, and one travels, as it were, back through that pattern of development to the starting point, though a contrasting perspective opens when one gets there.

14 If one looks at the progression from the literary archetypes, starting with the plot structures, character types, and thematic phases, and moves through the several stages of development, the first stage is not sheerly objective, because Frye is talking about plot as filtered already through what the reader perceives to be a plot structure. Each of his three stages is more subjective than the one before it. With the third stage, his archetypes are the *mythos* and the mythic world. Perhaps these are relatable to what Jung describes as, on the one hand, "darkly discerned potencies" and "world-pictures" on the other (*Two Essays*, 237). For both Jung and Frye, the destination is arrived at by moving

through and past these alternatives into what Jung calls a "virtual centre" and Frye on Jung calls "the real center" (*Two Essays*, 237; *NFCL* 118). When one does, the journey of individuation or the reader's literary odyssey is completed. In Jung, the conscious mind is entirely in rapport with the unconscious mind and one sees with the help of or through all one's psychological functions. We are led "back to ourselves" as a living being capable of spontaneously identifying with everything around us (*Two Essays*, 237). Both Jung and Frye end with entirely subjective and spontaneous or synchronic persons or readers. Jung's person and Frye's reader have in common that they have become entirely open to self-expressive possibilities.

15 *Two Essays*, 71 and 238-39; *Psychological Types*, 297-319.

16 *AC*, 161; *Two Essays*, 110. Frye uses the word "revelation," too, but not in the theory of myths. Rather, it comes at the end of the second essay. When he says that "art ... reveals ... in its own forms" and that it does not "represent a separate content of revelation," or an "existential world," he is more in keeping with Cassirer's view of "art" (*AC*, 125; Cassirer 1946a, 98). The "sensuous forms" of the mythic image and word, by their letting go of the effort to represent the real world, internalize these forms within the mind, so that they "become what they really are," namely, the "forms of the mind's [Jung would have said the self's] own self-revelation" (1946a, 99). Cassirer is perhaps a bit closer to Jung when he says that myth and language, when seen in their final influence upon art rather than in their original state, "point to a final community of function" (1946a, 84). There is a final "settlement" of archetypes into four functions" in Jung, as we have seen (Jung, 1966, 99 and 223).

17 Spring, in the seasonal sequence, features the birth of a comic society, which centers around a hero; summer brings the growth of an heroic individual; tragedy the attainment of his maturity with the recognition of the limits imposed upon man by the natural order in fall; and winter displays the final demise of the heroic ideal. In this sequence, recognition comes first; it ends with reversal. Initially, there is the "recognition of a newborn society rising in triumph around a still somewhat mysterious hero" (*AC*, 192). The span of that mysterious hero's life is the focus of romance (*AC*, 198). This hero becomes the tragic hero who dies, and he dies into a world that, whatever it is, is not ours, not our human world. Reversal of the heroic is completed in satire, which displays the "disappearance" or "tearing to pieces" of the hero: "heroism" or any "effective [human] action" is "absent, disorganized, or foredoomed to defeat," so that "confusion and anarchy

reign over the world" (*AC*, 192). The sequence, then, is Spenglerian: it moves from birth, through growth, maturity, to death.

18 See Freud, *Totem and Taboo* (New York: Norton, 1950), 77.

19 See *Two Essays*, 110.

Chapter Fourteen: Ricoeur and Frye on Myth

1 *Man*, N.S., 4 (1969), 336. All subsequent citations are to this page. For a list of other surveys of myth studies, see *Philosophy, Religious Studies, and Myth*, Robert A. Segal, editor. New York: Garland Publishing, 1996, x-xi.

2 Wendy Doniger O'Flaherty, "Inside and Outside the Mouth of God: The Boundary Between Myth and Reality," *Daedalus* 109 (spring 1980), 93.

3 Gerald Bruns, *Hermeneutics Ancient and Modern* (New Haven: Yale University Press, 1992), 240. Subsequent citations are to this text.

4 Gilbert Murray, Preface to Aristotle's *On the Art of Poetry*, tr. Ingram Bywater (London: Oxford University Press, 1920), 6.

Chapter Fifteen: Biblical Hermeneutics and Frye

1 Frank Kermode, "Northrop Frye and the Bible" in *Omnium Gatherum*, ed. Susan Duick and others (Gerrards Crossing, Buckinghamshire, England: Colin Smythe, 1989), 76. Subsequent citations are to this essay.

2 See Frederic Jameson, *The Political Unconscious* (Ithaca: Cornell University Press, 1981); and Christopher Wise, "Jameson / Frye / Medieval Hermeneutics," *Christianity and Literature* 41 (spring 1992), 313-33.

3 *Origen*, tr. Rowan A. Greer (New York: Paulist Press, 1979), 178-88. Subsequent references are to this text. For a brief discussion and evaluative bibliography, see Brevard S. Childs, *Biblical Theology of the Old and New Testaments* (Minneapolis: Fortress Press, 1993), 33-36.

4 Paul Ricoeur, *Essays on Biblical Interpretation*, editor Lewis S. Mudge (Philadelphia, Fortress Press, 1980), 49-72. Subsequent citations are to this essay.

5 In *The Great Code* (xix and 235), Frye cites three particular works that have influenced his book: Gadamer's *Truth and Method*, Walter Ong's *The Presence of the Word: Some Prolegomena for Cultural and Religious History* (New Haven: Yale University Press, 1967), and Ricoeur's *The Conflict of Interpretations: Essays in Hermeneutics*, editor Don Ihde (Evanston: Northwestern Press, 1974). The last contains the essay "Preface to Bultmann."

6 His chapter has a three part structure: an introduction (178-80), body (180-85), and conclusion (185-88). The introduction consists of what we might call a four-cell typology. Readers are placed in four classes according to their institutional setting or their place outside or inside the church. Two groups are excluded and the other two are his weak or simple and cultivated readers. Or again, the contrast is between literalists and typological readers. His chapter is addressed only to this last class of readers (180), though part of his rhetorical purpose is to invite his weak readers or literalists to become strong readers in accordance with his motif that reading Scripture is a developmental process.

7 Origen: "Scripture [is to be understood] according to the spiritual meaning [not] the sound of the letter" (180). The body of his chapter presents a sequence of points.

BIBLIOGRAPHY

Robert D. Denham's *Northrop Frye: An Annotated Bibliography of Primary and Secondary Sources* (Toronto: University of Toronto Press, 1987) is the standard bibliography. It is updated by the section, "Frye Bibliography," in his semi-annual *Northrop Frye Newsletter* 1 (Fall 1988-). A joint project, by the Frye Centre at Victoria University and the University of Toronto Press, for *The Collected Works of Northrop Frye*, has already begun (see Newsletter 7 [Fall 1996], 35). General editor Alvin A. Lee "plans to have three volumes published each year over the course of the next decade." The first two volumes, *The Correspondence of Northrop Frye and Helen Kemp*, have already been published. The third volume will consist of Frye's student papers at Victoria and Emmanuel Colleges and essays from 1932-1938. "Frye's writings on critical theory and mythology" are to be edited by Joseph Adamson; his writings "on the Bible and religion" are to be edited by Alvin A. Lee and Jean O'Grady. For a list of the editions of Frye's books, see Robert D. Denham's "Appendix" in *The Legacy of Northrop Frye*, eds. Alvin A. Lee and Robert D. Denham (Toronto: University of Toronto Press, 1994), 339-53.

Frye, with the help of Jay Macpherson, compiled "Myth and Myth Criticism: An Introductory Bibliography" to accompany his "Literature and Myth," in *Relations of Literary Study: Essays on Interdisciplinary Contributions*, ed. James Thorpe (New York: Modern Language Association, 1967), 27-55. While his bibliography is thirty years old, it is far more helpful than others. For a list of surveys and bibliographies on myth, see the "Series Introduction" by Robert Segal in *Theories of Myth* (New York: Garland, 1996), x-xi. The series contains reprints of much of the primary literature of early twentieth century myth theory. It consists of *Psychology and Myth*; *Anthropology, Folklore and Myth*; *Philosophy, Religious Studies, and Myth*; *Literary Criticism and Myth*; *Ritual and Myth*; *Robertson Smith, Frazer, Hooke, and Harrison*; and *Structuralism in Myth: Levi-Strauss, Barthes, Dumézil, and Propp*. They were published in 1996.

Abrams, M. H. "Anatomy of Criticism." *University of Toronto Quarterly* 28 (January 1959), 190-96.

Ackerman, Robert. *J. G. Frazer: His Life and Work*. Cambridge: Cambridge University Press, 1987.

_____. *The Myth and Ritual School: J. G. Frazer and the Cambridge Ritualists*. Theorists of Myth, Vol. 2. New York: Garland Publishing, 1991.

Adams, Hazard. *Antithetical Essays in Literary Criticism and Liberal Education*. Tallahassee: Florida State University Press, 1990.

_____. *Philosophy of the Literary Symbolic*. Tallahassee: University Presses of Florida, 1983.

Adamson, Joseph. *Northrop Frye: A Visionary Life*. Toronto: ECW Press, 1993.

Altieri, Charles. "Northrop Frye and the Problem of Spiritual Authority." *PMLA* 87 (October 1972), 964-75.

Auden, W. H. *The Enchafed Flood*. Charlottesville: University Press of Virginia, 1950.

Auerbach, Erich. *Mimesis: The Representation of Reality in Western Literature*. Princeton: Princeton University Press, 1953.

_____. *Scenes from the Drama of European Literature: Six Essays*. New York: Meridian Books, 1959.

Ayre, John. "The Mythological Universe of Northrop Frye." *Saturday Night* 88 (May 1973), 19-24.

_____. *Northrop Frye: A Biography*. Toronto: Random House of Canada, 1989.

Balfour, Ian. *Northrop Frye*. Twayne's World Author Series, 806. Boston: Twayne Publishers, 1988.

Bashford, Bruce. "Literary History in Northrop Frye's *Anatomy of Criticism*." *Connecticut Review* 8 (October 1974), 48-55.

Bate, Walter Jackson. *The Burden of the Past and the English Poet*. Cambridge: Harvard University Press, 1970.

Bates, Ronald. *Northrop Frye.* Canadian Writers Series, No. 10. Toronto: McClelland and Stewart, 1971.

Battestin, Martin C. *The Providence of Wit: Aspects of Form in Augustan Literature and the Arts.* Oxford: Clarendon Press, 1974.

Black, Max. *Models and Metaphors: Studies in Language and Philosophy.* Ithaca: Cornell University Press, 1962.

Blodgett, E. D. Review of *The Secular Scripture. Canadian Review of Comparative Literature* 4 (Fall 1977), 363-72.

Bloom, Harold. *The Anxiety of Influence: A Theory of Poetry.* 2nd ed. New York: Oxford University Press, 1997 [1973].

_____. *A Map of Misreading.* New York: Oxford University Press, 1975.

_____. "A New Poetics." *Yale Review* 47 (September 1957), 130-133.

_____. *Ruin the Sacred Truths: Poetry and Belief from the Bible to the Present* (Charles Norton Lectures, 1987-1988). Cambridge: Harvard University Press, 1989.

_____. *Shelley's Mythmaking.* Yale Studies in English, No. 141. New Haven: Yale University Press, 1959.

_____. *The Western Canon: The Books and School of the Ages.* New York: Harcourt Brace, 1994.

Blumenberg, Hans. *Work on Myth,* tr. Robert M. Wallace. Cambridge: MIT Press, 1985.

Brockway, Robert W. *Myth from the Ice Age to Mickey Mouse.* Albany: State University of New York, 1993.

Bruns, Gerald. *Hermeneutics Ancient and Modern.* New Haven: Yale University Press, 1992.

Buckley, Jerome Hamilton. *The Triumph of Time: A Study of Victorian Concepts of Time, History, Progress, and Decadence.* Cambridge: Harvard University Press, 1966.

Buechner, Frederick. *Telling the Truth: The Gospel as Tragedy, Comedy, and Fairy Tale.* New York: Harper & Row, 1977.

Bultmann, Rudolf, and others. *Kerygma and Myth: A Theological Debate,* ed. Hans-Werner Bartsch, tr. Reginald H. Fuller. New York: Harper, 1961.

Burke, Kenneth. *Attitudes Toward History*. Boston: Beacon Press, 1961.

_____. "The Encyclopaedic, Two Kinds of." *Poetry* 91 (February 1958), 320-28.

_____. *A Grammar of Motives*. New York: Prentice-Hall, 1945.

_____. *The Rhetoric of Religion: Studies in Logology*. Boston: Beacon Press, 1961.

Campbell, Joseph. *The Hero with a Thousand Faces*. New York: Pantheon, 1949.

Caserio, Robert. *Plot, Story, and the Novel*. Princeton: Princeton University Press, 1979.

Cassirer, Ernst. *An Essay on Man: An Introduction to a Philosophy of Human Culture*. New Haven: Yale University Press, 1944.

_____. *The Individual and the Cosmos in Renaissance Philosophy*, tr. Mario Domandi. New York: Harper & Row, 1963.

_____. *Kant's Life and Thought*, tr. James Haden. New Haven: Yale University Press, 1981.

_____. *Language and Myth*, tr. Susanne K. Langer. New York: Harper, 1946.

_____. *The Logic of the Humanities*, tr. Clarence Smith Howe. New Haven: Yale University Press, 1961.

. *The Myth of the State*. New Haven: Yale University Press, 1946b.

_____. "Mythic, Aesthetic, and Theoretical Space," tr. Lerke Holzwarter Forster and Donald Phillip Verene. *Man and World* 2 (1969), 3-17.

_____. *The Philosophy of Symbolic Forms I: Language*, tr. Ralph Manheim. New Haven: Yale University Press, 1953.

_____. *The Philosophy of Symbolic Forms II: Mythical Thought*, tr. Ralph Manheim. New Haven: Yale University Press, 1955.

_____. *The Philosophy of Symbolic Forms III: The Phenomenology of Knowledge*, tr. Ralph Manheim. New Haven: Yale University Press, 1957.

_____. *The Philosophy of the Enlightenment*, tr. Fritz C. A. Koelln and James P. Pettegrove. Princeton: Princeton University Press, 1951.

_____. *The Platonic Renaissance in England*, tr. James P. Pettegrove. Austin: University of Texas Press, 1953.

_____. *The Question of Jean-Jacques Rousseau*, tr. Peter Gay. New York: Columbia University Press, 1954.

_____. *Symbol, Myth, and Culture: Essays and Lectures of Ernst Cassirer 1935-45*, ed. Donald Phillip Verene. New Haven: Yale University Press, 1979.

Cave, Terence. *Recognitions: A Study in Poetics*. Oxford: Clarendon Press, 1988.

Chase, Richard. *The Quest for Myth*. Baton Rouge: Louisiana State University Press, 1949.

Childs, Brevard S. *Biblical Theology of the Old and New Testaments*. Minneapolis: Fortress Press, 1993.

_____. *The Book of Exodus: A Critical, Theological Commentary*. The Old Testament Library. Philadelphia: Westminster Press, 1974.

_____. *Introduction to the Old Testament as Scripture*. Philadelphia: Fortress Press, 1979.

_____. *Myth and Reality in the Old Testament* (Studies in Biblical Theology, No. 27). Naperville, IL: Alec R. Allenson, 1960.

_____. *The New Testament as Canon: An Introduction*. Valley Forge, Pennsylvania: Trinity Press International, 1994.

Cochrane, Charles Norris. *Christianity and Classical Culture: A Study of Thought and Action from Augustus to Augustine*. London: Oxford University Press, 1940.

Cohen, J. M. *Robert Graves*. New York: Grove Press, 1961.

Cook, David. *Northrop Frye: A Vision of the New World*. New York: St. Martin's Press, 1985.

Cook, Eleanor and others, eds. *Centre and Labyrinth: Essays in Honour of Northrop Frye*. Toronto: University of Toronto Press, 1983.

Cooper, Lane. *An Aristotelian Theory of Comedy*. New York: Harcourt Brace, 1922.

Cornford, Francis M. *The Origin of Attic Comedy.* Cambridge: Cambridge University Press, 1914.

Crossan, John Dominic. *The Dark Interval: Towards a Theology of Story.* Niles, IL: Argus, 1975.

Crouzel, Henri. *Origen.* San Francisco, Harper & Row, 1989.

Culler, A. Dwight. *The Victorian Mirror of History.* New Haven: Yale University Press, 1985.

Culler, Jonathan. *Structuralist Poetics: Structuralism, Linguistics and the Study of Literature.* Ithaca: Cornell University Press, 1975.

Curtius, Ernst Robert. *European Literature in the Latin Middle Ages.* London: Routledge, 1953.

Czarnecki, Mark. "The Gospel According to Frye." *Maclean's* 5 (April 1982), 40-44.

Dale, Peter Allan. *The Victorian Critic and the Idea of History.* Cambridge: Harvard University Press, 1977.

Dante. *The Convivio.* London: Dent, 1912.

Daniélou, J. *From Shadows to Reality: Studies in the Biblical Typology of the Fathers,* London: Burns and Oates, 1960.

_____. *Origen.* New York: ET, 1953.

DeMaria, Robert, Jr. "The Ideal Reader: A Critical Fiction." *PMLA* 93 (May 1978), 463-74.

Denham, Robert D. "Anti anaesthetics; Or, The Turn of the Freudian Crews." *Centrum* 1 (Fall 1973), 105-22.

_____. "Common Cause: Notes on Frye's View of Education." *CEA Critic* 42 (November 1979), 23-28.

_____. "Frye and the Social Context of Criticism." *South Atlantic Bulletin* 39 (November 1974), 63-72.

_____. "Frye's Theory of Symbols." *Canadian Literature* 66 (Autumn 1975), 63-79.

_____. "Introduction." *Northrop Frye on Culture and Literature: A Collection of Review Essays,* ed. Robert D. Denham. Chicago: University of Chicago Press, 1978, 1-64.

_____. "The No-Man's Land of Competing Patterns." *Critical Inquiry* 4 (Autumn 1977), 194-202.

_____. *Northrop Frye: An Annotated Bibliography of Primary and Secondary Sources.* Toronto: University of Toronto Press, 1987.

_____. *Northrop Frye and Critical Method.* University Park: Pennsylvania State University Press, 1978.

_____. "Northrop Frye and Rhetorical Criticism." *Xavier University Studies* 11 (Spring 1972), 1-11.

_____. "The Religious Base of Northrop Frye's Criticism." *Christianity and Literature* 42 (Spring 1992), 241-54.

_____. "Science, Criticism, and Frye's Metaphysical Universe." *South Carolina Review* 7 (April 1975), 3-18.

_____, and Thomas Willard, eds. *Visionary Poetics: Essays on Northrop Frye's Criticism.* New York: Peter Lang, 1991.

Douglas, Mary. "Judgments on James Frazer." *Daedalus* 107 (Fall 1978), 151-64.

Duncan, Joseph E. "Archetypal Criticism in English, 1946-1980." *Bulletin of Bibliography* 40 (December 1983), 206-30.

Eaves, Morris, and Michael Fischer, eds. *Romanticism and Contemporary Criticism.* Ithaca: Cornell University Press, 1986.

Eggers, Walter, and Sigrid Mayer. *Ernst Cassirer: An Annotated Bibliography.* New York: Garland Publishing, 1988.

Eliade, Mircea. *Cosmos and History: The Myth of the Eternal Return*, tr. Willard R. Trask. New York: Harper, 1954.

_____. *Myth and Reality*, tr. Willard R. Trask. New York: Harper & Row, 1963.

_____. *Patterns in Comparative Religion*, tr. Rosemary Sheed. New York: Sheed and Ward, 1958.

_____. *The Sacred and the Profane: The Nature of Religion*, tr. Willard R. Trask. New York: Harper and Row, 1959.

Eliot, T. S. *Selected Essays.* New York: Harcourt, Brace and World, 1932.

_____. *Selected Prose of T. S. Eliot*, ed. Frank Kermode. London: Faber and Faber, 1975.

Feldman, Burton, and Robert D. Richardson. *The Rise of Modern Mythology 1680-1860.* Bloomington: Indiana University Press, 1972.

Fennelly, John F. *Twilight of the Evening Lands: Oswald Spengler a Half Century Later.* New York: Brookdale Press, 1972.

Finholt, Richard. "Northrop Frye's Theory of Countervailing Tendencies: A New Look at the Mode and Myth Essays." *Genre* 13 (Summer 1980), 203-57.

Fisch, Harold. *A Remembered Future: A Study in Literary Mythology.* Bloomington: Indiana University Press, 1985.

Fischer, Klaus P. *History and Prophecy: Oswald Spengler and the "Decline of the West."* Denham, NC: Moore Publishing Company, 1977.

Fletcher, Angus. *Allegory: The Theory of a Symbolic Mode.* Ithaca: Cornell University Press, 1964.

Fraser, Robert. *The Making of "The Golden Bough": The Origins and Growth of an Argument.* New York: St. Martin's Press, 1990a.

_____, ed. *Sir James Frazer and the Literary Imagination: Essays in Affinity and Influence.* New York: St. Martin's Press, 1990b.

Frazer, James George. *Folk-lore in the Old Testament: Studies in Comparative Religion, Legend and Law.* 3 volumes. London: Macmillan, 1918.

_____. *The Golden Bough: A Study in Magic and Religion.* Abridged edition. London: Macmillan, 1922.

_____. *The Golden Bough: A Study in Comparative Religion.* 3rd ed. 12 volumes. London: Macmillan, 1911-15.

_____, tr. Apollodorus. *The Library.* Loeb Classical Library, 2 volumes. London: William Heinemann, 1921.

Frei, Hans W. *The Eclipse of Biblical Narrative: A Study in Eighteenth and Nineteenth Century Hermeneutics.* New Haven: Yale University Press, 1974.

Freud, Sigmund. *The Standard Edition of the Complete Psychological Writings of Sigmund Freud,* eds. James Strachey and others. 24 volumes. London: Hogarth Press and the Institute of Psycho-Analysis, 1953-1974.

Froelich, Karlfried, ed. and tr. *Biblical Interpretation in the Early Church.* Sources in Christian Thought. Philadelphia: Fortress Press, 1984.

Frye, Northrop. "Allegory," in *Encyclopedia of Poetry and Poetics*, eds. Alex Preminger and others. Princeton: Princeton University Press, 1965. Pp. 12-15.

_____. *Anatomy of Criticism: Four Essays*. Princeton: Princeton University Press, 1957.

_____. *The Bush Garden: Essays on the Canadian Imagination*. Toronto: Anansi, 1971.

_____. *Creation and Recreation*. Toronto: University of Toronto Press, 1980.

_____. *The Critical Path: An Essay on the Social Context of Literary Criticism*. Bloomington: Indiana University Press, 1971.

_____. *Divisions on a Ground: Essays on Canadian Culture*, ed. James Polk. Toronto: Anansi, 1982.

_____. *The Double Vision of Language, Nature, Time, and God*. Toronto: University of Toronto Press, 1991.

_____. *The Educated Imagination*. Bloomington: Indiana University Press, 1966.

_____. *The Eternal Act of Creation: Essays, 1979-90*, ed. Robert D. Denham. Bloomington: Indiana University Press, 1993.

_____. *Fables of Identity: Studies in Poetic Mythology*. New York: Harcourt, Brace and World, 1963.

_____. *Fearful Symmetry: A Study of William Blake*. Princeton: Princeton University Press, 1947.

_____. *Fools of Time: Studies in Shakespearean Tragedy*. Toronto: University of Toronto Press, 1967.

_____. *The Great Code: The Bible and Literature*. New York: Harcourt Brace Jovanovich, 1982.

_____, with Sheridan Baker and George W. Perkins. *Harper Handbook to Literature*. New York: Harper & Row, 1985.

_____. "Literary Criticism," in *The Aims and Methods of Scholarship in Modern Languages and Literatures*, ed. James Thorpe. New York: Modern Language Association, 1963. Pp. 57-69.

_____. "Literature and Myth," in *Relations of Literary Study: Essays on Interdisciplinary Contributions*, ed. James Thorpe. New York: Modern Language Association, 1967. Pp. 27-55.

_____. *The Modern Century*. Toronto: Oxford University Press, 1967.

_____. *Myth and Metaphor: Selected Essays, 1974-1988*, ed. Robert D. Denham. Charlottesville: University of Virginia Press, 1990.

_____. "Myth and Poetry," in *The Concise Encyclopedia of English and American Poets and Poetry*, eds. Stephen Spender and Donald Hall. New York: Hawthorn Books, 1963. Pp. 225-28.

_____. *The Myth of Deliverance: Reflections on Shakespeare's Problem Comedies*. Toronto: University of Toronto Press, 1983.

_____. *A Natural Perspective: The Development of Shakespearean Comedy and Romance*. New York: Columbia University Press, 1965.

_____. *Northrop Frye in Conversation* [an interview with David Cayley]. Concord, Ontario: House of Anansi, 1992.

_____. *Northrop Frye on Culture and Literature: A Collection of Review Essays*, ed. Robert D. Denham. Chicago: University of Chicago Press, 1978.

_____. *Northrop Frye on Education*. Ann Arbor: University of Michigan Press, 1988.

_____. *Northrop Frye on Shakespeare*, ed. Robert Sandler. New Haven: Yale University Press, 1986.

_____. *Reading the World: Selected Writings, 1935-1976*, ed. Robert D. Denham. New York: Peter Lang, 1990.

_____. *Reflections on the Canadian Literary Imagination: A Selection of Essays by Northrop Frye*, ed. Branko Gorjup. Rome: Bulzoni Editore, 1992.

_____. "Response." *Eighteenth-Century Studies* 24 (Winter 1990-91). Pp. 243-49.

_____. *The Return of Eden: Five Essays on Milton's Epics*. Toronto: University of Toronto Press, 1965.

_____. *The Secular Scripture: A Study of the Structure of Romance*. Cambridge: Harvard University Press, 1976.

_____. *Spiritus Mundi: Essays on Literature, Myth, and Society*. Bloomington: Indiana University Press, 1976.

_____. *The Stubborn Structure: Essays on Criticism and Society*. Ithaca: Cornell University Press, 1970.

_____. *A Study of English Romanticism.* New York: Random House, 1968.

_____. *T. S. Eliot.* Edinburgh: Oliver and Boyd, 1963.

_____. *The Well-Tempered Critic.* Bloomington: Indiana University Press, 1963.

_____. *Words with Power: Being a Second Study of "The Bible and Literature."* New York: Harcourt Brace Jovanovich, 1990.

_____. *A World in a Grain of Sand: Twenty-Two Interviews with Northrop Frye,* ed. Robert D. Denham. New York: Peter Lang, 1991.

Fussell, Paul. *The Great War and Modern Memory.* New York: Oxford University Press, 1975.

_____. *Samuel Johnson and the Life of Writing.* New York: Harcourt Brace Jovanovich, 1971.

Gadamer, Hans-Georg. *Hans-Georg Gadamer on Education, Poetry, and History: Applied Hermeneutics.* Albany: State University of New York Press, 1992.

_____. *Philosophical Hermeneutics,* ed. and tr. David E. Linge. Berkeley: University of California Press, 1976.

_____. *The Relevance of the Beautiful and Other Essays.* Cambridge: Cambridge University Press, 1986.

_____. "Religious and Poetical Speaking" in *Myth, Symbol, and Reality,* ed. Alan Olson. Notre Dame: University of Notre Dame Press, 1980. Pp. 86-98.

_____. *Truth and Method.* 2nd edition. New York: Crossroad, 1991.

Gay, Peter. "The Social History of Ideas: Ernst Cassirer and After" in *The Critical Spirit: Essays in Honor of Herbert Marcuse,* eds. Kurt H. Wolff and Barrington Moore, Jr. Boston: Beacon Press, 1967. Pp. 106-20.

Gillespie, Gerald. "Bible Lessons: The Gospel According to Frye, Girard, Kermode, and Voeglin." *Comparative Literature* 38 (1986), 289-97.

Girard, René. "Lévi-Strauss, Frye, Derrida and Shakespearean Criticism." *Diacritics* 3 (Fall 1973), 34-38.

Golden, Leon. "Aristotle, Frye, and the Theory of Tragedy." *Comparative Literature* 27 (Winter 1975), 47-58.

Gombrich, E. H. *Art and Illusion: A Study in the Psychology of Pictorial Representation*. Bollingen Series XXXV, 5. New York: Pantheon, 1961.

_____. "Freud's Aesthetics." *Encounter* 26 (January 1966), 36.

Gomperz, Theodor. *The Greek Thinkers: A History of Ancient Philosophy*. 4 volumes. London: John Murray, 1901-12.

Goodin, George. *The Poetics of Protest: Literary Form and Political Implication in the Victim-of-Society Novel*. Carbondale: Southern Illinois University Press, 1985.

Goodman, Nelson. *Ways of Worldmaking*. Indianapolis: Hackett Publishing Company, 1978.

Gottfried, Rudolf B. "Our New Poet: Archetypal Criticism and *The Faerie Queene*." *PMLA* 83 (October 1968), 1362-77.

Grady, Wayne. "The Educated Imagination of Northrop Frye." *Saturday Night* 96 (October 1981), 19-28.

Graf, Fritz. *Greek Mythology: An Introduction*. Baltimore: Johns Hopkins University, 1993.

Graves, Robert. *The White Goddess: A Historical Grammar of Poetic Myth*. London: Faber and Faber, 1948.

Gunn, Giles. *The Interpretation of Otherness: Literature, Religion, and the American Imagination*. New York: Oxford University Press, 1979.

Hahn, Lewis Edwin, ed. *The Philosophy of Paul Ricoeur*. Library of Living Philosophers, Vol. 22. Chicago: Open Court, 1995.

Hair, Donald S. *Domestic and Heroic in Tennyson's Poetry*. Toronto: University of Toronto Press, 1981.

Hamilton, A. C. *Northrop Frye: Anatomy of his Criticism*. Toronto: University of Toronto Press, 1990.

_____. "Northrop Frye and the Literary Canon." *English Studies in Canada* 19 (June 1993), 179-93.

_____. "Northrop Frye and the Recovery of Myth." *Queen's Quarterly* 85 (Spring 1978), 66-77.

_____. "Northrop Frye on the Bible and Literature." *Christianity and Literature* 42 (Spring 1992), 255-76.

_____. "Northrop Frye: The Visionary Critic." *CEA Critic* 42 (November 1979), 2-6.

Hanson, R. P. C. *Allegory and Event: A Study of the Sources and Significance of Origen's Interpretation of Scripture.* London: SCM Press, 1959.

Hardin, Richard F. " 'Ritual' in Recent Criticism: The Elusive Sense of Community." *PMLA* 98 (October 1983), 846-862.

Hart, Jonathan. *Northrop Frye: The Theoretical Imagination. Critics of the Twentieth Century.* London: Routledge, 1994.

Hartman, Geoffrey. *Beyond Formalism: Literary Essays 1958-1970.* New Haven: Yale University Press, 1970.

_____. *Criticism in the Wilderness: The Study of Literature Today.* New Haven: Yale University Press, 1980.

_____. "The Culture of Criticism." *PMLA* 99 (May 1984), 371-397.

_____. *The Fate of Reading.* Chicago: University of Chicago Press, 1975.

Hilles, Frederick W. "The Plan of Clarissa." *Philological Quarterly* 45 (January 1966), 236-48.

Homans, Peter. *Jung in Context.* Chicago: University of Chicago Press, 1979.

Hopper, Stanley Romaine. *The Way of Transfiguration: Religious Imagination as Theopoiesis*, eds. R. Melvin Keiser and Tony Stoneburner. Louisville: Westminster Press, 1992.

Hughes, H. Stuart. *Oswald Spengler: A Critical Estimate.* Rev. edition. New York: Scribner's, 1952.

Hughes, Peter. "Vico and Literary History." *Yale Italian Studies* 1 (Winter 1977), 83-90.

Hyman, Stanley Edgar. *The Tangled Bank: Darwin, Marx, Frazer and Freud as Imaginative Writers.* New York: Atheneum, 1974.

Jaspers, Karl. *Way to Wisdom: An Introduction to Philosophy*, tr. Ralph Manheim. New Haven: Yale University Press, 1954.

Jaynes, Julian. *The Origin of Consciousness in the Breakdown of the Bicameral Mind.* Boston: Houghton Mifflin, 1976.

Jemielity, Thomas. *Satire and the Hebrew Prophets.* Louisville: Westminster/John Knox Press, 1992.

Jenkyns, Richard. *The Victorians and Ancient Greece*. Cambridge: Harvard University Press, 1980.

Jones, Ernest. *The Life and Work of Sigmund Freud*. 3 volumes. New York: Basic Books, 1953-57.

Josipovici, Gabriel. *The Book of God: A Response to the Bible*. New Haven: Yale University Press, 1988.

_____. *The Lessons of Modernism*. Totowa, NJ: Rowman and Littlefield, 1977.

_____. *The World and The Book*. London: Macmillan, 1971.

Jung, C. G. *The Collected Works of C. G. Jung* (Bollingen Series XX). 20 volumes. Princeton: Princeton University Press, 1953-1979.

_____. *Memories, Dreams, Reflections*, ed. Aniela Jaffé, trs. Richard and Clara Winston. New York: Vintage Books, 1962.

_____. *The Portable Jung*, ed. Joseph Campbell. New York: Viking Press, 1971.

_____. *Psychological Types*. Bollingen Series XX, Vol. 6. Princeton: Princeton University Press, 1971.

_____. *Two Essays on Analytical Psychology*. Bollingen Series XX, Vol. 7. New York: Pantheon Books, 1966.

Kennengiesser, Charles and William L. Petersen, eds. *Origen of Alexandria*. Notre Dame: University of Notre Dame Press, 1986.

Kent, Thomas L. "The Classification of Genres." *Genre* 16 (Spring 1983), 1-20.

Kermode, Frank. *An Appetite for Poetry*. Cambridge: Harvard University Press, 1989.

_____. *The Art of Telling*. Cambridge: Harvard University Press, 1983.

_____. "The Children of Concern." *English Studies in Canada* 19 (June 1993), 195-99.

_____. *The Classic*. London: Faber and Faber, 1975.

_____. *Continuities*. London: Routledge, 1968.

_____. *The Genesis of Secrecy: On The Interpretation of Narrative*. Cambridge: Harvard University Press, 1979.

_____. *History and Value*. Oxford: Clarendon Press, 1988.

_____. "Northrop Frye and the Bible" in *Omnium Gatherum: Essays for Richard Ellmann*, Susan Duick and others. Gerrard's Cross, Buckinghamshire: Colin Smythe, 1989. Pp. 71-79.

_____. *Poetry, Narrative, History*. Oxford: Basil Blackwell, 1990.

_____. *Puzzles and Epiphanies: Essays and Reviews 1958-61*. London: Routledge, 1962.

_____. "Reading Shakespeare's Mind." *New York Review of Books* 9 (October 12, 1967a), 14-17.

_____. [Review of *Anatomy of Criticism*]. *Review of English Studies* 10 (August 1959), 317-23.

_____. *The Sense of an Ending: Studies in the Theory of Fiction*. New York: Oxford University Press, 1967b.

_____. *Shakespeare, Spenser, Donne*. New York: Viking Press, 1971.

Kierkegaard, Soren. *Repetition: An Essay in Experimental Psychology*, tr. Walter Lowrie. New York: Harper & Row, 1964.

Kincaid, James. *Tennyson's Major Poems: The Comic and Ironic Patterns*. New Haven: Yale University Press, 1975.

Kockelmans, Joseph. "On Myth and Its Relationship to Hermeneutics." *Cultural Hermeneutics* 1 (1973), 47-86.

Kostelanetz, Richard. "The Literature Professors' Literature Professor." *Michigan Quarterly Review* 17 (Fall 1978), 425-42.

Krieger, Murray, ed. *Northrop Frye in Modern Criticism: Selected Papers from the English Institute*. New York: Columbia University Press, 1966.

Krois, John Michael. *Cassirer: Symbolic Forms and History*. New Haven: Yale University Press, 1987.

Lampe, G. W. H., and K. J. Woollcombe. *Essays on Typology. Studies in Biblical Theology*. London: SCM Press, 1957.

Langbaum, Robert. *The Modern Spirit: Essays on the Continuity of Nineteenth and Twentieth Century Literature*. New York: Oxford University Press, 1970.

Langer, Susanne K. *Feeling and Form: A Theory of Art Developed from Philosophy in a New Key*. New York: Scribner's, 1953.

_____. *Philosophy in a New Key: A Study in the Symbolism of Reason, Rite, and Art.* New York: New American Library, 1951.

Larsen, Stephen, and Robin Larsen. *A Fire in the Mind.* New York: Doubleday, 1991.

Laustner, M. L. W. *Thought and Letters in Western Europe: A. D. 500 to 900.* Ithaca: Cornell University Press, 1931.

Leclercq, Jean. *The Love of Learning and the Desire for God: A Study of Monastic Culture.* New York: Fordham University Press, 1961.

Levy, G. R. *The Sword from the Rock: An Investigation into the Origins of Epic Literature and the Development of the Hero.* London: Faber and Faber, 1963.

Lewis, C. S. *The Discarded Image: An Introduction to Medieval and Renaissance Literature.* Cambridge: Cambridge University Press, 1964.

Lewis, R. W. B. *The American Adam: Innocence, Tragedy, and Tradition in the Nineteenth Century.* Chicago: University of Chicago Press, 1955.

Liddell-Hart, Basil Henry. *Strategy.* New York: Praeger, 1954.

Lodge, David. *After Bakhtin: Essays on Fiction and Criticism.* London: Routledge, 1990.

Louth, Andrew. *Discerning the Mystery.* Oxford: Clarendon Press, 1983.

Lovejoy, Arthur. *The Great Chain of Being: A Study of the History of an Idea.* Cambridge: Harvard University Press, 1936.

Lubac, Henri de, S. J. *Exegese Medievale: les quatres sens de l'Ecriture.* 4 volumes. Paris: Aubier, 1959-64.

_____. *Histoire et Espirit.* Paris: Aubier, 1950.

Lynch, William, S. J. *Christ and Apollo: The Dimensions of the Literary Imagination.* New York: Sheed & Ward, 1960.

McConnell, Frank. "Northrop Frye and *Anatomy of Criticism.*" *Sewanee Review* 92 (Fall 1984), 622-29.

_____. *Storytelling and Mythmaking: Images from Film and Literature.* New York: Oxford University Press, 1979.

McKeon, Michael. *The Origins of the English Novel: 1600-1740.* Baltimore: Johns Hopkins University Press, 1987.

McLuhan, Herbert Marshall. "Inside Blake and Hollywood." *Sewanee Review* 55 (October-December 1947), 710-15.

———. *From Cliché to Archetype.* New York: Viking Press, 1970.

MacIntyre, Alasdair. *After Virtue: A Study in Moral Theory.* 2nd ed. Notre Dame, IN: University of Notre Dame Press, 1984.

Male, Emile. *The Gothic Image: Religious Art in France of the Thirteenth Century.* New York: Harper and Row, 1958.

Malraux, André. *The Voices of Silence.* Princeton: Princeton University Press, 1978.

Manganaro, Marc. *Myth, Rhetoric, and the Voice of Authority: A Critique of Frazer, Eliot, Frye, and Campbell.* New Haven: Yale University Press, 1992.

Mattingly, Harold. *Roman Imperial Civilisation.* New York: Norton, 1957.

Meier, C. A. *Soul and Body: Essays on the Theories of Carl Jung.* Santa Monica, CA: Lapis Press, 1986.

Miller, J. Hillis. "But Are Things as We Think They Are?" *TLS* (October 9-15, 1987), 1104-5.

Moynihan, Robert. *A Recent Imagining.* Hamden, CT: Archon Books, 1986.

Murray, Gilbert. "Excursus on the Ritual Forms Preserved in Greek Tragedy" in Jane Harrison, *Themis.* Cambridge: Cambridge University Press, 1912. Pp. 341-63.

———. *Euripides and His Age.* London: Oxford University Press, 1965.

———. Preface to Aristotle, "*On the Art of Poetry*," tr. Ingram Bywater. London: Oxford University Press, 1920.

Myers, I. B. *Manual.* Princeton: Princeton University Press, 1962.

Nelson, Cary. "Reading Criticism." *PMLA* 91 (October 1976), 801-815.

Niebuhr, H. Richard. *Christ and Culture.* New York: Harper and Row, 1951.

O'Flaherty, Wendy Doniger. "Inside and Outside the Mouth of God: The Boundary Between Myth and Reality." *Daedalus* 109 (Spring 1980), 93-125.

O'Hara, Daniel. *The Romance of Interpretation: Visionary Criticism from Pater to de Man*. New York: Columbia University Press, 1985.

Ong, Walter J. *The Presence of the Word: Some Prolegomena for Cultural and Religious History*. New Haven: Yale University Press, 1970.

_____. "Synchronic Present: The Academic Future of Modern Literature in America." *American Quarterly* 14 (Summer 1962), 239-59.

Page, Fred. *Spinning Yarns: Weaving Identity and Integrity into Christian Life Through Remembering Stories of the Presence and Providence of God*. Unpublished dissertation. University of Dubuque Theological Seminary, 1990.

Peterson, R. G. "Critical Calculations: Measure and Symmetry in Literature." *PMLA* 91 (May 1976), 367-75.

Pratt, Annis. *Dancing with Goddesses: Archetypes, Poetry, and Empowerment*. Bloomington: Indiana University Press, 1994.

Raglan, Lord. *The Hero: A Study in Tradition, Myth, and Drama*. New York: Vintage, 1956 [1936].

Rank, Otto. *The Myth of the Birth of the Hero and Other Writings*. New York: Vintage Books, 1959.

Reagan, Charles E. *Paul Ricoeur: His Life and His Work*. Chicago: University of Chicago Press, 1996.

Rebhorn, Wayne A. "After Frye: A Review Article on the Interpretation of Shakespearean Comedy and Romance." *Texas Studies in Literature and Language* 21 (Winter 1979), 553-82.

Reed, John R. *Victorian Conventions*. Athens: Ohio University Press, 1975.

Riccomini, Donald R. "Northrop Frye and Structuralism: Identity and Difference." *University of Toronto Quarterly* 49 (Fall 1979), 33-47.

Ricoeur, Paul. *The Conflict of Interpretations: Essays in Hermeneutics*, ed. Don Ihde. Evanston: Northwestern University Press, 1974.

_____. *Essays on Biblical Interpretation*, ed. Lewis S. Mudge. Philadelphia, Fortress Press, 1980.

_____. *Fallible Man*. New York: Fordham University Press, 1986.

_____. *Figuring the Sacred: Religion, Narrative, and Imagination*, ed. Mark I. Wallace. Mineapolis: Fortress Press, 1995.

229

_____. *Freud and Philosophy: An Essay on Interpretation.* New Haven: Yale University Press, 1970.

_____. *Hermeneutics and the Human Sciences: Essays on Language, Action and Interpretation,* ed. J. B. Thompson. Cambridge: Cambridge University Press, 1981.

_____. *History and Truth.* Evanston: Northwestern University Press, 1965.

_____. *Interpretation Theory: Discourse and the Surplus of Meaning.* Fort Worth: Texas Christian University Press, 1976.

_____. "Myth: Myth and History," in *The Encyclopedia of Religion.* Vol. 10. New York: Macmillan, 1987.

_____. *Oneself as Another,* tr. Kathleen Blamey. Chicago: University of Chicago Press, 1992.

_____. *The Philosophy of Paul Ricoeur: An Anthology of His Work,* eds. Charles E. Reagan and David Stewart. Boston: Beacon Press, 1978.

_____. *A Ricoeur Reader: Reflection and Imagination,* ed. Mario J. Valdés. Toronto: University of Toronto Press, 1991.

_____. *The Rule of Metaphor: Multi-Disciplinary Studies in the Creation of Meaning in Language,* tr. R. Czerny. Toronto: Toronto University Press, 1978.

_____. *The Symbolism of Evil.* Religious Perspectives, No. 17, tr. E. Buchanan. New York: Harper & Row, 1967.

_____. *Time and Narrative,* tr. K. McLaughlin, and D. Pellauer. 3 vol. Chicago: University of Chicago Press, 1984-88.

Rieff, Philip. Introduction to Sigmund Freud, *General Psychological Theory.* New York: Collier Books, 1963.

Robertson, D. W., Jr. *A Preface to Chaucer: Studies in Medieval Perspectives.* Princeton: Princeton University Press, 1962.

Ruland, Vernon, S. J. *Horizons of Criticism: An Assessment of Religious-Literary Options.* Chicago: American Library Association, 1975.

Ruskin, John. "Of Kings' Treasures" (1864) in *The Genius of John Ruskin,* ed. John D. Rosenberg. Boston: Houghton Mifflin, 1963, 296-314.

Russell, Ford. "*Pride and Prejudice*: Verbal Performance versus Conversation." *Dibrugarh University Journal of English Studies* [India] 6 (1987), 1-14.

_____. Review of *Myth and Metaphor*. *Christianity and Literature* 40 (Summer 1991), 396-98.

_____. "Satiric Perspectives in Rochester's *A Satyr against Reason and Mankind*." *Papers on Language and Literature* 22 (Summer 1986), 245-53.

Ruthven, K. K. *Myth*. London: Methuen, 1976.

Salusinszky, Imre. *Criticism in Society*. New York: Methuen, 1987.

Scarborough, Milton. *Myth and Modernity: Post-Critical Reflections*. Albany: State University of New York Press, 1994.

Schilpp, Paul Arthur, ed. *The Philosophy of Ernst Cassirer*. (*The Library of Living Philosophers*, volume 6.) Evanston, IL: The Library of Living Philosophers, 1949.

Schwartz, Sanford. "Reconsidering Frye." *Modern Philology* 78 (February 1981), 289-95.

Scruton, Roger. *The Philosopher on Dover Beach: Essays*. New York: St. Martin's Press, 1990.

Seamon, Roger. "Poetics against Itself: On the Self-Destruction of Modern Scientific Criticism." *PMLA* 104 (May 1989), 294-305.

Simonetti, Manlio. *Biblical Interpretation in the Early Church: An Historical Introduction to Patristic Exegesis*. Edinburgh: T. and T. Clark, 1994.

Smalley, Beryl. *The Study of the Bible in the Middle Ages*. 2nd ed. Oxford: Clarendon Press, 1941.

Smith, William Robertson. *The Prophets of Israel and Their Place in History*. New York: Appleton, 1882.

Spengler, Oswald. *The Decline of the West*, ed. Arthur Helps, tr. Charles Francis Atkinson. Abridged edition. New York: Oxford University Press, 1991.

_____. *The Decline of the West*, tr. Charles Francis Atkinson. 2 volumes. New York: Alfred A. Knopf, 1926-1928.

_____. *Letters of Oswald Spengler: 1913-1936*, ed. and tr., Arthur Helps. New York: Knopf, 1966.

Tillich, Paul. *A History of Christian Thought: From Its Judaic and Hellenistic Origins to Existentialism*, ed. Carl E. Braatan. New York: Simon and Schuster, 1967.

Tillyard, E. M. W. *The Elizabethan World Picture.* London: Macmillan, 1943.

Todorov, Tzvetan. *Literature and Its Theorists.* Ithaca: Cornell University Press, 1987.

Toliver, Harold. *The Past that Poets Make.* Cambridge: Harvard University Press, 1981.

Toynbee, Arnold. *A Study of History.* Abridged ed. 2 volumes. New York: Oxford University Press, 1957.

Trigg, Joseph Wilson. *Origen: The Bible and Philosophy in the Third-Century Church.* Atlanta: John Knox Press, 1983.

Turner, Frank M. *The Greek Heritage in Victorian Britain.* New Haven: Yale University Press, 1981.

Van Ghent, Dorothy. "Introduction," to Joseph Conrad, *Nostromo.* New York: Holt, Rinehart and Winston, 1961. Pp. vii-xxv.

_____. "Keats' Myth of Letters." *Keats-Shelley Journal* 3 (Winter 1954), 7-25.

_____. *Keats: The Myth of the Hero*, rev. Jeffrey Cane Robinson. Princeton: Princeton University Press, 1983.

Vansina, Frans D. *A Primary and Secondary Systematic Bibliography of Paul Ricoeur 1935-1984.* Louvain-la-Neuve: Editions Peeters, 1985.

Vickery, John B. *Robert Graves and the White Goddess.* Lincoln: University of Nebraska Press, 1972.

_____. *The Literary Impact of "The Golden Bough."* Princeton: Princeton University Press, 1973.

Vieth, David M. "Towards an Anti-Aristotelian Poetic: Rochester's *Satyr against Mankind* and *Artemisia to Chloe*, with Notes on Swift's *Tale of a Tub* and *Gulliver's Travels*." *Language and Style* 5 (1972), 123-45.

Walker, Steven F. *Jung and the Jungians on Myth: An Introduction.* Theorists of Myth, Vol. 4. New York: Garland Publishing, 1995.

Watts, Alan W. *Myth and Ritual in Christianity.* Boston: Beacon Press, 1968.

Weston, Jesse L. *From Ritual to Romance*. Princeton: Princeton University Press, 1993 [1920].

Wheelwright, Philip. *The Burning Fountain: A Study in the Language of Symbolism*. Bloomington: Indiana University Press, 1954.

_____. *Metaphor and Reality*. Bloomington: Indiana University Press, 1962.

_____, ed. *The Presocratics*. New York: Odyssey Press, 1966.

White, Hayden. *Metahistory*. Baltimore: Johns Hopkins University Press, 1973.

Whitehead, Alfred. *Science and the Modern World*. New York: New American Library, 1948.

Whitman, Cedric H. *Homer and the Heroic Tradition*. New York: Norton, 1965.

Wimsatt, William K., Jr., and Cleanth Brooks. *Literary Criticism: A Short History*. New York: Vintage Books, 1967.

Wise, Christopher. "Jameson/Frye/Medieval Hermeneutics." *Christianity and Literature* 42 (Spring 1992), 313-33.

Wolfflin, Heinrich. *Principles of Art History: The Problem of the Development of Style in Later Art*. New York: Dover, 1950.

Wollheim, Richard. *Art and Its Objects: An Introduction to Aesthetics*. New York: Harper and Row, 1968.

LIST OF FRYE'S REFERENCES
TO MODERN MYTH THEORISTS

Many of Frye's references are no more than passing allusions. His later references often iterate earlier items.

Fearful Symmetry (1947)
Bryant, Jacob: 173-75
Casaubon, Edward (fictional mythographer in George Eliot's novel
    Middlemarch): 173
Davies, Edward: 173-75
Frazer, James: 174
Freud, Sigmund: 233, 301
Ruskin, John: 98, 411, 422

Anatomy of Criticism (1957)
Bachelard, Gaston: 358
Bodkin, Maud: 358
Burke, Kenneth: 358
Campbell, Joseph: 361
Cassirer, Ernst: 10, 350
Cornford, Francis M.: 46, 357
Fergusson, Francis: 358
Frazer, James: 10, 108-09, 148, 193, 361, 362
Freud, Sigmund: 6, 10, 72, 111, 192, 193, 196, 214, 277, 291, 359, 361
Gaster, Theodor: 360, 361
Harrison, Jane: 361
Jung, Carl: 6, 10, 72, 108, 111, 192, 193, 196, 214, 277, 291, 359, 361
Murray, Gilbert: 187, 361
Raglan, F. R. R. S.: 361
Rank, Otto: 361
Ruskin, John: 9, 10, 36, 93, 114, 154, 198, 267, 328, 341
Silberer, Herbert: 359

Spengler, Oswald: 160, 343
Weston, Jesse: 361
Wheelwright, Philip: 358

Northrop Frye on Culture and Literature (published in 1978, but its
    reviews were mostly written in the 1950s)
Casaubon, Edward (fictional mythographer in Eliot's *Middlemarch*):
    234
Cassirer, Ernst: 67-75, 111
Dumézil, Georges: 101
Eliade, Mircea: 98-106
Frazer, James: 67, 81, 84-94, 99-100, 101, 123-24, 125
Freud, Sigmund: 67, 75, 89, 90, 93, 94, 100, 117, 118, 119, 121, 123,
    174, 175, 199, 214, 219
Graves, Robert: 230-36
Jung, Carl: 95-98, 101, 106, 116-29, 174
Knoll, Max: 97
Langer, Susanne: 111-16
Malinowski, Bronislaw: 86
Mannhardt, Wilhelm: 85, 86
Neumann, Eric: 96
Nordau, Max: 96
Plesner, Helmuth: 96-97
Ruskin, John: 200, 201
Schmidt, Father Wilhelm: 101
Silberer, Herbert: 125
Smith, William Robertson: 85, 86
Spengler, Oswald: 76-83, 133-34, 141, 145, 146, 184
Tylor, Edward B.: 100, 101
van der Leeuw, Gerhardus: 97
Vico, Giambattista: 141, 145, 146

Fables of Identity (1963)
Cassirer, Ernst: 15, 249
Eliade, Mircea: 30
Frazer, James: 16, 17
Freud, Sigmund: 36, 66, 227, 228, 246

Vico, Giambattista: 14

The Stubborn Structure (1970)
Frazer, James: 189, 190, 260, 261, 269
Freud, Sigmund: 5, 29, 30, 32, 39, 54, 80, 133, 158, 180, 184, 215,
    222, 255, 293
Graves, Robert: 116, 190, 268
Jung, Carl: 82
Langer, Susanne: 46
Spengler, Oswald: 184

The Critical Path (1971)
Bodkin, Maud: 16
Bryant, Jacob: 98
Frazer, James: 99
Freud, Sigmund: 18, 22, 99, 126, 141-42, 165
Jung, Carl: 16, 18
Levi-Strauss, Claude: 145
Ruskin, John: 98, 101
Vico, Giambattista: 34, 38, 54, 93

The Bush Garden (1971)
Frazer, James: 88, 119
Freud, Sigmund: 21, 93, 230, 236

The Secular Scripture (1976)
Freud, Sigmund: 57, 58, 122
Graves, Robert: 70, 120, 154, 172, 192, 193
Jung, Carl: 57
Ruskin, John: 121, 177
Weston, Jesse: 121, 192

Spiritus Mundi (1976)
Frazer, James: 111, 112, 114, 116
Freud, Sigmund: 107, 115
Graves, Robert: 112
Jung, Carl: 116, 117, 119

INDEX

Dante, x, 22, 25, 46, 51, 58,
76, 78, 104, 115, 130
Decline of the West, 6, 13, 15,
21, 24, 26-28, 32-34, 36, 40-
41, 45, 55
DeMaria, Robert, 106, 113
Demeter, 35
Denham, Robert D., xiv-xv, 6,
12, 152
Dickens, Charles, 5, 92
Dionysian, 44-45
displacement, 82, 84-85, 89-
90, 92, 106
Donne, John, 5
Double Vision, 12, 56, 150
Dying God, x

Educated Imagination, 5, 12,
51
Eliade, Mircea, 132, 134
Eliot, George, ix, xi, 18
Eliot, T. S., 12, 91
Essay on Man, 62, 67, 73, 82,
215
Eternal Act of Creation, 115

Fables of Identity, xiii, 4, 11-
12, 19, 25, 27, 30, 36, 63,
96, 114
Fearful Symmetry, xii, xiv, 9-
10, 15-19, 137
Finnegans Wake, 92
Fischer, Klaus P., 26
Four Zoas, 18
Fraser, Robert, 34
Frazer, James George, ix-xvi,
6, 13-19, 25-26, 32, 34-42,

44-46, 49, 52-55, 59, 61, 69,
72, 83, 86, 96, 126-127,
129, 133, 136-137, 139-140,
148, 152
Freud, Sigmund, x, xii-xv, 11,
16, 18-19, 59, 61, 71-72, 82-
83, 86-90, 92, 103, 117-118,
127, 132-133, 136-137, 139-
140

Gadamer, Hans-Georg, ix, xv-
xvi, 46, 50-51, 59, 72, 133,
151-152
Goethe, 28, 30, 44-45, 56
Golden Bough, xiii, 6, 13-14,
16, 18, 32, 34-40, 45, 96
Graves, Robert, x, 96
Great Code, xi-xii, 9-11, 29,
49, 63, 75-76, 98, 134, 137,
140-143, 148, 150-152

Hamilton, A. C., xiv-xvi, 24,
33, 65, 104, 127, 129, 152
*Harper Handbook to
Literature*, 89, 122
Hegel, G. F. W., 75
Heraclitus, 26
hermeneutics, Biblical or
medeival, ix-xi, xiv, 51, 81,
138, 141-142, 145-146, 148-
150, 152
*History of the Decline of
Antiquity*, 26
Hugo, Victor, 46
Hyman, Stanley, 137

Ibsen, Henrik, 5